VIF Perspective

A POLITICAL ECONOMIC APPROACH TO RECLAIMING INDIA

Editor

C D Sahay

Vitasta

LET KNOWLEDGE SPREAD

Published by
Renu Kaul Verma
Vitasta Publishing Pvt Ltd
2/15, Ansari Road, Daryaganj
New Delhi - 110 002
info@vitastapublishing.com

In association with
Vivekananda International Foundation
3, San Martin Marg, Chanakyapuri, New Delhi 110021

ISBN 978-93-86473-38-7

First Edition 2019
MRP ₹695

VIF Editorial Committee: CD Sahay, Arvind Gupta, Lt Gen Gautam Banerjee
Cover and layout by Vits Press
Printed by Vikas Computer and Printers

CONTENTS

List of Contributors

Ambassador Prabhat Prakash Shukla is an Indian Foreign Service officer. He has served in diplomatic assignments in Brussels, London and Kathmandu and as the Indian Ambassador to Russia. He was Diplomatic Adviser to the Prime Minister from 1996 to 2000. He is currently on the Advisory Board of the Vivekananda International Foundation, New Delhi.

Dr Anantha Nageswaran is a Co-Founder and Member of Investment Board at Aavishkaar Venture Management Services. Dr Nageswaran serves as the Regional Head of Investment Consulting with Credit Suisse in Singapore. He is also a Co-Founder of Takshashila Institution. Dr Nageswaran holds a Master's in Business Administration and a doctoral degree in Finance from the University of Massachusetts, Amherst, US.

Dr Suhas P Wani is Director, Research Programme Asia, and Director, ICRISAT Development Centre at International Crops Research Institute for the Semi-Arid Tropics (ICRISAT),Telangana State, India. He is an authority in the area of watershed management, wastewater treatment and safe re-use in agriculture, integrated soil fertility management and climate resilient agriculture. Recipient of many international awards, he has published more than 500 research papers and written several books.

Dhirendra Singh was a member of the Indian Administrative Service (Karnataka Cadre). He retired as Union Home Secretary in 2005. Post-retirement, he was a Member of the Commission on Centre-State Relations. In Karnataka, he headed the Departments of Planning and Finance, Agriculture, Horticulture, Animal Husbandry, Forestry and Fisheries, Rural Development and Panchayati Raj, thus having a ring side view on matters concerning agricultural production and river water usage. He is a member of the Executive Council of the VIF.

Ambassador Dinkar Srivastava is a former Indian Foreign Service Officer whose last assignment was as India's Ambassador to Iran. He is currently Senior Fellow and Cluster Head at VIF.

Col DP Kumar Pillay, Shaurya Chakra is a combat veteran from the Brigade of Guards, decorated for conspicuous gallantry. He has served in the Planning and International Cooperation Division of the Ministry of Defence and in the National Security Council Secretariat. Currently, he is a research fellow at the Institute of Defence Studies And Analyses (IDSA), New Delhi. Col Pillay holds a PhD from Panjab University.

HK Varma has more than 38 years of working experience in various aspects of water resources planning, development and management while working in Central Water Commission

(CWC) and Water and Power Consultancy Services (India) Limited (WAPCOS) and the Asian Development Bank (ADB). Presently, he is the Executive Director, International Commission on Irrigation and Drainage (ICID).

Avinash C Tyagi has vast experience in dealing with various facets of water resources management, hydrologic observation, disaster risk management, inter-state water dispute resolution, and international policy making. He served as Commissioner of Policy Planning in the Ministry of Water Resources and Director,Water and Climate Wing at the World Meteorological Organisation (WMO). He has also been the Secretary General, International Commission on Irrigation and Drainage (ICID).

Vikas Khitha is Chief Executive – Power Development and is also the Head – Special Initiatives (Construction) in Larsen & Toubro Limited.

Partha Pratim Mitra is a former Indian Economic Service Officer in the Government of India. He is an expert on matters of Rural Development, Social Justice, Banking, Economic Affairs, Commerce and Industry.

Jandhyala BG Tilak, former Vice Chancellor, National University of Educational Planning and Administration, is currently a Distinguished Professor at the Council for Social Development, New Delhi. He has also been on the teaching faculty of the University of Virginia and the Hiroshima University, besides being on the research staff of the World Bank.

Dr Arpita Mitra has a doctoral degree in History from Jawaharlal Nehru University, New Delhi. She has been a Fellow (2015-2017) at the Indian Institute of Advanced Study, Shimla, and is presently an Associate Fellow at the VIF.

Foreword

Vivekananda International Foundation (VIF) is a prominent and distinctive think tank, based in Delhi. Guided by the message of Swami Vivekananda (1863-1902), the VIF conducts research on a wide range of subjects covering international relations, national security, foreign policy, issues of defence, governance, economics, history and civilisation. The objectives of the VIF's research are to promote nation building, encourage harmony in diversity, prioritise conflict avoidance and generate environmental awareness. An able team of researchers, defence, security and foreign policy experts, prominent academicians and eminent citizens helps the VIF in its activities. The VIF's messages are reflected in its regular publications.

In 2017, the VIF started a series of publications under the general title of 'VIF PERSPECTIVE'. The books bring together thoughtful essays and articles on a variety of subjects, ranging from India's Nuclear Deterrence to Climate Change. National security cannot be constrained to merely military and sovereignty issues. The concept of national security is evolving and becoming broader. Addressing non-traditional issues, such as climate change and agriculture productivity, to name a few, are vital in the overall context of national security.

The VIF is happy to offer to the readers, a volume titled, *A Political Economic Approach To Reclaiming India*, edited by Shri CD Sahay. Essays in the volume focus on issues of economic security, health, food, water, skills development and education, and highlight the urgent need to address these in the context of national security. The essays have been written by eminent experts with deep understanding of the subjects they deal with.

I am confident that the present volume will contribute to the ongoing debate on how issues of economy and governance are becoming important in the context of national security, and how these should be addressed.

Dr Arvind Gupta
Director
Vivekananda International Foundation
Delhi, August 2018

Editor's Note

The basic objective behind bringing out the VIF PERSPECTIVE is to generate and stimulate well informed debate in shaping opinion on a wide range of issues of current relevance that directly or otherwise impact India's quest for economic prosperity with equity, her emergence as a major power in the sub-continent and beyond, wellbeing of its citizens in a peaceful environ both internally and in the regional context.

In this issue of the PERSPECTIVE, we continue that exercise, focusing on two critically important aspects of Economy and Governance. Very briefly, Prabhat Shukla, in his article highlights the impact of the US policies in the late 1940s and beyond, under which it designed and managed the global economic system in a way that served its economic and strategic interests. He suggests that Indian policy-makers need to shed the Nehruvian paradigm and move to a low-tax, lightly-regulated economy and allow the Rupee to strengthen.

Anantha Nageswaran examines the profound changes to the Indian economy under the National Democratic Alliance (NDA) Government and recommends that policy bias against capital and 'capriciousness of the taxman' must end to encourage sustainable growth.

Moving on to some of the important developmental issues that call for effective governance, Suhas Wani and Dhirendra Singh address the agrarian crises with reference to the Prime Minister's clarion call to double the farmers' income by 2022 as an important policy initiative for poverty alleviation. In their view, a consortium approach involving public and private institutions, and the corporates along with State agricultural universities, will go a long way in empowering the farmers.

On a related aspect of management of water resources, a team of experts led by Dhirendra Singh and including Avinash Tyagi, Harish Kumar Varma and Vikas Khitha look at the availability of water from 23 river basins, recommending a wide range of practical measures to prevent wastages and better utilisation.

Partha Mitra focuses on another flagship initiative of the Modi Government relating to skill development. He has tried to identify the reasons for India's poor districts remaining backward, and suggested designing India's skills and employment strategies based on available natural resources for human resource development.

Dr DPK Pillay's article takes up the issue of making affordable healthcare available to all, particularly in the rural areas. Given India's dismal standing under several health indices, he suggests major overhaul in public healthcare system under the 'Ayushman Bharat' initiative that holds considerable promise.

DP Srivastava laments the low research and development (R&D) expenditure, the perpetuating technology dependence and poor competitiveness of Indian companies in global market. Highlighting the urgent need for indigenous R&D, he calls for reinforced efforts on the part of the Government and the corporate sector in the R&D sector.

Prof Tilak, in his article on education, highlights the critical importance of inculcating value based education for building a humane society, by focusing on core universal human values of *Satya* (truth), *Dharma* (righteousness), *Shanti* (peace), *Ahimsa* (non-violence) and *Prema* (love). The rapid growth in the Indian education system in the post-independence era has also brought in the profit-seeking private educational institutions that did not pay due emphasis on moral and ethical issues, thus suggesting the need for basic reforms.

Lastly, Arpita Mitra, in an interesting article, recounts the recent evidences on the River Sarasvati that challenges the hypothesis of an Aryan invasion/immigration in the Indus Valley Civilisation (IVC) and recommends corrective measures to amend the existing narratives in our history textbooks.

We believe that, in these article, we have covered some of the pressing challenges of nation building in its various facets and put forward some fresh ideas. We promise to maintain this dialogue with our readers through regular compilation of VIF PERSPECTIVEs in the months ahead.

Before I conclude, I would like to thank our distinguished authors for contributing well researched articles on a wide range of issues. I would also like to express my appreciation and gratitude to the entire VIF team for their unstinted support, without which it would not have been possible to bring out this publication.

CD Sahay

Editor, VIF Perspective and Senior Fellow, VIF

New Delhi, August 2018

Where Economics & Strategy Intersect

A Political Economy Approach to Global Power

Prabhat P Shukla

The United States, since the late 1940s, designed and managed the global economic system in a way that served its economic and strategic interests. It thus examined the major turning points in this post-War history to demonstrate how strategy and economy mesh.

To this end, the US has used its power as the issuer of the international reserve currency, the Dollar, and its position as the export destination of first resort to shift the patterns of global capital flows and trade. Over time, this has led to the growth, by turns of the European Economic Community, and then Japan. Finally, from the early 1990s until 2008, it was China that enjoyed an enabling environment created by the US.

This pattern has led to misunderstanding of the nature of global power, and facile conclusions that one or other growth area was about to displace the US as the primary power in the world. It did not happen, and it will be the same with China. The brief message for Indian policy-makers in the face of the global structural changes described is that similar changes are also required for managing the Indian economy. We need to shed the Nehruvian paradigm and move to a low-tax, lightly-regulated economy, and allow the Rupee to strengthen.

How Economics shaped post-WWII World

THIS essay attempts to understand the role of economic power in shaping the world since World War II. It focuses on the main strand of economic developments over this period, and it is important to clarify what it does not do. It does not look at subsidiary (or, at best, parallel) processes, important though they also were, processes such as the Cold War or the limited détente that began in the early 1970s. It also ignores the quiet struggle between the United Kingdom (UK) and the United States (US) over economic influence until about the mid-1960s.

This point may require elucidation. It is not that the Cold War or détente were less important. But their importance lay in the military and strategic arenas–the détente of the 1970s was of historic significance, but that was because of the cross-recognition of the two Germanies (thus ending the uncertainty of the early 1960s when Kennedy, Khrushchev, and Erhard led the US, Soviet Union and West Germany, respectively) and of the Oder-Neisse frontier; and, of course, the limitation of nuclear arms. But from the economic point of view, these processes were put in the shade by the much bigger magnitudes of capital flows in the West and among the oil producers. Equally, it ignores the emerging challenges to the US domination of the World Economy in recent years. It does not, thus, look at the Chinese

Belt and Road Initiative (that has been done separately), or the emergence of crypto currencies, nor does it look at the Russian (and possibly Chinese) drive for a gold-backed alternative to the US dollar. All these are unquestionably important, but at the moment, their success is far from assured. There is time before these need to be the subjects of detailed study.

Phase I: European Recovery & US External Imbalances

The study begins with the European Recovery Programme, or the Marshall Plan, as it is more commonly known, which ran from 1948 to the end of 1951. By way of backdrop, the Bretton Woods institutions–the International Monetary Fund (IMF) and the World Bank–had been established and had placed the US Dollar at the centre of the international financial system. It was the only currency that was convertible into gold at a fixed price ($35 per ounce) and all other currencies were fixed in relation to the dollar. Devaluations beyond a narrow range could only be done with the IMF permission where the US had veto voting power and were only permitted in cases of 'fundamental disequilibrium' which was not defined.

The Marshall Plan Aid turned out to be necessary because the European recovery after the war was slow in coming. By 1946-47, there were signs of serious unrest and the fear of Communist advances if the economies of the countries were not to show some quick and substantial improvement. Two features of the Marshall Plan Aid are worth highlighting. First, it was large. The total value over the period 1948 to 1952 was approximately $12.5 billion (in current dollars, a bit over $450 billion, using gold prices as the convertor). The US Gross Domestic Product (GDP) in 1952 was a little under $60 billion. What this did was to leave little American assistance for other countries–a point frequently made by the US officials in discussions with other countries, including India.

The second feature was that it marked the line of cleavage in the Cold War. The countries that accepted the aid were: Austria, Belgium, Denmark, France, Greece, Iceland, Italy, Luxembourg, the Netherlands, Norway, Portugal, Sweden, Switzerland, Turkey, and the UK, as well as the bi-zone of Germany, later to become the Federal Republic of Germany (FRG). Those countries that rejected the US assistance were: the Soviet Union, Albania, Bulgaria, Czechoslovakia, Hungary, Poland, Romania and of course, the Soviet part of Germany, later to become the German Democratic Republic (GDR). These countries formed the Warsaw Pact and the Soviet-led economic cooperation arrangement under the Council for Mutual Economic Assistance (COMECON). Finland, despite being a capitalist country, also refused the Marshall Plan aid. It became a byword through the Cold War for sensitivity to the Soviet concerns, and gave the term 'Finlandisation' to the discourse during those years. Yugoslavia, a part of the Communist International (Commintern) in 1948, initially rejected the Marshall Plan aid but, in 1949, asked to be included. It did then receive the US assistance, but outside of the Marshall Plan aid.

These European countries also committed to accept the 'friendly advice' of the US to develop economic integration among themselves, including West Germany. This served the dual purpose of tying the FRG with the West economically, which was a major goal, because the country had not yet been taken into the North Atlantic Treaty Organization (NATO)– that was to happen in 1955, after the failure of the European Defence Community. The second major objective was to find a large enough economic area to absorb the investment already made in the oil industry in West Asia, including the pipelines that were to transport Saudi and other oil into Europe. The important thing in this connection to note is how the money was used. Over 10 percent was spent on oil imports, almost entirely from the Middle East, and a slightly smaller amount was spent on transport–also oil fired, or undergoing conversion from coal to oil.[1]

This marked the beginning of a three-way economic commitment involving the US, those parts of Europe that accepted the Marshall Plan Aid, and West Asia, with Saudi Arabia at its centre. A little bit of background to this development may add clarity as regards to the drivers of these changes.

As far back as December 1943, while the World War II was still on–but after the German surrender at Stalingrad had determined the outcome, and the Teheran Conference between Roosevelt, Stalin and Churchill had just ended–the oil company California Arabian Standard Oil Co (known as 'ARAMCO' since January 1944) requested the US Administration for permission and backing to supply oil from Saudi Arabia to West European markets. In short order, this request was approved and finance amounting to a maximum of $160 million was also provided to be repaid over a period of 25 years. Certain conditions were attached, including building up a reserve, and that ARAMCO would not sell oil to any party deemed inimical to the US interests by the State Department.[2]

By April 1944, the policy was elaborated in greater detail. The Inter-Divisional Petroleum Committee of the State Department announced its aims with regard to the Middle East oil in the following terms:

- *Facilitation, by international agreement and otherwise, of substantial and orderly expansion of production in Eastern*

Hemisphere sources of supply, principally in the Middle East, to meet increasing requirements of post-war markets.

- *Removal, by international agreement and otherwise, of impediments to the exploitation of Middle Eastern concessions held by the United States' nationals.*[3]

The phrase 'by international agreement and otherwise' catches the eye–diplomat-speak for the use of coercion if persuasion were not to work. And it was used on a regular basis–in Syria in 1949, in Iran in 1953, in the Suez in 1956, to name a few. But the more important purpose of discussing the role of oil is to bring out its importance for the US, an aspect that will feature in a bigger way in the discussion of developments in the international economy in the late 1960s and early 1970s.

It would be helpful to quantify this emerging triangular relationship. European imports of crude in the period of the Marshall Plan Aid were as follows:

Year	Imports of Crude
1947	5 million tons
1948	11 million tons
1949	29 million tons
1950	31 million tons
1951	54 million tons

European refining capacity showed a similar increase. It rose from 24 million tons in 1948 to 40 million tons in 1950, and to 77 million tons by 1952.[4] All the oil came from wells owned by the US, British and the British-Dutch oil companies. Most of the refining was done in refineries with the same ownership pattern, and the same went for the retail distribution.

For the nonce, the European Recovery Programme (ERP) served its purposes as per its intended design. It integrated

Germany; it moved the European economies from coal as the primary fuel to oil, and it drew a line of cleavage between the Soviet bloc and the Western bloc. There were problems of course, most notably the Dollar shortage caused by the fact that the US was running persistent surpluses with the Europeans, who were unable to make the settlements in their balance of payments. Accordingly, the US extended regular loans to the countries amounting to another roughly $9 billion over a period of eight years, from 1952 to 1960.

By this latter date, the success of the ERP was well-established and the member-states were running surpluses with the rest of the world, so that they could make their currencies convertible on current account. In 1957, six of the leading countries of the ERP–France, West Germany, Italy, Belgium, the Netherlands and Luxembourg-set up the European Economic Community (EEC) and, thus, began a period of changing trade patterns between the US and Europe and, by extension, in the global economy.

The reason was that, as the European surpluses grew, and with it, the fear that the US dollar would face devaluation pressures, countries such as France asked to redeem their dollar holdings into gold. This was the period of fixed exchange rates, and dollar convertibility into gold at the fixed parity of $35 per ounce. This faced the US with a double dilemma–how to preserve the Bretton Woods system, with fixed exchange rates and convertibility into gold, and yet fix the persistent and growing trade deficits. At the same time, they also wanted to provide for the growing liquidity needed to finance the rapidly growing global trade–growing faster by a factor of two to three than the global output. The table below illustrates the scale of the US deficits between 1959 and 1973.

Table 1: The US Balance of Payments, 1959–1973 (in $ billion)[5]

Year	Trade Balance	Current Balance	Basic Balance
1959	0.91	-2.14	-2.00
1960	4.89	1.80	-3.20
1961	5.57	3.07	-3.11
1962	4.52	2.46	-3.69
1963	5.22	3.20	-5.04
1964	6.80	5.79	-6.19
1965	4.95	4.29	-6.19
1966	3.82	1.94	-4.12
1967	3.80	1.54	-5.36
1668	0.64	0.96	-1.08
1669	0.61	-1.63	-2.27
1970	2.16	-0.32	-3.02
1971	-2.72	-0.91	-6.27
1972	-6.99	-9.81	-1.67
1973	0.62	0.67	-2.52

Source: US Department of Commerce, Survey of Current Business.

Phase II: The Oil-Finance Cycle and Financialisation

In actual fact, as the US archives show, the problem between Europe (and, increasingly, Japan) on the one hand and the US on the other was more acute than the figures suggest, for the deficits of the US with those countries were larger. Several ideas were at this stage floating in the Nixon administration by 1969, but the dominant theme was that a devaluation of the dollar was the way to fix the persistent trade deficit. After an initial minor adjustment, which did not yield the desired result, President Nixon took the step, in August 1971, of taking the US dollar off gold, and imposed domestic price controls as well as import tariffs of 10 percent across the board.

The availability of monetary gold was the obvious constraint on the issuance of dollars in the period when the dollar was linked to gold, for that was the second problem in using the dollar as the international currency for financing trade. It is revealing, therefore, that the South Africans were running their mines at full capacity. Figure 1 shows that, in 1970, South Africa had the highest gold production in its history. This amount, 1,000 tons in 1970, represented two-thirds of the world gold production at that time. But even this amount was not sufficient to meet the requirement and it tapered off once the gold window closed.

Figure 1: South African Gold Production 1940 - 2012[6]

In the event, this did not help the external balance except for a short while, and the downward pressure on the US dollar continued. The US was not the only major economy facing difficulties. The UK, which had already once devalued the Pound in 1967, continued to face balance of payments difficulties, and decided to let its currency float in 1972. The Japanese and the Swiss followed a few months later and, by 1973, most of the major currencies were floating, including the US dollar, though the Europeans maintained a band within which their currencies could float against one another.

In parallel with this process, a few others were also in train, and would collectively transform the global economy, and the US role in its management.

Three processes are discussed next. None of them would have been possible but for the freedom given to the dollar by the abandonment of the gold standard, and the floating of exchange rates. The three processes were:

(i) Increase in oil prices driven by the Organisation of Petroleum Exporting Countries (OPEC);

(ii) Loosening of the US monetary policy, with the US dollar freed from the constraints of maintaining any parity with either gold or other currencies; and

(iii) Rise in the role of the banks to deal with the flow of petro-dollars into the European money markets, overwhelmingly into London.

The rise in oil prices began in the late 1960s, when Libya began its hard bargaining with Occidental Petroleum Corporation. As an independent company, it enjoyed little official support, and was heavily dependent on Libyan oil as its only major source of crude. Its leverage was further increased by the difficulties created by Nasser over the Suez Canal in 1967, leaving Libya and Algeria as the only two countries that could supply oil to Europe without needing to transit the Suez Canal.

Colonel Gaddafi, who had taken over Libya in a coup in September 1969, finally succeeded in raising the tax payments charged to Occidental on its oil. One after another, the other oil companies agreed to the higher taxes, which then fed back into arrangements in the Persian Gulf producers. This started a chain of increasing demands, which culminated in the Tehran Agreement of 1971 that saw an increase of some 50 percent (from 80 cents a barrel to $1.25 per barrel) in the amount of tax paid by the oil companies to the oil producer countries. This was accompanied by a programme of annual increases all the way to 1975.

This is what led the US State Department oil expert, James Akins, to remark, '*With the possible exception of Croesus, the world will never have seen anything quite like the wealth which is flowing and will continue to flow into the Persian Gulf.*'[7] The Akins article is remarkably prescient on a subject notoriously hard to predict, and is recommended to the inquisitive reader–not only for the information it provides on oil politics, but equally for the way it leads to the other two aspects mentioned above. For he goes on to examine how the massive surpluses that the OPEC was going to earn could be utilised.

And that brings in the US financial and monetary response to these developments. It would be useful to pause, though, and stress that all this was happening before the October 1973 Yom Kippur War upset even these arrangements, and led to a partial embargo and hence still higher prices for oil. This, in turn, provided even higher surpluses for the OPEC, especially the Arab, countries.

Why this becomes important to note is that, after the US abandoned the gold standard in August 1971, Paul Volcker–then the Under Secretary for International Affairs at the Treasury–remarked at one of the meetings of a working group that the developing countries would have to bear the burden of adjustment, given the policies the West was following. The exact quote is in the third person in a report from a staffer from the office of the Presidential Assistant for International Economic Affairs: '*Paul noted that both the OECD and the US ideas of equilibrium call for the LDCs to bear a significant part of the adjustment burden!*'[8]

Table 2: Global Current Account Balances 1973 to 1980[9]

	1973	1974	1975	1976	1977	1978	1979	1980
Industrial Countries	11.3	-9.6	19.4	-0.5	-4.6	30.8	-7.8	-44.1
OPEC	6.2	66.7	35.0	40.0	31.1	3.3	68.4	112.2
LDCs	-8.7	-42.9	-51.3	-3.9	-28.6	-37.5	-57.6	-82.1

Source: IMF Annual Report, various issues.

And so indeed it turned out.

Table 2 shows the nature and magnitude of the current account deficits the least developed countries had to face throughout the 1970s and beyond.

The loose monetary policy that marked the 1970s has been well-documented. President Nixon was facing re-election in 1972 and needed positive economic results after the upheavals described above. He, therefore, appointed a new Federal Reserve Chairman, Arthur Burns, who loosened M1(measures of money supply denoted by 'M1', 'M2' etc.) from $228 billion to $249 billion between December 1971 and December 1972. The previous 12-month period under the long-serving Chairman, William McChesney Martin, saw a move from $198 billion to $203 billion.

The essence of the loose monetary policy became clear towards the end of the decade, as inflation rose to 14 percent by 1979, but allowed two large oil price hikes to be absorbed by the global economy–with the developing countries being the exception, which indeed had to bear the burden of the changing economic strategies. How they coped with the burden is the third part of the changes that followed the abandonment of the Bretton Woods arrangements in the early 1970s.

This was the role of the private commercial banks in the handling of the unprecedented funds that accrued to the oil exporters. Since the end of the war, the job of transferring capital was left to governments, as the Marshall Plan Aid itself showed, or to the World Bank and the IMF. At this stage, an informal consensus emerged among the financial managers of the world–the IMF, Organization for Economic Cooperation and Development (OECD), and the main central banks–that the handling of these large funds would be left to the private banks, as they–the governments or the international financial institutions–could not do the same job adequately. The traditional lenders, particularly the IMF, were constrained by quota limits and conditionalities. In point of fact, even the banks were uncertain about their ability to handle and recycle such large amounts of capital. The geographical location of the recycling centre was to be the City of London, because both continental Europe and the US had fairly tight banking regulations, which would not permit the free-wheeling practices that made such recycling possible. Thus, the Eurodollar market was unleashed–though it had existed on a small scale since at least the late 1950s.

A recent book by Carlo Edoardo Altamura, titled *European Banks and the Rise of International Finance* provides useful insights into the process. The main driver was the British financial establishment, led by the Bank of England, which recognised that the City of London was singularly well-placed to provide the banking services needed to undertake the task of recycling. The interesting insight the book provides is that even the banks were not quite sure they could cope with the challenge of recycling. The following quote from one of the British members of the Trilateral Commission, Sir Philip de Zulueta, to the Governor of the Bank of England is illustrative: *'At the Brussels meeting, we had among other things a discussion about the re-cycling of the Arab oil money. The bankers present, of whom the most important were David Rockefeller himself and Alan Hockin (Executive Vice President of the Toronto Dominion Bank) but included some Europeans, expressed considerable worry about the capacity of the private banking system to re-cycle the extra Arab oil money into medium term credits...*'[10]

Among other issues, the bankers were concerned about the maturity mismatch, since the deposits were short-term, the loans 'medium to long' term, and the straight fact that many of the countries to which loans were advanced were poor credit risks. But in a pattern that was to repeat itself in the early 2000s, there was no better option, as the surpluses kept pouring in. The only safeguard adopted was syndication–loans to developing countries were divided up among a number of banks and these syndicated loans parcelled out the credit risks among the participant banks.

To sum up, the situation that the US and the developed world faced in the early 1970s involved some tough choices. The dollar was in an unsustainable position, being both a national currency and an international one. The demands of the latter meant that the US had to run persistent deficits on its balance of payments; in addition, because trade was rising several times faster than global GDP, the issuance of dollars had to be faster than the national growth would warrant. Inflation, and hence, depreciation, was built into this system. Moreover, the US was running consistent deficits on its balance of payments, and so there was always a downward pressure on the currency.

The only way to control the situation was to go the way Nixon chose, or to curtail the money supply and induce a recession, which is how the issue was faced down by Federal Reserve Chairman Volcker in the late 1970s, which is discussed below.

For once, the decision was to accommodate the rise of the

petro-dollar, and its recycling through the Eurocurrency markets. This, in turn, meant the financialisation of the US economy, and the empowerment of the commercial banks in a way that had not been seen since the Great Depression.

It also meant empowering Europe in a way not seen since the war. Those with long memories will recall the public and sharp airing of differences in the 1970s between the Europeans, particularly the French, on the one side and the Americans on the other. Authors like Mary Kaldor wrote 'The Disintegrating West', as a harbinger of things to come, with Europe emerging as an independent force, equal to the US, in international affairs. And a young economist, Fred Hirsch, spoke of the need for a 'controlled disintegration' of the global economy as a legitimate aim for the 1980s.

Phase III: Controlled Integration of the Global Economy

The riposte was not long coming, and it was Volcker again who set the stage. Fittingly or not, he delivered the first Fred Hirsch Memorial Lecture in 1978, Hirsch having died in January the same year, aged 47. Instead of controlled disintegration, Volcker spoke of the need for a 'managed integration' of the global economy. He was then the President of the New York Federal Reserve Bank, and shortly to be appointed Chairman of the Federal Reserve Board. In arguing for managed integration, he conceded that the US was no longer the dominant economic presence, but argued that a coordinated approach with Japan and Europe would best serve the interests of the three, also making the point that such an approach would avoid currency volatility and at the same time prevent unhealthy competition between the three for advantageous positions in the developing countries. Also noteworthy is the following passage: '*For one thing we have learned that even large exchange rate changes have not been nearly as effective as hoped in achieving adjustment of long-standing imbalances in current account positions. Where clear improvements have been made, they can be traced to changes in relative demand pressures, or to structural changes such as North Sea oil.*'[11]

This relative demand management was the tool that he was to employ to good effect upon taking over at the Federal Reserve Bank, for that was the result of his shift towards money supply targeting, causing interest rates to rise to 20 percent by the end of 1980. The stated aim was to end the high inflation, which was 14 percent at its peak in the late 1970s. It also had the effect of breaking the oil-finance recycling as many of the developing countries in Latin America and East European countries, to which smaller amounts were extended, were unable to service the loans. Figure 2, taken from an IMF study, shows the result of this monetary tightening.

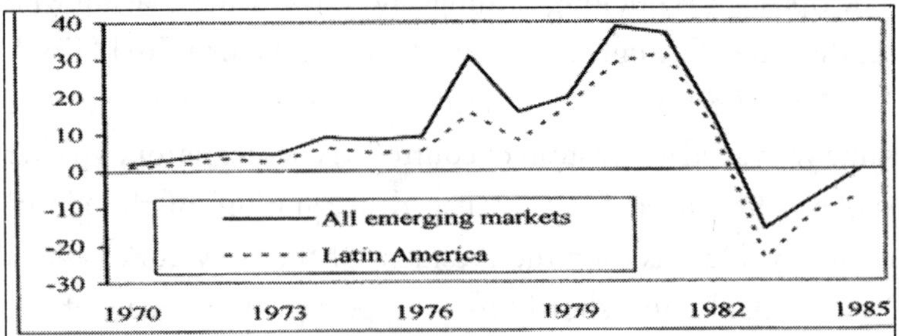

Source: World Bank, Global Development Finance.
Bank flows include short-term financing.

Figure 2: Bank Flows to Emerging Markets 1970–1985 (in US$ billions)[12]

The implications of this monetary tightening for Europe were spelt out by an ex-President of France, who was well-versed in the ways of high finance, Giscard d'Estaing, in an article in *Foreign Affairs,* written in 1983, at a time when the US recovery was well underway: '*Traditionally a US recovery has fuelled exports of developing countries, increasing their orders of equipment goods from countries such as Japan, Germany and France, and the interdependence between European countries has led to diffusion in Europe of these expansionary forces, thereby sustaining the world recovery. This time, and due to the international debt crisis, developing countries will not be in a position to benefit fully from the US recovery.*'[13]

This passage also provides some insight into the active diplomacy then underway on the North-South Dialogue. Evidently, the European economies were at risk of an economic 'decoupling' because of the policies adopted in the US. Of course, these policies also affected the US itself in a long-term way, and it would be well to spell out some of features of the new economy that was slowly taking shape.

The most important feature was the decline of the traditional manufacturing industries and rise of international finance as the new driver of the economies of many of the developed countries. Here is how Altamura, already quoted above, puts it: '*After the end of the gilded age of Fordist capitalism, a new compact for growth had to be found. The compact that started to take place in the Western world (Europe for the purpose of our work) in the early 1970s, after the crumbling of Bretton Woods and, particularly, after the first oil shock, was a compact based on less and less regulation on financial movements and institutions. It was based on the centrality of the banking and financial sector as opposed to the public hand and industrial sector as the engines of growth, and, finally, was based on the collusion between controllers and controlled, which increased the moral hazard.*'[14]

The result of this empowerment of the banks was that the commercial banking sector in the US grew by orders of magnitude over the period 1978 to 2007. The commercial banking sector held assets of $1.2 trillion in 1978, equivalent to 53 percent of GDP. The assets rose to $11.8 trillion in 2007 or 84 percent of GDP.

Over the same period, investment banks grew even faster, from $33 billion (1.4 percent of GDP) to $3.1 trillion (22 percent of GDP). Profitability in the sector grew significantly and more rapidly than in other corporate sectors combined, as shown in Figure 3.

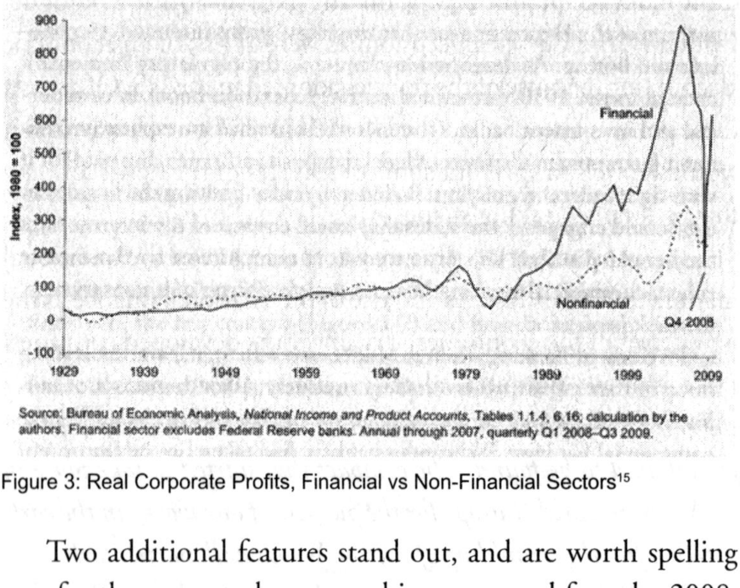

Source: Bureau of Economic Analysis, *National Income and Product Accounts*, Tables 1.1.4, 6.16; calculation by the authors. Financial sector excludes Federal Reserve banks. Annual through 2007, quarterly Q1 2008–Q3 2009.

Figure 3: Real Corporate Profits, Financial vs Non-Financial Sectors[15]

Two additional features stand out, and are worth spelling out, for they were to be repeated in aggravated form by 2008. The first was the emergence of large-scale global surpluses, which could not be productively employed in the country, or countries, originating them. These were the OPEC member-states at this time. Having no place to deposit these surpluses, such as the IMF, or even the Bank for International Settlements (BIS), all the countries concerned agreed that it was best for the private banks accept these funds and utilise them where possible. In the 1970s, the focus of these deposits was the offshore commercial banks. By the 2000s, however, the US financial services industry had been liberalised to an extent where they could handle the funds onshore.

The second feature was the recycling of these funds to countries, some of which were questionable credit risks. As the amount of surpluses grew, the banks were perforce looking at riskier investments. The same was to happen in the 2000s, of course, and that is what gave rise to the subprime loans. The difference was that, in 1979, Volcker could apply the brakes on the oil-finance cycle by curtailing money supply, and the US economy could take the shock because its own exposure was limited to offshore commercial banks, and the debtors were also foreign countries. Three decades later, it was a different story.

But all that was still to come. In the 1980s, the Mexican default in the summer of 1982 forced the hand of the US financial establishment to ease up on money supply, and that began a financial bull run that has continued–with occasional hiccups–to this day. For comparison, the Dow Jones Industrial Average (DJIA) ranged between 600 and 1000 from 1965 to 1982. It was a little above 700 in August 1982, when the New York Federal Reserve Bank announced that it was abandoning monetary targeting. Twenty years later, it was above 10,000.

Figure 4 shows the DJIA growth, from year 1900 to 2014, in graphic form.

This twenty-year period also saw a few significant changes in the global economy. The most important, without question, was the relative decline of Europe, and the rise of Asia, as it also became the most important trade partner of the US. And within that process, the world saw the rise of Japan in the 1980s, and its stagnation from the mid-1990s.

A second feature was the liberalisation of the US financial

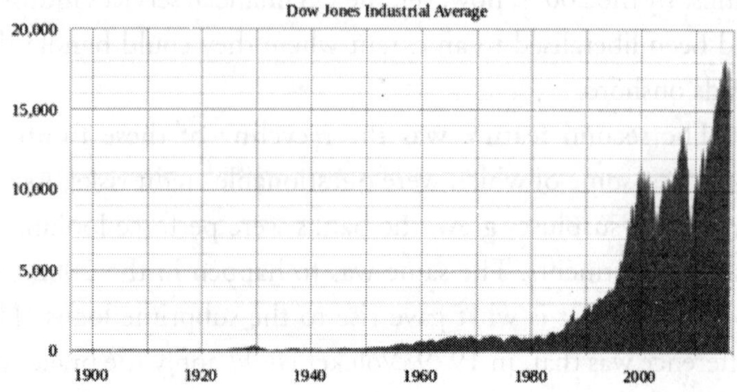

Figure 4: Dow Jones Industrial Average 1900 - 2014

sector. The improbable reality of the US economy up to the 1970s was that it was heavily controlled and regulated–a result of the post-1929 experience and the New Deal regulation. Banks were divided into commercial and investment functions under the Glass-Steagall Act of 1933. Regulation Q set limits on the interest they could pay on deposits, and they could not cross state borders. In addition, other measures, such as the Bank Holding Act and the Interest Equalisation Tax, were further constraints. The process of removing these began in the 1980s, which gradually eroded, and finally repealed Glass-Steagall and also, along the way, permitted the growth of moral hazard. The Savings & Loans bailout in the late 1980s cost the taxpayer some $125 billion. Later, in 1998, saving Long-Term Capital Management (LTCM) was similarly helped out by the New York Federal Reserve Bank, though no public funds were used. Nonetheless, several analysts noted that the New York Federal Reserve Bank had brokered a better deal for the LTCM shareholders than would have been possible without such intervention. And there was, of course, the bailout of Bear Stearns by the New York Federal Reserve Bank, whose role was described by Volcker as *'actions that extend to the very edge of its lawful and implied powers'.*

Phase IV: Growth Shifts to Asia

Meanwhile, the real economy was also undergoing shifts of an unprecedented magnitude. With Europe struggling after the Latin American debt crisis–several commentators described the situation as 'Eurosclerosis' while Asia was gaining economic heft. In the 1980s, Japan was the fast-rising economy, and the usual spate of writing ensued describing Japan as the coming economic leader of the world.

As is well-known, that did not happen. And the reasons for that not happening are well-documented, and deserve treatment in some detail. The first point to note is that the Japanese economy did not stagnate from the late 1980s. Though it is frequently believed that the crash of the stock market at the end of December 1989, when the Nikkei was close to 40,000, marked the downturn. In actual fact, Japan's GDP continued to grow until 1995. It was \$3.0 trillion in 1989, and reached \$5.3 trillion in 1995.

The cause of the stalling may be found in the rise of China, and this came about in three stages - the devaluation of the Yuan and the simultaneous rise in the Yen; the Asian Financial Crisis; and the entry of China in the World Trade Organisation at the end of 2001.

The devaluation of the Yuan by nearly 50 percent (from 'Y5.8 to \$1' to 'Y8.7 to \$1') on 1 January 1994 had the effect of making asset prices and labour costs significantly cheaper for foreign investors. Table 3, sourced from Asian Development Bank (ADB) *Key Indicators of Developing Asian and Pacific Countries* for various years, provides an indication of how Foreign

Direct Investment (FDI) behaved over the period just before, and just after the devaluation, and how the Asian Financial Crisis affected the region in terms of FDI flows. It suggests a clear movement of FDI into China in ever-growing amounts, and either stagnant, or diminishing investment into other South-East Asian countries. The partial exceptions are Singapore and, to a lesser extent, Thailand.

Table 3: Total Net Foreign Direct Investment (in US$ million)[3]

Countries	1990	1995	1997	1998	2007
East Asia					
China, People's Rep. of	2,657.0	33,849.0	41,673.7	41,118.1	121,418.3
Hong Kong, China	...	...	...	-2,220.0	6,712.0
Korea, Rep. of	-263.1	-1,776.2	-1,605.2	672.8	-13,696.7
South Asia					
India	96.0	2,143.0	3,562.0	2,480.0	15,545.0
Sri Lanka	41.6	53.1	429.8	193.0	548.0
South-East Asia					
Indonesia	1,093.0	3,742.0	4,677.0	-241.0	1,164.2
Malaysia	2,332.0	6,642.0	6,787.7	2,708.0	-2,561.7
Philippines	528.0	1,361.0	1,113.0	1,592.0	-514.0
Singapore	3,541.0	4,748.0	2,849.1	5,148.9	11,837.0
Thailand	2,402.0	1,183.0	3,298.0	7,360.0	7,819.4
Vietnam	120.0	1,780.0	2,220.0	1,671.0	6,550.0
Developed Member Countries					
Australia	4,272.4	2,792.5	3,819.2	1,889.0	1,624.7
Japan	-48,968.9	-22,591.0	-22,767.8	-20,960.2	-50,999.5
New Zealand	...	49,84.3	2,120.1	-1,31.7	821.3

Table 4: China's Inward FDI and Exports by Foreign Funded Enterprises (Nominal), 1995-2005[16]

Year	FDI (in $ bn)	Total Exports (in $ bn)	Exports by FFEs (in $ bn)	Share of FFE Exports (in %)
1995	37.52	148.78	46.88	31.51
1996	41.73	151.05	61.51	40.72
1997	45.26	182.79	74.90	40.98
1998	45.46	183.71	80.96	44.07
1999	40.32	194.93	88.63	45.47
2000	40.72	249.20	119.44	47.93
2001	46.88	266.10	133.24	50.07
2002	52.74	325.60	169.99	52.21
2003	53.51	438.23	240.31	54.84
2004	60.63	593.33	338.59	57.07
2005	60.33	761.95	444.18	58.30

Table 4 also shows the effects of this large-scale FDI into China over a period of one decade, from 1995 to 2005.

Table 4 shows the growing importance of FDI in China's export performance. Enterprises with foreign funding contributed 31 percent to China's exports in 1995, just as the boom was starting. By 2005, when the boom was in its peak years, their contribution was 58 percent.

But an even more striking pattern, where the direction of trade flows, is also taken into account. Table 5, sourced from ADB (*op. cit.*), reveals the shift between 1990 and 2007 in the direction of exports. It shows a major shift in Chinese exports towards the US and Europe, with both doubling (or better) in percentage terms, which was obvious in absolute terms, given the huge increase in China's export quantities. For almost all other countries, the opposite process is underway. Exports to both the above destinations decline, while exports within Asia go up significantly, which mostly means to China. Only

Table 5: Direction of Trade: Merchandise Exports (percent of total merchandise exports)

Country of Origin	To Asia		To Europe		To North and Central America	
	1990	2007	1990	2007	1990	2007
China, People's Rep.	67.7	40.8	14.7	23.5	10.0	22.9
Korea, Rep. of	34.0	51.4	15.5	16.1	33.4	17.5
India	21.0	32.6	47.2	23.4	16.3	17.6
Indonesia	64.3	60.8	12.8	13.3	13.9	12.5
Malaysia	58.0	57.1	16.6	13.5	18.1	17.3
Singapore	47.1	64.7	17.2	11.3	23.0	11.6
Thailand	37.8	54.1	25.3	15.5	25.3	14.5
Vietnam	39.1	36.8	48.1	23.1	0.6	25.0
Australia	50.4	60.5	17.1	12.5	12.9	7.6
Japan	26.1	42.8	23.0	16.8	36.3	24.9
New Zealand	30.4	32.4	21.7	15.3	16.9	15.7

India and Indonesia provide some partial exceptions, but not very significant in the quantitative terms. In plain language, China has become the funnel through which raw materials and intermediate goods are finished and exported to the US and Europe.

Table 6 shows the changing pattern of imports and the direction of trade, which is equally revealing. The imports of all countries, except China, go up from Asia, and down from the US and Europe. China's imports from all three regions declined, which indicates that it was importing ever larger amounts from other sources–mostly oil and other raw materials not covered in the three jurisdictions included in these tables. Here, then, we have the new pattern that emerged over the period from the mid-1990s to the mid-2000s, which brings out the nature and source of China's huge current account surpluses. To go further,

Table 6: Direction of Trade: Merchandise Imports (percent of total merchandise imports)

Country of Origin	To Asia		To Europe		To North and Central America	
	1990	2007	1990	2007	1990	2007
China, People's Rep. of	48.4	40.4	24.1	14.5	15.8	9.4
Korea, Rep. of	33.5	46.7	13.1	12.6	25.3	12.0
India	17.3	29.9	41.3	21.6	12.9	9.2
Indonesia	43.4	70.7	22.5	8.4	13.7	5.1
Malaysia	50.6	60.3	17.9	13.2	18.1	11.6
Singapore	48.2	54.4	15.9	14.1	16.9	13.5
Thailand	53.3	56.4	19.7	11.0	12.1	7.6
Vietnam	34.1	69.1	21.3	10.4	0.4	3.9
Australia	32.4	49.0	27.5	23.8	26.4	14.8
Japan	25.1	40.8	19.8	13.4	27.2	14.0
New Zealand	24.0	42.0	25.0	17.7	20.0	11.5

the bulk of the surpluses arose from exports to two destinations, the US and the EU. The US alone accounted for over 25 percent of total exports in 2005, and for 18 percent as recent as 2016.

Phase V: Unsustainable Surpluses Again

Thus, in the real economy, China was running up surpluses of a magnitude that even the Japanese–in their halcyon days–did not enjoy, leading to unprecedented surplus accumulation by China. At the same time, the OPEC countries were also enjoying a sustained rise in oil prices, which were to peak at over $140 per barrel (Brent) in 2008. Croesus was left far behind. A revealing datum is the figure for money supply in the US. M3 is the broadest measure commonly used, and it captures the newer forms of money market funds, as well as external sources. In the US Fed data, they also used to show the figures for non-M2 M3, and this figure, which captured these new sources rose from one percent in 1959 to 35 percent in 2006.

Once again, the global economy was faced with excessive surpluses and nowhere to be used. During this time, the bulk of the monies were deposited in the US banks, particularly in the Wall Street banks, now freed from all constraints. They had also developed new and unregulated instruments with which to recycle these colossal amounts. Inevitably, this required dropping diligence standards for evaluating loan recipients. And this time, instead of syndicating loans, the safeguard employed was securitisation, in the form of Mortgage-Backed Securities, and other derivatives. Despite some efforts at regulating these activities, nothing was done to control them. It was in essence a repeat, with some change of technique and major actors, of the oil-finance recycling of the 1970s.

At least one person in a position of authority seemed to sense the dangers in the situation. When Fed Chair, Greenspan, began raising interest rates in 2004, he testified before the Senate, where he said, *inter alia*, 'We cannot be certain that this benign environment will persist and that *there are not more deep-seated forces emerging as a consequence of prolonged monetary accommodation*' (emphasis added).[17]

Given the elliptical way central bankers use language, it is hard to be certain as to the meaning of this sentence. His book, *The Age of Turbulence,* also does not clear up the meaning. But it would be a reasonable assumption that this was on his mind, in the same way that the excess liquidity in the global system was in the late 1970s. In fact, in later years, Greenspan has squarely blamed the global savings glut for the financial crisis.

And Greenspan did not confine himself to statements. In the subsequent meetings of the Fed Open Market Committee, interest rates were raised 17 times on the trot, in a sequence that seems unimaginable today. What is even more striking, in comparison, when the cycle of upward moves began in 2004, unemployment was at 5.6 percent, and core inflation between 1.5 and 2 percent–that is significantly worse in terms of unemployment, and not much different in terms of inflation as compared to the present situation. And yet, he raised rates, whereas today, there is a marked concern to hasten slowly, and then too with every mark of extreme reluctance.

Of course, there was in between the searing experience of the financial crisis, or the Great Recession, as it is coming to be called. Enough has been written about it, and this essay does not intend to cover that ground. Some of the major post-crisis features of the global economy are, however, worth highlighting. Arguably, the most important change has been the effect on global trade. This has led global growth since the late 1940s, and has registered a growth rate of 6.8 percent annually between 1985 and 2007. Post-crisis, it has slowed down and has barely kept pace with the global GDP growth, even falling below in some years, and going negative in years, such as 2015–in both value and volume terms.

In turn, this behaviour of global trade has meant that export-dependent economies have been adversely affected. As the world's leading exporter, China has faced serious challenges in maintaining its growth rate. And that brings in the major feature, the rapid growth in Chinese debt, as shown on Figure 5 for the period 2004-16.

The open indebtedness in China is now 250 percent of GDP, and there is more from the shadow system. The Chinese are themselves more open about their economic problems than much of the western conventional media. Thus, for instance, the

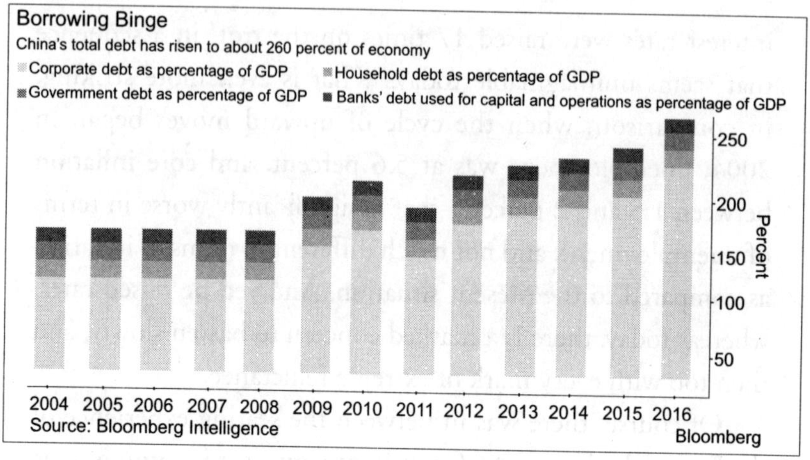

Figure 5: China's Total Internal Debt 2004 - 2016

Chair of the People's Bank of China described the latent risks in the financial system as '*hidden, complex, sudden, contagious and hazardous*'[18]. This came after warnings from the IMF and the BIS, as well as downgrades by some rating agencies regarding the very same issue–Chinese debt levels. This level of internal debt accumulation in such as short period of time is without precedence in the post-War history.

All of the above demonstrate not just the downside risks facing the Chinese economy in the post-crisis period; it also indicates the dependence of China on benign US policies, especially with regard to interest rates and trade. On the first count, higher interest rates will cause China also to tighten its debt issuance or risk a depreciation of the Yuan–and there are several well-known China bears who are shorting the currency. But it will also affect China's external debt, which is of the order of $1.5 trillion. This is why Fed Chair, Janet Yellen, finally broke her silence on the relevance of China in decision-making on interest rates in September 2015, when she decided against raising them and invoked China 16 times in her press conference.

This was in stark contrast for the Fed, which barely talked about global worries before.[19]

On the second count, China is even more dependent on the US for its continued growth. In 2016, for instance, China's export surplus with the US was of the order of $350 billion an dits overall surplus was $510 billion, so the US contributed just under 70 percent of China's trade surplus. This is in conformity with the long-term pattern of the US-China trade.

There is the counter-argument that 'China owns US debt', or that the 'US is addicted to Chinese debt'–suggesting that, due to mutual dependence, China also has leverage over the US. In fact, China owns a little less than 6 percent of the US Government debt, which is about the same as Japan. Adding corporate debt to the numbers puts Japan well ahead of China. Plus which, the various Quantitative Easings have shown that, in the final analysis, the US does not need any outsider to buy its bonds. At its peak, the Fed was buying (and 'twisting', that is, swapping maturities) a trillion dollars annually on its own. To prove the point, it may be recalled that China sold $188 billion of US Treasury's in 2016–with little effect on yields.

To offer some final thoughts, the above narrative has been aimed at showing that the US has ensured its economic domination of the global economy essentially through financial control, after the industrial domination was irretrievably lost in the late 1960s. The financial flows and the management of currencies enabled the US to direct its support through the process of 'managed integration', as described above. In turn, this brought the blessings of the US effective demand to the EEC, then to Japan and, finally, to China. This last phase is being played out now, and there are vested interests in keeping it going, just as there are–especially in the new Trump administration–forces that seek an altogether new system and pattern of international engagement.

It is early yet to discern the contours of this new pattern. But some tentative conclusions are possible. Firstly, the heavy reliance on trade-led global growth is under strain. It was breaking down anyway, even before 2017, but is now part of the strategy of the new US administration. This would have far-reaching implications for both the global value chains that emerged over the last two decades or so, and for the financialisation of the US (and Western more generally) economy that took shape under the oil-finance cycle.

The role of Brexit is also worth noting. The Eurocurrency markets depended on the City of London in order to function, and that was among the main drivers of the British entry into the EEC, as it was then called. Now, the pull-out of the UK from the EU could very well be the harbinger of a new financial system to displace the current one.

These are huge changes, and are calling forth huge opposition. The outcome of this struggle will determine the kind of world that emerges.

Conclusion

Some winding up remarks would be in order now. Perhaps, a good starting point would be to state what should be obvious from the foregoing, and that is the US is not in decline. Since the late 1960s, the US GDP share in the global output has been fluctuating between 22 and 24 percent. In 2016, it was 25 percent. One could argue about the nature and quality of the growth, but the basic fact cannot be controverted. The notion of decline has been linked to the undoubted rise of China. But China has filled the space vacated by the USSR, Europe, and

Japanese stagnation. China's growth, as has been argued in this essay, is itself dependent on the US policies of loose money, and open trade, especially its imports. This is changing, if the Trump administration follows through on its new economic approach. And so far, it gives every indication of being serious about this.

Equally, the US dollar is not under threat. Its role in international reserves remains unchanged, even enhanced. It accounted for 62 percent of international reserve holdings in 1996, and that has gone up slightly to 63 percent currently, as of end-2016. The Euro has increased slightly over the same period. The combined value of the D-mark, the French Franc, and the ECU was a little shy of 18 percent in 1996; it is 20 percent now. There is also the Greek debt issue, which has not yet been finally resolved. The IMF has not joined in yet, pending a review of the repayment programme of the government for sustainability. After satisfying itself on that score, it will join the assistance package in 2018.

The Chinese Yuan is in the one percent handle at present, but it has entered the Special Drawing Rights (SDR) basket only last year, so its future will need to be tracked. So far, though, China has maintained 'strict and tightening' capital controls, so it is unlikely that its share will rise significantly until capital controls are eased. Gold-backed movements are also worth monitoring, especially since China is now the largest gold producer in the world, and Russia and Uzbekistan are also among the top ten gold producers.

The foregoing analysis has also attempted to show the nature of the functioning of the global economy since the late 1940s. It has been an economy led and controlled by the US power, which has been sustained by increasing financialisation and the US dollar dominance, especially since the end of the Bretton

Woods arrangements in the early 1970s. It has also been a system where trade has acquired a leading role in fostering economic growth. And once again, as the export destination of first resort, the US has had the power to direct the speed of that economic growth. It has also used its pulling power to shift growth from one jurisdiction to another–Europe initially, then Japan and finally China.

All this has not been without external challenges, and internal doubt. As early as 1952, the incoming President Eisenhower team posed the problem inherent in international trade, that of persistent surpluses and deficits. The point was made in the following words: 'How is it expected that a world system of trade and payments, free of quantitative restrictions and exchange controls and with convertible currencies, would be kept in balance? In other words, what equilibrating forces are expected to operate so as to prevent persistent surpluses and deficits (not accounted for by normal capital flow)? Under the gold standard the notion was that an inflow of payments produced by an export surplus would tend automatically to increase prices in the surplus country and reduce prices in the deficit country, thus stimulating imports into the surplus country and deterring imports into the deficit country. Whatever may have been the validity of this notion in the past, it is clear that, under present and foreseeable circumstances, there is no direct or automatic connection between the inflow and outflow of payments and internal price levels.'[20]

This was written at a time when the US was running surpluses with the rest of the world, and so is all the more prescient. But once the tide turned and the US was facing the prospect of persistent deficits, the same problem was seen differently. Kissinger noted in a memo to President Nixon that 'the present monetary system puts very little real pressure on surplus countries to act short of intense political pressure from the rest of the world'.[21]

This indeed gets to the heart of the problem of international trade and finance. Surpluses are deemed as 'good' but deficits as 'bad'–and yet, you cannot have one without the other. And when the surpluses become as large as they did in the 1970s and in the early 2000s, the global economy faces the problem of how to utilise them. Both times, financial institutions found a way to put these surpluses to some use, and inevitably, they were economically unsustainable.

It appears possible that the new US Administration has understood that there are structural problems in the global economy and its management since the 1940s. The structure of the US economy itself has had perforce to change to accommodate these patterns of capital and trade flows, but this has come at a cost–frequent financial crises, poor job growth, and persistent deficits in the external balance, with corresponding volatility of the US dollar. The new economic team has openly rejected the long-standing commitment to free trade. They have also supported external policies–like the full-throated support of President Trump for Brexit, where as the earlier US President Obama had voiced open discouragement for it. It would be wise to prepare for a radical shake-up of the global economy.

One of the consequences that appears to be happening already, and even before the current US administration took office, is a slowdown in international trade. The period after 2012 saw stagnation, and even negative growth, especially in 2015, both in value and by volume. The situation has improved a little in recent years, but even now, the growth in trade is no faster than overall global growth. This is slow by historical standards, when trade has outstripped global growth by a factor of two or three.

This implies that domestic demand will grow in importance as a driver of growth. The Chinese leaders recognise this, and have been talking for the last ten years about the need to boost domestic demand. The results so far have fallen short. But India is in the happy situation of having one of the most buoyant domestic consumption economies in the world. The changes described in this essay suggest that India needs to nurture this and the best way is to reduce the burden of direct taxes–on income, on corporate profits, and on property-related transactions–and to reduce the burdens of regulations and inspection. Not only will this play to India's strengths, it will also provide a true free-market approach to managing the Indian economy, something that has long been promised, but not really delivered so far. The experience of several countries is that reducing taxes does indeed raise revenues after an initial dip, through better compliance, and through higher economic growth. The times are propitious for such an approach.

There is another insight that the history of the last seven decades has to offer–depreciating one's currency is no help in fixing an external imbalance. The US example also bears this out. In terms of gold prices, the US dollar has fallen from $35 per ounce, to close to $1,300 per ounce in 2016–and the US continues to run persistent deficits. And the US dollar has not weakened just in terms of gold; it has been all over the place against the currencies of its main trading partners, including periods of extended weakness to no avail.

India itself offers a compelling example. A dollar bought Rs 3.21 in 1947, whereas today it is in the range of Rs 69. That is a 20-fold decline, and there has been a similar decline vis-à-vis other currencies as well. Yet, we have run deficits in our balance of trade every year, except two in the 1970s. Indian policy-makers would be well-advised not to work to weaken the Indian Rupee since it will not help our external balance. The current US administration has, to boot, placed India on the watch list for policies that deliberately weaken the Indian Rupee. We have been buying over a billion US dollars per month for the past few years, whether intending to weaken the currency or not. But that has been the effect. And it has not helped our trade balance.

Finally, the inquisitive mind will be struck by the close linkages between the economics and politics. If the Marshall Plan aid divided Europe along the line of cleavage of East and West, the Yom Kippur War served to raise oil prices and the launch of the oil-finance cycle. Similarly, there is fertile ground for inquiry into the gold production and its link to the US dollar, to the US Interest Equalisation Tax, and perhaps even to apartheid. Similarly, the breaking of the oil-finance cycle in the early 1980s led to major pro-democracy movements in South America. The distinction almost universally drawn between the economic and the strategic domains is probably a misleading one–and that is what this essay has tried to demonstrate.

References

1 David S. Painter, 'Oil and the Marshall Plan', The Business History Review, 58 (3) Autumn, 1984, pp. 359-383.

2 Foreign Relations of the United States: Diplomatic Papers 1944, 'The Near East, South Asia, and Africa', The Far East Volume V, Doc 890F. 6363/91, 27 December 1943; and Doc 800. 6363/1515a, 3 March 1944.

3 Foreign Petroleum Policy of the United States: Memorandum by the Inter-Divisional Petroleum Committee of the Department of State, 1944811.6363/4-1144, 11 April 1944.

4 Jon Kimche, Seven Fallen Pillars, Secker & Warburg, London 1953, p. 21.

5 Keith Pilbeam, International Finance, Macmillan, UK, 1998.

6 South Africa Gold Production, https://commons.wikimedia.org/w/index.php?curid=30203661.

7 James Akins, 'The Oil Crisis: This Time the Wolf is Here', Foreign Affairs, April 1973.

8 Foreign Relations of the United States: Foreign Economic Policy: 1969-76, Volume III, 'International Monetary Policy, 1969-72', Document 173 of 1 September 1971.

9 Pilbeam, No. 5, p. 291.

10 Carlo Edoardo Altamura, 'European Banks and the Rise of International Finance: The post-Bretton Woods era' (Kindle Locations 3258-3262), Routledge Explorations in Economic History, Taylor and Francis, Kindle Edition.

11 Paul Volcker, 'The Political Economy of the Foreign Affairs', November 1978, p. 9, https://www.newyorkfed.org/medialibrary/media/research/quarterly_review/1978v3/v3n4article1.pdf.

12 Johannes Wiegand, 'Bank Recycling of Petro Dollars to Emerging Market Economies during the Current Oil Price Boom', IMF Working Papers, 08/180, https://www.imf.org/external/pubs/ft/wp/2008/wp08180.pdf .

13 Valery Giscard d'Estaing, 'New Opportunities and New Challenges', Foreign Affairs, Fall 1983.

14 Altamura, No. 10.

15 Johnson & Kwak, 13 Bankers, Vintage Books, New York 2011, pp. 59–61.

16 China Statistical Yearbook (1996-2006): National Bureau of Statistics of China; quoted in WeishiGu, Titus O Awokuse, Yan Yuan, 'The Contribution of Foreign Direct Investment to China's Export Performance', paper prepared for presentation at the American Agricultural Economics Association Annual Meeting, Orlando, FL, July 2008, p. 28.

17 New York Times, 21 July 2004.

18 China's Central Bank Chief Warns of 'Sudden, Contagious and Hazardous' Financial Risks, Bloomberg News, 4 November 2017, https://www.bloomberg.com/news/articles/2017-11-04/china-s-zhou-warns-on-mounting-financial-risk-in-rare-commentary .

19 Patrick Gillespie and Heather Long, @ CNN Money, 'Janet Yellen invokes China 16 times in 1 hour', 18 September 2015, http://money.cnn.com/2015/09/18/news/economy/china-yellen-global-economy-worry/index.html .

20 Foreign Relations of the United States: 1952-54, Volume I, Part 1, Economic and Political Matters, Document 16, dated 11 December 1952.

21 Foreign Relations of the United States: 1969-76, Volume III Foreign Economic Policy; International Monetary Policy, 1969-72, Document 124, dated 7 May 1969.

The Indian Economy: Casting Away the Structural Chains

Ananth Nageswaran

This paper takes a look at the profound changes to the Indian economy that have taken place since the NDA government came to office in 2014. Some of the policy initiatives such as demonetisation have been controversial not only because of their ham-handed execution, but also because policy signals have been confusing. After the initial hiccups, the country may be settling down with the Goods and Services Tax and with the operation of the Insolvency and Bankruptcy Code that would enable lenders to recover their dues from defaulting borrowers. The government has done well on financial inclusion as the bulk of the population now has bank accounts and uses them too. On the debit side, the recapitalisation of the banking sector was left too late and the crisis was an opportunity to reform the banking system.

That seems to have been missed. Further, the government has to address the policy bias against capital and scale and also the capriciousness of the taxman. Without both, sustainable growth will remain elusive.

A Year of Profound Changes

ON 8 November 2017, the world took note of the first anniversary of the 45th Presidency of the United States of America. India 'celebrated' or debated an anniversary of a different nature. On 8 November 2016, the Government of India had announced the withdrawal of two high-denomination notes–Rupees 500 and Rupees 1000. While there is some disagreement as to whether the withdrawal constitutes demonetisation in the strict sense, the fact is that the stock of these two denominations were demonetised. It was not an end for High Denomination Notes (HDN) in general because these two denominations were replaced with a new set of 500-Rupee and 2,000-Rupee (yes!) denomination notes. These two denominations constituted more than 85 percent of the notes or currency in circulation by value.

Within a few months, the Government of India introduced a much-needed regulatory bill for the Real Estate sector. It notified a legislation for facilitating insolvency and bankruptcy for those who are either unable or unwilling to repay their debt obligations. Then, in July 2017, it introduced a Goods and Services Tax (GST), replacing indirect taxes both in States and in the Union Government with a single GST. Hence, it has been a year of profound and long-lasting changes for the Indian economy. What do they collectively mean for the outlook for the Indian economy?

See-sawing Growth in Three Years

The withdrawal of the specified HDN constituted a huge liquidity shock to the economy, unsurprisingly, as they constituted a huge chunk of the currency in circulation by value. The economic growth rate predictably slowed in the first two quarters of the calendar year 2017. In the 12 months ending June 2017, growth rate of the real Gross Domestic Product (GDP) slowed to 5.7 percent. Statistically, it is impossible to quantify the impact of the withdrawal of the HDN on economic growth. Economic growth had already begun to slow from the 9.1 percent rate attained in the first quarter of 2016. The gradual slowdown in the growth rate from that level was due to a multiplicity of factors.

Before explaining that, we have to acknowledge here that the growth rate climbed from 6.1 percent in the quarter ending December 2014 to a high of 9.1 percent in the quarter ending March 2016, on the back of lower price of crude oil that boosted the government revenues and led to a higher government spending. Part of the effect was, of course, statistical.

In 2015, India's Central Statistical Organisation (CSO) changed the methodology of calculating economic growth, citing the availability of more granular information on businesses and had shifted the base year from 2004-05 to 2011-12. Growth rates from 2011-12 onwards were revised higher. However, due to the non-availability of historical data—CSO is unable to revise historical GDP data for the new base year 2011-12—it is hard to place these growth estimates in the historical context.

Now that we have explained the acceleration from 6.1 percent to 9.1 percent, how did the growth rate come down to 5.7 percent? As stated earlier, there is more than one explanation.

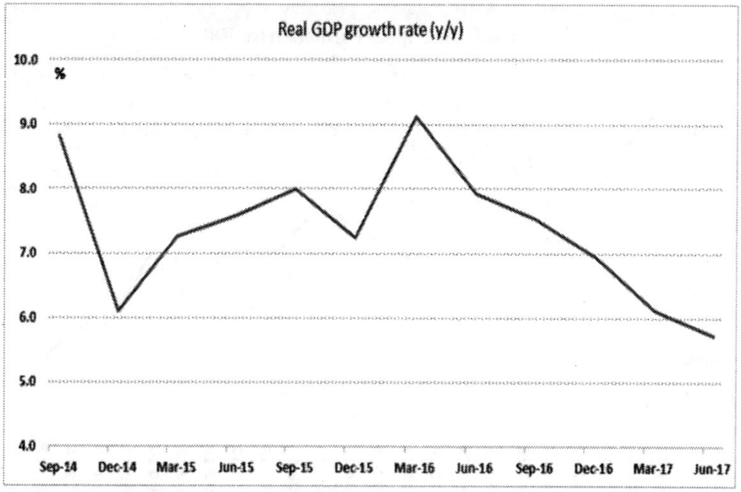

Source: Handbook of Statistics on the Indian Economy, Reserve Bank of India

Global growth had slowed in 2015 and it bottomed out only by mid-2016. Consequently, net exports were a drag on India's economic growth. The base effect of the crash in oil price had disappeared. More importantly, India was hobbled by the twin balance sheet problem. India's corporations were saddled with huge amounts of debt accumulated in the boom years preceding and following 2008, which was the year of the Global Financial Crisis (GFC). Most of these companies were concentrated in the infrastructure sectors–steel, cement, power and lately, telecom. The slowdown in India's economic growth rate from 2011 onwards until 2014 had upended their plans and left them with debt that they could not service. Naturally, they had no appetite for taking on new loans to make green-field investments and create assets on the ground. India's fixed capital formation had slowed from 33.0 percent of GDP in June 2013 to around 25.5 percent of GDP in March 2017.

Since the bulk of the debt had been taken from India's banks which are predominantly government-owned, the

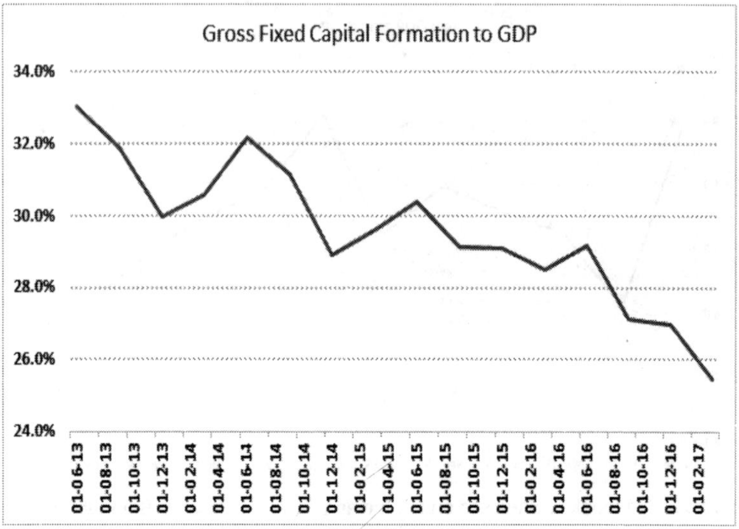

Source: Handbook of Statistics on the Indian Economy, Reserve Bank of India

banking system had been groaning under the burden of non-performing assets (NPA). In some cases, the bank capital had been fully eroded and provisioning was on the lower side. Banks had also resorted to restructuring their loans so that they would be treated as current. Hence, problem-recognition was slow. The Reserve Bank of India ended the official sanction of forbearance and directed banks to account for all their NPA by March 2017. This had the effect of slowing down credit growth in the country. Both demand for and supply of credit was under stress. Private sector banks, which were relatively less affected because they had not lent as much to corporations as government-owned banks had, continued to make personal loans for housing and automobile purchase, and there was a rapid increase in credit card debt. Overall bank credit growth to businesses of all sizes had slowed to a crawl. In general, in recent quarters, government spending and private consumption expenditure had shouldered the task of maintaining economic growth. With export demand absent and private sector investment spending held back by debt concerns, it was no surprise, therefore, that economic growth had decelerated for six quarters up to June 2017.

In the quarter ending September 2017, the economic growth rate, measured in constant 2011-12 prices, improved to around 6.3 percent (y/y). The biggest contributor to the improvement in the GDP growth came from a rebound in manufacturing. Manufacturing growth rebounded to 7 percent from a low of 1.2 percent in the second quarter. But, this is a puzzle considering that the index of industrial production went up only by 2.2 percent in the July-September quarter. Further, the rebound in manufacturing growth without an improvement in India's export performance is another source of anomaly. However, it is possible that India's economic growth is on an improving trajectory from here on. But, the firming trend in the global crude oil prices remains a risk. Another source of risk is correction in asset prices globally. That would undermine confidence and halt global growth in its tracks, snuffing out the chances of recovery in India's exports. However, an end to initial compliance issues with GST and banking recapitalisation can improve the domestic growth impulse. It is possible that the economic growth rate rebounds to between 6.5 percent and 7.0 percent in the coming quarters.

Demonetisation: Upfront Costs & Uncertain Future Benefits

Into this slowing growth dynamic, the government announced its unprecedented banning of HDN in November 2016. It is very difficult to pass a definitive judgement on the success or failure of the exercise because economic benefits, given sufficiently long time, might exceed the costs. However, near-term, the costs easily exceed the benefits. The government spelt out, as its objectives, the curbing of black money, corruption and terrorism. Subsequently, digitisation was added as a goal, more as an after-thought. If the exercise was about making it difficult to store ill-begotten wealth in cash or to use such cash for financing real estate transactions, the introduction and retention of currency note of the denomination of Rupees 2000 defeats the purpose.

It is often claimed that India has a low tax/GDP ratio and that there is a need to increase the tax ratio to meet the development expenditure. But, a quick perusal of World Bank data on this ratio for many developing countries suggests that India is far from being an outlier on this matter. Further, there is plenty of statistics put out by the government on the number of high income tax payers being disproportionately few[1]. However, tax compliance is a two-player game. Tax rates and tax administration matter as much as the tax morality of taxpayers. Internationally, there is evidence that reasonable tax rates and a tax administration that is not coercive or vindictive lead to, over time, enhanced tax compliance and revenues for the government. India has a long way to go with respect to both. According to the 'Ease of Doing Business' survey, India's overall tax incidence at 55.3 percent is among the highest in the world. It used to be above 60 percent until 2017 but the introduction of the GST has brought the tax incidence rate down. However, it is debatable if India's businesses see the benefits of the introduction of the GST yet.

Long Way to Go for GST to become 'GST'

GST, dubbed as the nation-wide 'single indirect tax', was introduced in July 2017. In theory, it should have facilitated the creation of a single market for goods and services in India by eliminating inter-state tax barriers. The initial months since the new tax had been introduced have witnessed considerable confusion, uncertainty and angst especially among small businesses. Not only have there been too many rates but the processes of filing returns and claiming input tax credits have proven to be daunting for many businesses, especially small and medium sized businesses. Further, given that a substantial chunk of daily consumption items have been exempted from the GST, the government has compensated by levying a GST rate of 28 percent on several items. The government has guaranteed a 14 percent compounded increase in annual revenues for five years to State governments, to make them give up their right to levy local sales tax, etc.

The design of the GST has featured an undue concern on ensuring revenue neutrality (that is, the expected revenue from the new tax should not be lower than the projected revenues from the taxes that were being withdrawn) rather than the tax being geared to facilitate enhanced economic activity, ushering in a genuine single market in the country. The consolation is that the government and the GST Council–the body that decides on the GST tax rates comprising State Finance Ministers and the Union Finance Minister–have proven responsive to complaints and have simplified procedures, lowered the rates and have removed exemption limits. However, more work remains to be done to make it a genuinely 'Good and Simple' Tax and a facilitator of a national market in India. But, the general direction appears to be right. However, it is difficult to estimate the growth impact of the original bad design of the tax and the duration of such impact. One can only hope that the damage is limited.

The Bright Side: Financial Inclusion

While the debate continues on the wisdom of demonetisation, its execution and on the design and implementation of the GST, the government seems to have done a good job with two other equally important reforms. One is the Financial Inclusion scheme–banking the unbanked. The '*Pradhan Mantri Jan Dhan Yojana*' (PMJDY) scheme undertaken in the initial months of the current government in 2014 was a massive success in enabling many millions of Indians to have a bank account in their names for the first time in their lives. With that, they will now be able to receive the cash transfers that they are entitled to, under various government schemes and subsidies. The success of the PMJDY in bringing banking services to many Indians will greatly facilitate government's efforts to transfer cash benefits to citizens in lieu of persisting with price-distorting subsidies.

It is similar to the mobile phone connectivity that India achieved for its citizens in the first decade of the millennium. An empirical study ('Bank Accounts for the Unbanked: Evidence from a Big Bang Experiment', May 2017) has shown that the PMJDY accounts are increasingly actively used over time: 'Seventy percent of the accounts migrate out of dormancy into active use. Second, activity levels in the PMJDY accounts increase over time, a pattern not necessarily seen in non-PMJDY accounts. In many specifications, activity increases in the PMJDY accounts relative to non-PMJDY accounts. These findings are especially stark given that non-PMJDY accountholders in our sample appear to be much poorer and have transaction sizes that are one order of magnitude smaller. Finally, we find that the active accounts experience significant increases in cash balances. Government direct benefit transfer aids but does not fully explain their usage. Overall, the data indicate that the unbanked learn by doing, and increase usage of accounts for transactions, liquidity management, and increasingly, balance accumulation.'

More good news is possible out of the successful financial inclusion initiative. Another paper ('Who wants to be an entrepreneur?', May 2016) suggests that 'financial development facilitates economic growth by moving workers out of less productive, informal entrepreneurial activity into formal jobs in more productive firms.' If this were to happen, India could reasonably aspire to resemble the prosperous high growth economies of the West. But it would take time and much more remains to be done to get from here to there. The important and underlying requirement is that productive firms create formal jobs. Unfortunately, it is not happening. It requires fixing two issues. Onc is the issue of non-performing assets (NPA) in the banking system and the other is the absence of dynamism in the formal business sector.

That a scheme like the PMJDY was required after five decades of public sector banking is testimony to the fact that the poorer sections of society were not able to access financial services adequately from the organised financial system. Therefore, if the government was keen to take credit for the successful implementation of the PMJDY, and correctly so, it must be prepared to take the blame for allowing NPAs in public sector banks to fester for three years. May be, just maybe, there is some light at the end of the tunnel now.

Easing the Exit from Debt

The second success of the government is in putting in place a framework for Insolvency and Bankruptcy. That is working well. Cases are being referred to the National Company Law Tribunal which adjudicates on bankruptcy cases. Assets owned by defaulting debtors are quickly disposed of and creditors' claims are settled. Creditors too must take a haircut on their claims and move on, instead of dragging the matter for years, keeping unviable and bad assets at inflated book values without providing for losses. All of this is in the process of becoming history.

Stung by the growth slowdown to 5.7 percent (as discussed earlier), the government has moved to announce a massive bank recapitalisation scheme. It should take care of the substantial portion of the requirements of government-owned banks, provided there is no fresh accretion to their NPA. The government has also announced that it would use the opportunity to strengthen the banking system and banks where the government owns the majority stake. However, Little details are available on that. It would be a pity if the opportunity were missed to recast the Indian banking system owned by the government.

Government ownership plagues governance of these institutions. Prudent commercial considerations seldom inform their lending decisions. Either they lack the skills to assess credit risk correctly or other considerations dictate the creation of bank assets. This is India's third NPA crisis in three decades. Often, crises are the only opportunity to abandon the old and failed ways and usher in desirable changes that strengthen the institutional infrastructure. With bond market developments in the country stymied by both the government's first and large claim on national savings and due to the private sector's penchant for negotiating loans with bankers on favourable terms, it is imperative that the banking sector be reformed and decoupled from the government–both in terms of ownership and management.

Long-term Priorities

The short-term growth setbacks caused by the withdrawal of HDN and the needlessly complicated design and introduction of the Goods and Services Tax may be ironed out over time. The bigger question is the long-run growth outlook. The chart below shows the compounded annual growth rate of Gross National Income per capita over a moving 5-year period. The growth momentum has slowed in recent years.

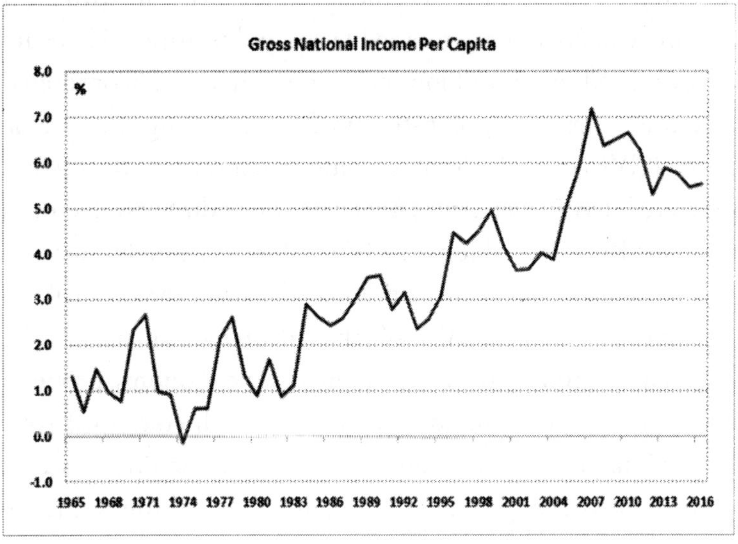

Source: World Bank

The challenge for the government is not only to restore growth but to sustain it. Among many things, it needs to address three things urgently. One is to eliminate the bias against bigness that has plagued Indian policymaking since Independence to the present day and, secondly, it has to ensure that its tax policies do not kill the economy in the process of extracting revenues for the government. The third issue is one of access to capital for small businesses. The government has a role in facilitating it but the responsibility lies with the private sector.

The Anti-big Bias

For that challenge to be met successfully, India needs to tackle the extreme fragmentation of its production–both in farms and factories. India's economic structure in farms and factories is fragmented, inefficient and primitive. The numbers are shocking and beyond belief. India cannot 'make it' with such extremely nano and micro-sized farms and factories. There are an estimated 63.4 million non-agricultural unincorporated enterprises (excluding construction) contributing gross value added (GVA) of Rs 11.5 trillion only. In contrast, only 189,468 registered (with the Annual Survey of Industries) factories generate Rs 11.6 trillion of GVA. More startlingly, just 4.1 percent of them have 500 or more workers and they contribute 60 percent of the GVA of the registered factories. The fragmented production structure makes the economy prone to overheating and stagflation–i.e. lower growth combined with higher inflation. Too few large enterprises in the private sector capture the banking sector. Too many small and unproductive enterprises are unable to respond to demand surges resulting in higher inflation. Current account and trade deficits widen, consequently, bringing pressure on the currency to depreciate. The solution is not to favour the current big firms but to favour potential enterprises becoming big or to encourage firms to start big. But, the policy making in India has an 'anti-big' bias.

The Economic Survey of India, 2012-13, featured a

rigorous discussion on India's demographic dividend and how it could be harnessed for the benefit of the country. That is feasible only if the youth have the right education and skills and can either be entrepreneurial or earn a living through employment. Typically, jobs are created when firms hire more as they grow in size. The shocking fact about India is that, in 35 years of existence, the productivity of a 35-year old firm merely doubles, while its headcount actually falls by a fourth, whereas a company in the United States in the same time period grows ten times, both in terms of operations and employment.[2] This is neither normal nor healthy. Therefore, it is natural for economists and policy makers to examine causes, which are multiple. Labour laws, rules and regulations matter, as do the costs of employing permanent workers, which in itself is a vast topic for discussion, and can't be dealt with justice in this paper.

The following table (figure 2.14) from the World Development Report, 2013, examines policies that encourage or condemn firms to stay small. It illustrates the government incentives dis-incentivising growth.

The Survey notes, 'Schemes and interventions based on tightly defined classifications create an incentive structure that might prevent firms from growing. Service tax exemptions for firms with less than Rupees 10 lakh revenue and exemption from central excise duty for firms with an annual turnover of less than Rupees 1.5 crore are examples of these schemes.'

Fast forward four more years and the newly constituted NITI-Aayog picks up the theme in its latest Enterprise Survey of Indian States on the ease of doing business in India.[3] The survey found that firms with hundred or more employees took significantly longer to get the necessary approvals, faced more regulatory obstacles and higher costs of compliance than

Figure 2.14: Government Incentives Dis-incentivizing Growth (list not exhaustive)

	SCHEME	DISCRIPTION	Availability of Incentives by Size of Organization			
			MICRO	SMALL	MEDIUM	LARGE
Non-Financial incentives	National Manufact. Competitiveness Programme	Assistance aimed at improving processes, design, technology	✔	✔	✔	✘
Non-Financial incentives	Government Purchase and Price Preference Policy for MSEs	358 items reserved for exclusive purchase from MSEs. 20% of annual value of goods and services purchased to be procured from MSEs.	✔	✔	✘	✘
Financial incentives	Credit Linked Capital Subsidy Scheme for Technology Upgrade	15% capital subsidy for Tech. Upgrade on term loan from approved inst.	✔	✔	✘	✘
Financial incentives	Credit Guarantee Fund Scheme for MSEs	Credit guarantee for collateral free loan for loans upto RS. 1 Cr.	✔	✔	✘	✘
Financial incentives	MSE-Cluster Development Programme	Training, tech etc. grant of 75% of project cost Tangible assets and infrastructure: grant of 80% of project cost	✔	✔	✘	✘
Financial incentives	Quality upgradation in MSEs-incentives for certification	Reimburse 75% of ISO cetification expenses (max. Rs. 75K one time)	✔	✔	✘	✘
Financial incentives	Micro Finance Programme	SIDBI supporting NGOs/ Micro Finance institution in providing loans	✔	✘	✘	✘

Source: Ministry of Micro, Small and Medium Enterprises

smaller firms. Tax regulations and environmental clearances were bigger obstacles for firms employing more than ten people. These things make it relatively hard for firms to grow in size.

In fulfilling large export orders, India's smaller factory sizes are big deterrent. A typical textile factory in India has about 150 people whereas a factory in Bangladesh has about 600 people. The Textile Commissioner said recently that India's textile industry would grow to a size of USD $250 billion in two years from the present size of USD $150 billion.[4] It is pertinent to note here that only two textile firms, Alok Industries and Arvind are big. Alok Industries had a turnover of little under USD $2 billion in the year ending March 2016, whereas Arvind had a turnover of around USD $800 million.

This fragmentation can be contrasted with the IT industry where billion dollar firms are numerous.

Importantly, the anti-big bias is in the minds. In a telling observation, an entrepreneur who runs an apparel sourcing company noted that, in China, 'The volumes are so high they do not start out thinking you are a crook. Here, it is exactly the opposite. You can price yourself out or you can time yourself out.'[5] The anti-big mind-set not just among politicians and senior policy makers but also in the operational layers of bureaucracy must be one of the biggest causal factors behind a vast proportion of enterprises remaining pygmies in India. On top of this, in recent years, the penchant of the political leadership to confer short-term (and long-term economically ruinous) fiscal benefits to the poorer segments of the population has meant that terrorism of the taxpayers that used to be the norm up to the Nineties has returned with a bang.

Tax Policies and Economic Activity

A 2015 World Bank paper on tax regimes in South Asia noted that generous corporate tax incentives require a higher tax rate compared to what would have been needed if all firms were subject to the same tax regulations. While tax incentives may benefit the privileged firms, they worsen the overall investment climate and put disproportionate pressure on a narrow range of taxpayers. Often, such tax incentives are offered to less productive firms or activities, dragging overall economic productivity down even as they introduce distortions and send the wrong message to productive and efficient firms.[6]

The policy implications are clear. India needs lower tax rates, higher tax thresholds, and a drastic and rapid elimination of ad-hoc tax exemptions and concessions. The government made a beginning in this direction in the budget for 2016-2017. It announced a gradual reduction in corporate income tax and phase-out of exemptions. The government has been going about it systematically, no doubt. It began by reducing the top corporate tax rate to 29 percent for companies with a revenue of Rupees 5 crore (50 million) in the 2016-17 budget. Further, the lower tax rate was also extended to manufacturing companies that did not avail of exemptions. Simultaneously, a time-table for phasing out exemptions was announced in the 2016-17 budget, in which the 25 percent tax rate was extended to companies with a turnover of less than Rupees 50 crore (500 million). Now, in the 2018-19 budget, the lower marginal tax rate for corporate income was extended to companies with an annual turnover of Rupees 250 crore (2.5 billion) or less. Hence, there has been a systematic approach to lowering the top marginal tax rate for corporate income. That is laudable.

However, two things stand out. One is the perception that the tax regime administration–capriciousness of the taxman–has worsened. Some go as far to say that it feels like the mindset of the 1970s has been brought back, when the taxmen presumed the guilt of the taxpayers to start with. Where does that perception originate? It originates in a few things: the headline-grabbing pursuit of black money, *benami* transactions; headlines on slapping of tax notices and fines on big foreign companies; the information that is being sought on wealth held in the Income-Tax return since the abolition of the wealth tax and its replacement by a surcharge on income tax and the imposition of Cess and Surcharges that make tax calculations complicated and also raise the effective tax rate.

Second, this government has imposed *Krishi Kalyan* cess, *Swachh Bharat* cess, Infrastructure cess, Clean Energy cess and in the budget presented on February 2018, it unified the cess on Primary and Secondary Education into a 'Health and Education' cess and raised the rate from 3 percent to 4 percent. What the government had sought to give away on the one hand through lower tax rates and higher personal tax exemption thresholds has been recouped through the levy of cess and surcharges. They are also cumbersome to calculate and they enhance the perception of harassment.

Perhaps, some of this has to do with the Economic Survey of 2015-16 that noted that, controlling for democracy and per capita GDP, India only had 4 percent of its citizens paying taxes whereas the proportion should be 23 percent. True, it takes two to tango and some taxpayers might be intrinsically opposed to the idea of paying taxes. They may go to any length to avoid paying taxes or even evade them. This has made tax collection a game of one-upmanship between the government and the citizen–as to who can go to what length to collect or to avoid paying taxes. The result is needless complexity and intimidating tax collection process.

The fact that GST had to be amended comprehensively within four months of introduction is an implicit admission that, in its initial design, it represented the triumph of the moral police and that of the bean counter. On 9 November 2016–the day after the Prime Minister had announced the withdrawal of HDN, we had noted, 'short-term liquidity squeeze could be severe and hence economic activity could suffer. Further, with the eventual design of the GST looking more complicated than originally envisaged and with the timelines getting shorter, uncertainty could be compounded. That risk is non-trivial. That is why the GST should have been more concerned with simplicity, ease of use and implementation rather than revenue considerations. Bold thinking was always needed and more so, in the light of this announcement.'

Tax is a contract between the citizen and the State. To a large extent, accountability and effectiveness in the utilisation of tax money for development purposes would go a long way in improving compliance. Second, with the availability of technology and with improvements in the field of data analytics, the government can afford to be trusting because it can also verify better than it used to be able to, if the trust is being exploited or taken advantage of. Put differently, the tax department can make self-compliance the norm and intervene in exceptional cases, dictated by the information at its disposal. Successful policymaking is as much about entrepreneurship and risk-taking as commercial businesses are. Crucially, it is also about finding the right balance between enabling and policing. The government must bet on economic activity and not on economic policing. A reasonable tax regime that is non-vindictive and non-usurious in its administration is the need of the hour in India.

Access to Working Capital

We should bear in mind that the problem of unproductive micro and small enterprises is not merely on account of government policies and attitudes in the government against size but it is also because the private corporate sector denies working capital to their small suppliers. The unequal balance of power between corporate buyers and small suppliers ensures that the latter are at the mercy of the former for payments against supplies. That often does not come on time and even palms have to be greased to get payments released. If the buyer is monopsony, then the supplier's bargaining position is even weaker. Nor can they afford to pursue legal remedies against recalcitrant corporate customers. Such remedies will be costly, protracted and may ruin the business too. 'Factoring' is the answer. SME suppliers discount their receivables and bills of exchange with banks who buy them (with or without recourse to the SME, in the event of non-payment) at a discount and then collect the proceeds from the corporate buyer.

The idea was included in the report of the Raghuram Rajan Committee on Financial Sector Reforms in 2008. Then, the RBI appointed a working group which submitted its report in November 2009. In 2014, the RBI issued a concept paper. Draft guidelines were issued followed by final guidelines. Receivables Exchange of India (RXIL), India's first Trade Receivables Discounting System (TReDS) started operating only in January 2017. The time taken underscores the glacial pace at which crucial reforms that would lift the economy on to a higher growth path are pursued. The world over, on providing working capital to small suppliers, things are moving much faster.[7]

Six months after its commencement in January 2017, hurdles to the smooth of functioning of the RXIL are emerging. Companies are wary of uploading invoices lest competitors come to know about their suppliers. Second, this is important, 'since TReDS is a transparent system, they (companies) necessarily would have to settle the suppliers' invoices within 45 days of acceptance of goods/services rendered'. The government deserves credit for insisting that public sector enterprises should mandatorily register themselves in the TReDS platform. It has done so as part of its recent policy package on recapitalisation of banks and on infrastructure investment. The government and the RBI must find ways to drag the private sector to be part of the platform such that one of the biggest hurdles that prevent small firms from growing is removed.

Converting Potential into Sustained Performance

On 16 November 2017, Moody's Investor Services upgraded India's sovereign credit rating from Baa3 to Baa2. It is the first rating upgrade for India in fourteen years.[8] In doing so, Moody's recognised the importance of bank credit growth for India's growth story and the significance of the government's decision to recapitalise banks. Importantly, Moody's said that India's public debt profile was unlikely to deteriorate. That is a statement of confidence on India's future growth trajectory. That reinforces what the International Monetary Fund had noted too. As part of its annual consultations and assessment of its member countries, the Fund publishes the 'Article IV' report. It projects the public debt and deficits of member countries as part of the exercise. India's public debt and deficit profile over the next several years is in sharp contrast to China's profile. See the tables below. They tell their own story.

The table for **China**:

Memorandum Items	2012	2013	2014	2015	2016	2017*	2018*	2019*	2020*	2021*	2022*
Nominal GDP (bn RMB)7/	54,099	59,696	64,718	69,911	74,631	81,344	81,364	95,919	104,067	112,608	121,482
Augmented debt (% GDP)8/	44.1	48.1	52.3	58.2	62.2	68.1	73.2	78.1	83.1	87.6	91.5
Augmented net lending/ borrwing (%GDP)8/	-5.1	-7.6	-7.2	-8.4	-10.4	-10.6	-10.8	-11.1	-11.2	-11	-10.7
Augmented fiscal balance (%GDP)9/	-7.8	-10.3	-9.8	-10.2	-12.4	-12.6	-12.6	-12.6	-12.6	-12.3	-11.9

*Projected figures

Source: People's Republic of China 2017 Article IV consultation—press release; staff report; and statement by t executive director for the People's Republic of China, International Monetary Fund, August 2017 (Table 1, page 4

The table for **India:**

Fiscal position (% GDP)	2012/13	2013/14	201415	2015/16	2016/17*	2017/18*	2018/19*	2019/20*	2020/21*	2021/22*
Central government balance 4/	-5.1	-4.6	-4.2	-4.1	-3.8	-3.7	-3.5	-3.3	-3.0	-2.8
Central government balance 4/	-7.5	-7.6	-7.3	-7.0	-6.8	-6.6	-6.2	-5.8	-5.5	-5.2
Central government debt 5/	69.1	68.0	68.3	69.8	69.7	68.6	66.9	64.8	62.7	60.5

*Projected figures

Source: India 2017 Article IV consultation—press release; staff report; and statement by the executive director for India, International Monetary Fund, February 2017 (Table 7, page 62.

As for the growth outlook, given India's demographic advantage and the substantial scope for productivity improvement in India's fragmented farm and factory sectors, it should be possible to grow the economy at a nominal rate of around 12 percent annually for over a decade or more. However, it won't come easily. The government can facilitate that by focusing on liberalising higher education, on reducing corporate taxes as promised and by actually recapitalising banks. Of course, addressing some of the issues identified earlier such as continued simplification of GST would help. Notwithstanding these, India faces more challenges than East Asian nations faced in their development phase.

Conclusion

In the twentieth century, success stories of economic development were to be found in East Asia and they rode the manufacturing wave, producing for the advanced world. Whether India can hope to repeat it is a question that is not answered easily. Trade protectionism is on the rise and global growth, on average, has slowed. With aging populations, productivity in the western world is on the decline. Information technology industry, which has been India's growth engine in the first decade of the new millennium, is undergoing profound transformation. Further, the advent of robotics and artificial intelligence has unpredictable consequences for reviving the manufacturing sector. Among other things, it raises a different set of skill demands on the population. Education has to be re-thought. Then, there are health and environment concerns. Recent pollution level in the national capital underscores the enormity of the challenges that India faces on both the fronts. Therefore, successful economic development and the achievement of middle-income status in the twenty-first century are arguably considerably more difficult than they were in the previous two centuries. Hence, the burden on the political leadership today is immeasurably greater than it has ever been. Not only should they sustain their focus and energies, but also keep themselves open to honest and competent advice. That is what would increase the chances of the government prioritising and addressing the right issues which have been discussed in this note.

Tamil sage, Thiruvalluvar, had dedicated one chapter (10 couplets or 'Kural', from 441 to 450) to the idea of surrounding oneself with wise men, who would keep the kings grounded and ensure they ruled the kingdom well, in the interests of the subjects. Four of his couplets are translated as follows:

A king wise enough to have men of greater wisdom than he to advise him shall be a powerful ruler. (Kural 444)

Where the king's counsellors possess the courage to reprove him, when necessary, nothing on earth can bring about such a king's ruin. (Kural 447)

Without courageous counsellors to point out his faults and so protect him, a king will ruin himself, even without foes. (Kural 448)

It is foolish surely to incur enmity of many foes, but 10 times worse to lose righteous friends. (Kural 450)

References

1 Arun Jaitley, Union Budget Speech 2017-18, 1 February 2017, available at http://indiabudget.nic.in/ub2017-18/bs/bs.pdf .

2 World Development Report 2013 (World Bank) cited in "Comparison of Labour Laws: Select Countries", Occasional Paper No. 160, Export-Import Bank of India, August 2013.

3 NITI Aayog & IDFC Institute, 2017, Ease of Doing Business–An Enterprise Survey of Indian States, Executive Summary and Chapter 9 August 2017.

4 Economic Times, India Times, 2017, Textile Industry Size to Touch $250 Billion in 2 Years, Says Official, 4 July 2017 (http://economictimes.indiatimes.com/articleshow/59443523.

5 Jacob, R., 2016, Will Garment Factories Move to Vietnam?, Business Standard, 2 March 2016 (http://www.business-standard.com/article/opinion/rahul-jacob-will-garment-factories-move-to-vietnam-116030201031_1.html)

6 Reva, A., 2015, Toward a More Business Friendly Tax Regime: Key Challenges in South Asia, Policy Research Working Paper 7513, Equitable Growth, Finance and Institutions Global Practice Group, The World Bank Group.

7 https://www.economist.com/news/finance-and-economics/21730150-squeezed-suppliers-and-big-corporate-buyers-stand-benefit-technology

8 https://www.moodys.com/research/Moodys-upgrades-Indias-government-bond-rating-to-Baa2-from-Baa3--PR_374998

Food Security and Farmers' Livelihoods

Suhas P Wani and Dhirendra Singh

To address the agrarian crises, Honourable Prime Minister of India has given a clarion call to double the farmers' income by 2022. A National Workshop was conducted at Vivekananda International Foundation (VIF), New Delhi, on 15 and 16 March 2017, jointly organized by ICRISAT, VIF and TAFE. Based on the recommendations from the workshop deliberations, KISAN-MITrA initiative for doubling the farmers' incomes was launched as a pilot project in Vidarbha region of Maharashtra and Bundelkhand region of Uttar Pradesh. Adopting holistic, science-led, value chain approach based on the ago-ecological potential and market information has been recommended for doubling the farmers' incomes. ICRISAT-led consortium has identified pilots of 5000 ha in each of the 18 targeted districts in Maharashtra and Uttar Pradesh. The consortium of public-

private institutions and corporates along with State Agricultural Universities are being formed to empower the farmers for doubling their incomes.

India can be a Powerhouse of Growth

INDIA, with 142 million hectares of arable land in 137 million farm households, with 46 of the 60 soil types in the world, along with 15 agro-climatic zones, varying from arid to humid tropics, hot arid deserts to cold deserts, and a varying annual rainfall–as high as 11,873 mm at Mawsynram, Meghalaya, to as low as 166 mm at Jaisalmer, Rajasthan–provides great opportunity to become powerhouse of growth to achieve food, nutrition and income security for the 1.3 billion plus population, leading to stable national security. India is the largest producer of spices, pulses, milk, tea, cashew and jute; and is the second largest producer of wheat, rice, fruits, vegetables, sugarcane, cotton and oilseeds. Agriculture remains the livelihood for 56 percent of the Indian population, with an average land holdings of 1.16 ha, with 85 percent of the holdings belonging to small and marginal farmers (< 2 ha land holding). The marginal and small farmers contribute to 55 percent of the total food grain production and 65 percent in fruits and vegetables. Inspite of these remarkable figures, agriculture contributes only 16 to 17 percent to the national Gross Domestic Product (GDP) value. However, 55 percent of the total cultivated area is still under rain-fed agriculture. With the stagnant growth rate of 3.1 percent, achieving food, nutrition and income security for the ever-growing population in India remains a major concern. The Prime Minister of India has envisioned doubling the farmers' income by 2022. A national workshop on Doubling Farmer's Income KISAN–MITrA (Knowledge-based Integrated Sustainable Agriculture Network–Mission India for Transforming Agriculture) through scaling-up was conducted at Vivekananda International Foundation in March 2017. The key strategy for doubling the farmers' income by 2022, and for reducing rural poverty, is to produce the food that market needs through agriculture as a business approach and to enhance the usage efficiency of scarce water resources, which have significantly fallen in sixty years–from a high of 5,177 m^3 in 1951 to 1,820 m^3 in 2011 per capita–with an alarmingly projected dwindling per capita availability of 1,341 m^3 in 2025 and 1,140 m^3 by 2050.

Changing climate, increasing weather variability, changing food habits, water scarcity and land degradation pose severe challenges for food and nutritional security for India's growing population. By reducing the cost of cultivation, increasing productivity and getting remunerative market prices for farmers through appropriate market linkages, and reduced post-harvest losses and risks, would result in increased individual incomes and, therefore, reduced poverty in the farming community.

The large-scale adoption with enabling institutions and policies would aid integrated science-led approaches, imbedded with public-private-producer partnerships. Together, this multi-disciplinary team, through partnerships, can implement and monitor the progress of doubling farmers' income in each state of India.

Goal

The overall goal of the March 2017 National Workshop was to improve the livelihoods of farmers by doubling their income in order to overcome the challenges faced by the farming community in India.

Objectives of the Workshop

- To brainstorm the challenges, opportunities, innovations, enabling policies, institutions and strategy for doubling farmers' income in different agro-eco regions of India;
- To develop a framework, including implementation strategy and monitoring and evaluation, for unlocking the potential of agriculture in India to double farmers' income;
- To prepare a blueprint strategy for the Vidarbha region of Maharashtra and for the Bundelkhand region of Uttar Pradesh as an exemplar; and
- To identify the potential consortium partners and funding agencies for implementing the pilot projects, with holistic strategy for doubling farmers' income in target regions of Maharashtra and Uttar Pradesh.

Expected outputs

- To distil the document on challenges, opportunities, innovations, enabling institutions and policies needed to unlock the potential of Indian agriculture for doubling farmers' income to improve farmers' welfare.
- Come up with a detailed strategy for implementing the innovations, along with monitoring and evaluation mechanisms, and institutional mechanisms for scaling-up the Vidarbha and Bundelkhand pilots.
- Identify potential private partners to fund as well as implement the Vidarbha and Bundelkhand pilots as a model for scaling-up.
- Provide a summary on the recommendations for the policy-makers and proceedings of the workshop as a reference for doubling farmers' income.

To begin with, a pilot for Vidarbha region of Maharashtra and Bundelkhand region of Uttar Pradesh as 'sites of learning' were proposed. With vagaries of climate, there is a need to develop agro-eco-region, specific climate resilient agri-food systems through moisture-conservation practices along with a watershed development programme that involves the use of check dams, storage structures, field bunds, gully plugs and gabions, and other soil and water conservation structures to help make a difference in the regions.

The introduction of climate-resilient food systems as per the agro-eco-region potential, such as millets-pulses based and other climate-smart crop systems, and allied practices, such as horticulture, fisheries, livestock etc., to help the farmers to realise better net incomes are required as adaptation measures to cope with impacts of climate change and a growing water scarcity in the country. Also, introduction of mechanisation and hassle-free financial support, marketing facilities and inputs support in convergence mode (single window system) and collective action through Farmer Producer Organizations (FPOs), for increasing profitability for the farmers are proposed. Creating awareness about health and nutritional benefits of crops like millets, pulses, vegetables and fruits, through effective mass and local media, to bring change in the consumer preferences and promotion of value-addition through entrepreneurship development through collectivisation (SHGs, NGOs, FPOs) are the key strategies for both these regions.

The use of technology and tools that help with agro-eco-region-based land use planning and weather-based Agro Met advisory services help the farmer chose the right crop for the right area and also help reduce the weather and market related risks.

The use of improved drought-tolerant cultivars, improved rainwater conservation and its efficient use, integrated pest management (IPM), crop diversification with vegetables, post-harvest systems, mechanisation and use of Information Communication Technology (ICT) in agriculture, along with value chain approach and market linkages, can also help achieve double farmers' income in these regions. The use of plant tissue culture, genomics and marker-assisted breeding and genetically modified (GM) technology can also play a role in increasing productivity, food security and income for the farmers in these regions. Most importantly, bridging the yield gaps through scaling-up of integrated and science-led innovations, to increase productivity and reducing cost of production, along with value-chain approach with market linkages, would help in increasing profitability for doubling the farmers' income. This new way of doing farming that produces what market needs will help as a business model to be developed.

Subsequent to the March 2017 National Workshop, doubling farmer's income activities have been initiated in both Vidarbha and Bundelkhand regions. The following sections highlight the progress made in these two regions and the interventions implemented since Rabi 2017.

Bundelkhand Region

In the Bundelkhand region of Uttar Pradesh, nearly 70 percent of the population is dependent on agriculture and allied sectors, such as livestock-based activities for their livelihoods. Approximately 33 percent of total geographical area is covered by degraded forest, grazing land and wasteland (UPWSRP, 2001).The Bundelkhand region is a hot spot of water scarcity, land degradation and is vulnerable to climate variability. A diverse cropping system is followed in the region.

Groundnut, black gram, sesame, millets, pigeon-pea and mentha are the main crops cultivated during *Kharif*, whereas wheat, chickpea, barley, mustard and lentils are grown during *Rabi* season.

Due to uncertain and erratic rainfall, poor groundwater recharge, high temperature, agricultural productivity in this region is very poor (0.2 to 2.0 tonne per ha). Most of the areas are cropped singly under rain-fed conditions. In addition, in absence of water and fodder availability, especially during summer, milch animals, especially cows, are left abandoned, which leads to the *Anna Pradha* system. Due to *Anna Pradha*, a large number of animals are left unattended in different villages. This creates problems for the farmers as they graze openly into the fields. Due to this, farmers are forced to leave their field fallow in the *Kharif* season despite having moderate to good rainfall. Farmers are largely dependent on *Rabi* crops, as wheat and chickpea are their staple food as well. Important crops and yield levels in the Bundelkhand region are listed in Table 1.

Large Yield Gaps to be Bridged

Important crops in the Bundelkhand region show low yield levels compared to state and national levels (Table 1), indicating large yield gaps, which could be reduced with science-led holistic farmer centric interventions.

Weather Variability and Climate Change

An area of about 581,000 ha in Uttar Pradesh under semi-arid moist climate has shifted towards drier side–both semi-arid dry and typic-arid climates.

Jalaun and Jhansi districts have witnessed great changes in their climate types. Jalaun district has lost all its 2,33,000 ha of semi-arid moist areas to become drier and added 1,67,000 ha

Table 1: Important crops and yield levels - Bundelkhand

Crop	Region	Year 2014- 2015				Yield (kg/ha)	
		Area (Lakh ha)	Per-cent to India	Produc-tion (Lakh tonnes)	Per-cent to India	2014 - 15	2010 to 2014 Mean
Rice	**Bundelkhand**	**0.70**	**0.16**	**1.14**	**0.11**	**1481***	**1480***
	Uttar Pradesh	58.7	13.4	122	11.7	2082	2293
	India	439	100	1048	100	2390	2380
Maize	**Bundelkhand**	**0.22**	**0.24**	**0.22**	**0.09**	**1318***	**1650***
	Uttar Pradesh	7.1	7.69	12.8	5.39	1791	1662
	India	92.6	100	237	100	2557	2563
Pearl	**Bundelkhand**	**0.32**	**0.45**	**0.28**	**0.31**	**882***	**1050***
	Uttar Pradesh	9.5	13.4	18.1	20	1899	1877
	India	71.2	100	90.5	100	1272	1181
Sorghum	**Bundelkhand**	**0.62**	**1.17**	**0.58**	**1.15**	**854***	**1065***
	Uttar Pradesh	1.6	3.1	1.6	3.23	994	
	India	53	100	50.5	100	953	
Sorghum	**Bundelkhand**	**0.56**	**1.51**	**0.12**	**0.43**	**281***	**769***
	Uttar Pradesh	2.9	7.74	1.7	6.26	606	899
	India	37.1	100	27.8	100	750	731
Pigeon-pea	**Bundelkhand**	**0.54**	**1.15**	**0.41**	**0.63**	**713***	**813***
	Uttar Pradesh	1	2.09	0.8	1.28	857	948
	India	46.8	100	65.6	100	1400	1378
Groundnut	**Bundelkhand**	**2.25**		**0.47**		**164***	**165***
Sesamu	**Bundelkhand**	**8.73**	**2.83**	**12**	**1.35**	**1309***	**2181***
Wheat	Uttar Pradesh	98.5	31.8	252	28.4	2561	2988
	India	309	100	889	100	2872	3060
Chickpea	**Bundelkhand**	**3.7**	**4.52**	**0.85**	**1.19**	**304***	**770***
	Uttar Pradesh	5.6	6.81	3.8	5.31	683	948
	India	81.9	100	71.7	100	875	939
Barley	**Bundelkhand**	**0.45**		**0.67**		**1531***	**2231***
Lentils	**Bundelkhand**	**1.51**		**0.4**		**299***	**602***

*Simple mean of 7 districts yield (kg/ha)

area to semi-arid dry type climate. It is challenging to see that an area of 66,000 ha has shifted to typic-arid climate from the semi-arid moist climate. Perhaps, this is the first time that 'typic-arid' climate is seen in the Jalaun district. Hamirpur district has also witnessed about 2,000 ha area of typic-arid climate. Jhansi district shows a large shift of an area of 2,13,000 ha of semi-arid moist type to semi-arid dry type climate. Lalitpur and Chitrakoot districts also show increasing dryness. Out of seven districts, only two districts–Mahoda and Banda–show slight increase in wetness. Identifying and promoting suitable climate-resilient crops, cultivars and management practices are must for doubling farmers' incomes.

Water Scarcity

Long-term data show that annual average rainfall decreased from 950 mm, during the 30-year period of 1944-1973, to an average of 847 mm during the next 30-year period of 1974-2004. This reduction was mainly due to decreased number of low (0-10 mm) and medium rainfall (30-50 mm) events. Similarly, the total number of rainy days in a year has also decreased. As a result, groundwater levels in open/dug wells (4-8 m deep) depletes rapidly after the monsoon and local communities suffer from water scarcity, especially in summer. The region has experienced severe drought conditions in the last six out of ten years. Promoting low-cost water harvesting, as per the water-balance approach, while considering topography, soil type and land use at the pilot sites, with improvement in the water-use efficiency, are considered as important strategies for drought proofing.

Widespread Land Degradation

Land degradation is a major challenge for increasing productivity in the Bundelkhand region. As in other drylands, in addition to macro nutrients, the deficiencies of micro and secondary nutrients have emerged, which need to be addressed. The key issues include: Detailed diagnosis of soil fertility constraints; rejuvenating degrading soils; soil C-building; and policies to promote soil test-based integrated nutrient management and streamlining soil-plant-water diagnostic services. For example, none of the laboratories in the Bundelkhand region is equipped to analyse 'B' in soil. Similarly, Jalaun, Hamirpur and Chitrakoot laboratories are not equipped to analyse other micronutrients as well.

Fitting in Suitable Varieties and Cropping Systems

The cropping intensity of this region is averaging approximately 110 percent, with predominance of single cropping, grown completely under rain-fed conditions. There is a need to shift towards climate-resilient, low-water requiring, crops and varieties. Crop intensification in Bundelkhand will be intended to give a wider choice in the production of a variety of crops in a given area so as to expand production related activities on various crops and also to reduce risk. Ensuring availability of high quality seeds of high-yielding crops cultivars, through on-farm seed production, is the key.

System Context Productivity

Looking at crops in isolation is not the right strategy; instead improving the system productivity should be the strategy. The key components, with wide scope,include an improvement in the livestock productivity, horticulture, agro-forestry and other livelihood options. Livestock plays a very important role in Bundelkhand, as more than 50 percent households in the region have *milch* animals (cows or buffaloes) or small ruminants.

However, milk productivity from these animals is very poor (2-5 Litres/day). Fodder availability during the post-monsoonal season declines drastically, especially during the dry years and, therefore, promoting quality annual/perennial fodder is one low-hanging technology among other interventions. Agro-forestry and horticulture has great potential for higher and sustained crop production and farm income. There is good scope to promote low-water requiring trees (*babool*, *teak*, *amla, jamun, tamarind, etc.*) and shrubs (*ber*, *karanda, etc.*) for addressing nutritional security and generating additional income with available resources without much investments.

Value-addition and Marketing

The key challenge and opportunity of the project is to identify and develop select value-added products specific to the region and establish market linkages with urban and semi-urban niche markets. Farm level processing is an opportunity to enhance farmers' incomes. Collectivisation of producers to harness synergies is the proposed pathway.

ICT and Extension System

In the Bundelkhand region, the extension system has limited penetration due to lack of sufficient grass root level extension functionaries to work at village level. Along with human resources, the major concern is lack of trained human power at grass root level for ensuring effective extension services. ICT is a promising option to monitor and evaluate day-to-day activities and strengthen the capacity of local extension agents by providing easy access to required information.

Seeing is Believing

There are isolated success stories, but for the implementation, there need to be 'sites of learning' in each district of the operational model for increasing productivity and farmers' income.

Following a meeting held under the Chairmanship of Agriculture Production Commissioner at Jhansi on 27 May 2017, the ICRISAT-led consortium has initiated interventions in the Bundelkhand region's seven districts (Lalitpur, Jhansi, Jalaon, Hamirpur, Mahoba, Banda and Chitrakoot). For operationalisation of the initiative, the team has been in touch with the DoA officials and other stakeholders regularly. In this context, a multi-disciplinary team of scientists has frequently visited the region.

Representative Pilot Sites & Enabling Institutions

Following a meeting with all the concerned officers in Lucknow on 4 May 2017 and meeting with the Agriculture Production Commissioner (APC), enabling institutions at State i.e. State Level Co-ordination Committee (SLCC) chaired by the APC, were formed. For convergence of primary sector activities in all the districts, district level coordination committees (DLCCs), chaired by District Magistrate (DM), were formed vide Government Order, dated 1 October 2017. A meeting of the officials from all seven districts was held by the APC and PS on 31 October 2017 at Jhansi.

The ICRISAT team between 28 May and 3 June 2017 identified pilot sites in seven target districts after discussions with different stakeholders, including JDAs, DDAs, AOs and farmers in all districts (Ref. Table 2 and Photo 1).

Table 2. Representative pilot sites across 7 districts in Bundelkhand

District	Pilot Block	Tentative Selected Villages	Cropping Pattern
Lalitpur	Talbehat	Poora-Birdah	Groundnut, Blackgram, Maize (kharif season- K); Peas, Wheat, Mustard (Rabi season-R)
Jhansi	Babina	Imiliya, Raja Kheda, Bachhauni, Rajapur, Raska, Taidol & Tiletha, Baral	Groundnut, Mungbean, Blackgram, (K); Wheat, Chickpea, Mustard (R)
Jalaun	Mahiva	Hydalpur, Noorpur, Naserpur	Peas, Mentha, vegetables (K); Wheat, chickpea (R)
Hamlr-pur	Sumerpur	Nazarpur, Sumerpur	Mustard, wheat, sesame (R)
Mahoba	Charkari	Chandopura, Nathupura, Patehpura Bajaria,	Peas, Blackgram, sesame (K); Wheat (R)
Banda	Thindwari	Palra, Benda, Thind-wari,	Pigeonpea, sesame (K); Chickpea, lentil, peas, wheat (R)
Chitra-koot	Karwi	Gowda, Rowli Kalyanpur	Munbean, Pigeonpea, sesame (K); Wheat, peas, chickpea, Lentil (R)

Photo 1. Discussions between ICRISAT scientists and DDAs/officials for pilot sites identification and project implementation

Soil Sampling and Analysis

During the field visit, stratified soil samples were collected from farmers' fields in pilot sites and analysed in the state-of-the-art laboratory at ICRISAT.

Tables 3a and 3b summarise the results of the analyses on soil samples recovered from the Bundelkhand region. Photo 2 illustrates the soil sampling work undertaken in the field.

The results indicate the farmers' field are widely degraded in soil organic 'C' (Nitrogen depletion) and available nutrients. Available 'P' deficiency was observed in soil samples sourced from four out of the seven districts and, similarly, 'K' deficiency was observed in soil samples from three out of the seven districts.

By contrast, there are widespread deficiencies of secondary nutrient 'S' (50%-100% deficient fields) and micronutrients Zn (33%-100%) and 'B' (0%-88%). There are emerging deficiencies of micronutrients like Fe (0%-100% deficient fields) and Mn (0%-50% deficient fields). Farmers are not aware of secondary and micro nutrient deficiencies and do not add these nutrients into their fields. However, a systematic detailed soil health mapping is to be undertaken to look into more detailed findings and spatial variability from field to field.

Table 3a. Soil fertility status of farmers' fields in Bundelkhand region - % deficient fields

	Percent Fields With Low Org C	Percent Fields Deficient in Available Nutrient Contents									
District	**OC**	**P**	**K**	**Ca**	**Mg**	**S**	**Zn**	**B**	**Fe**	**Cu**	**Mn**
Lalitpur	**50**	**75**	0	0	0	**75**	**100**	**75**	**100**	0	50
Jhansi	13	0	**50**	0	0	**88**	**63**	**88**	0	0	0
Jalaon	**100**	29	0	0	0	**100**	**100**	**71**	29	0	0
Hamirpur	**75**	0	0	0	0	**100**	**100**	0	75	0	25
Mahoba	25	**50**	**75**	0	0	**50**	**75**	25	25	0	25
Banda	**83**	0	0	0	0	**100**	33	17	17	0	**50**
Chitra-koot	**75**	**50**	25	0	0	**100**	**75**	**75**	25	0	25

Table 3b. Soil fertility status of farmers' fields in Bundelkhand region–average soil parameters

Available Nutrient Contents (mg / kg)													
				P	**K**	**Ca**	**Mg**	**S**	**Zn**	**B**	**Fe**	**Cu**	**Mn**
Lalitpur	8.12	0.17	0.50	4.42	122	4038	357	5.64	0.30	0.48	3.10	0.73	2.15
Jhansi	7.60	0.15	0.75	10.82	102	2356	333	6.35	0.76	0.38	9.00	1.04	9.22
Jalaon	7.71	0.14	0.35	6.17	172	2777	416	5.39	0.34	0.52	4.49	0.72	9.53
Hamirpur	8.46	0.17	0.41	17.97	143	2057	513	5.29	0.42	0.84	4.77	1.28	2.31
Mahoba	8.49	0.32	0.59	4.66	59	2245	366	19.61	0.46	0.56	6.13	0.99	5.39
Banda	7.95	0.13	0.37	9.77	205	3185	809	4.44	0.70	0.61	7.49	1.03	5.34
Chitra-koot	7.98	0.16	0.40	5.28	85	1682	303	6.44	0.53	0.37	8.72	0.95	13.86

Photo 2. Selection of soil sampling from farmers' fields across 7 districts in Bundelkhand

Partnerships with NGOs and Research Institutes

In order to reach out to a large number of farmers in 5,000 ha pilot sites across seven districts and harness the synergies of regional/national partners, the ICRISAT mapped and reached out for potential partnerships. Between 28 June 2017 and 2 July 2017, the team identified five NGO partners to support the implementation of the KISAN MITrA initiative across the seven districts in Bundelkhand.

The ICRISAT team has also taken into loop national prominent institutes, such as CAFRI and IGFRI, for collective working and interacted with the ICAR-CAFRI Director, Dr OP Chaturvedi, and the Principal Scientist, Dr RV Kumar, in IGFRI, which they agreed in principle. A consortium of IT service-providing companies as well as other corporate partners is being formed to work in both the pilot states.

Orientation & Farmer Meetings for *Rabi* 2017-18

To implement the selected need-based interventions during *Rabi* 2017-18, a team of scientists visited the districts, between 8 and 15 October 2017, and oriented the NGO partners and farmers through meetings at pilot sites about the protocols of participatory trials and demonstrations (Photo 3).

Photo 3. Farmer meetings in villages across 7 districts in Bundelkhand

Participatory Trials during *Rabi* 2017-18

As entry point interventions, the ICRISAT has arranged to provide drought tolerant chickpea (JG 11) seeds, deficient secondary and micronutrients (zinc, sulphate, borax), PGP cum nutrients (aquasap) for participatory trials and demonstrations in the pilot sites.

Table 4. Detail of trials initiated in pilots across seven districts in Bundelkhand

District	No of trials initiated	Villages
Lalitpur	32	Poora-Birdah
Jhansi	60	Imiliya, Rajapur, Raska, Taidol & Tiletha, Baral
Jalaun	46	Naserpur,
Hamirpur	24	Kalla, Viharevar, Kalimati, Saukar, Simnaudi, Dhanpura
Mahoba	30	Chandpur, Nathopura
Banda	60	Palra, Benda
Chitrakoot	53	Gowda, Rauli Kalyanpur,
Total in Bundelkhand	**305**	

Trials were initiated in pilots across all seven districts. The details of the current trials held on 25 October 2017 are summarised in Table 4.

Photo 4 shows farmers' participatory demonstration on improved chickpea cultivar (JG 11) along with balanced fertiliser application and intercrop with mustard in Bundelkhand.

Interventions in Pipeline

Taking into account the short sowing window, mechanisation is to be piloted on the sites on sharing basis.

- Zero till crop planters are ordered and are to be placed soon, one in each pilot.
- Recycling of wastes is to be promoted through aerobic composting for building soil 'C'. This has advantage to start the composting process as and when required and as per water availability.

This proposal is targeted to showcase the science-led innovations and technologies, aimed to double the farmers' income, and strengthening of the ecosystem services for achieving agricultural sustainability of the Bundelkhand region of Utter Pradesh.

Major growth engines that will come into picture are listed as under:

- Soil-test based integrated nutrient management and soil C-building through recycling wastes;
- Rainwater conservation (including de-silting of existing structure and renovation of traditional water bodies);
- Mechanisation through custom hiring centres (CHCs);
- High yielding, nutritious and drought/climate-resilient crops/cultivars;
- Strengthening seed production system;

- Dual purpose cultivars, fodder production, thorn-less cactus etc.;
- Crop diversification, using high-value crops;
- Rehabilitation of wasteland and promotion of agro-forestry/horticulture system;
- Livelihood improvement interventions through skill development; and
- Farmers-producer organisation and market linkages.

Photo 4. Farmers' participatory demonstration on improved chickpea cultivar (JG 11) along with balanced fertilizer application and intercrop with mustard in Bundelkhand, UP

Vidarbha Region

Climate change in India is real and it is one of the major challenges faced by Indian Agriculture, more so in the semi-arid tropics (SAT) of the country, including the Vidarbha region of Maharashtra. Historical weather data of the Vidarbha region over 53 years (1961–2013), using the revised water-budgeting approach of Thornthwaite and Mather (1955) in the periods 1961-1990 and 1991-2013 are presented in Figure 5.

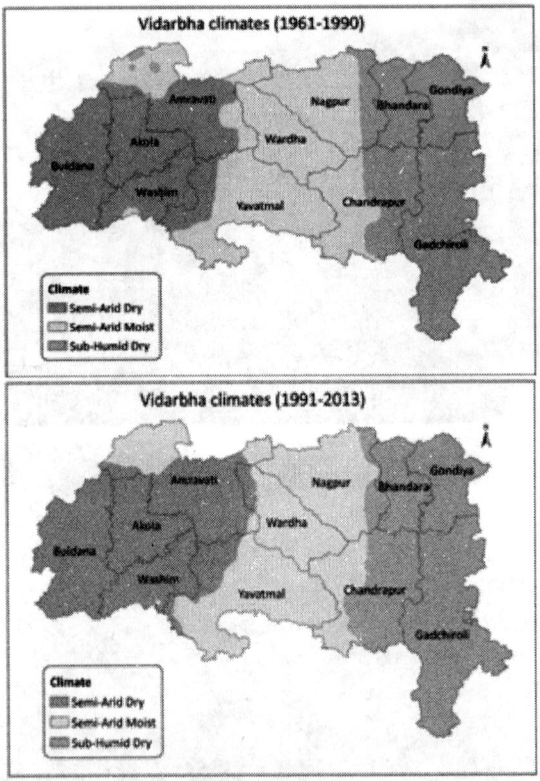

Figure 5: Changes in Climate Types in Vidarbha

The major issues related to weather and climate variability that need to be considered in developing a strategy for bringing improvements in agriculture sector in Vidarbha are as follows:

a) Uncertainty in rains for rain-fed crop sowing;
b) Uneven distribution of rainfall during the southwest monsoon period;
c) Dry spells and droughts in the cropping season;
d) High temperatures and low humidity during break monsoon in the crop season;
e) Heavy rainfall leading to flooding;
f) Fluctuations in temperatures during *Rabi* crop season;
g) Less information on climate change assessment, impacts and adaptation strategies specific to Vidarbha region; and
h) Limited awareness among farmers on weather and climate variability and change.

To discuss the KISAN MITrA initiative, a meeting was attended in Mumbai, on 10 August 2017, by Dr Suhas Wani, Director Asia Regional Program, ICRISAT and Dr KV Raju, Principal Scientist, ICRISAT with Chief Minister of Maharashtra, State Agriculture Minister and Cabinet Minister, Agriculture, with the Department of Agriculture (DoA) officials along with a team of World Bank aided project on Climate Resilient Agriculture (POCRA). The concept strategy for KISAN MITrA or doubling farmers' income initiative in the Vidarbha region of Maharashtra, covering eleven districts was presented by Dr Wani. The Chief Minister appreciated the initiative and advised the officials to take it forward and integrate the POCRA activities in the KISAN MITrA initiative.

Another meeting was conducted, on 16 September 2017, at Pune under the chairmanship of Mr Bijay Kumar, Principal Secretary and Mr Sachindra Pratap Singh, Commissioner of Agriculture.

On 26 September 2017, a meeting was held in Nagpur, which was attended by the divisional level agricultural department officials - JDAs, DSAO, SDAO and TAOs–of Amravati and Nagpur. Following these meetings, the ICRISAT has initiated interventions in the eleven districts of the Vidarbha regions–Amravati, Akola, Buldhana, Bhandara, Chandrapur, Gadchiroli, Gondia, Nagpur, Yavatmal, Wardha and Washim.

Large Yield Gaps to be Bridged

A quick analysis of important crops in Vidarbha showed low yield levels compared to the state and national levels (Table 5).

Water Scarcity

Amravati district has witnessed great changes in climate types with increase in the semi-arid dry area by about 138,000 ha. Wardha district also has witnessed increase in the semi-arid dry areas by about 64,000 ha. Washim, Yavatmal and Akola have also increased their semi-arid dry climates by about 10, 7 and 2 thousand hectares, respectively. Nagpur and Bhandara districts have also experienced increased dryness in areas of about 90,000 ha and 1,000 ha, respectively. If this trend continues, utmost care needs to be taken for identifying and promoting suitable crop cultivars, and management practices, for climate resilient agricultural productivity leading to the challenging task of doubling farmers' incomes by the year 2022.

Widespread Land Degradation

In addition to macro nutrients, the deficiencies of micro and secondary nutrients have emerged which need to be addressed. The key issues include: detailed diagnosis of soil fertility constraints, rejuvenating degrading soils, soil C-building, policies to promote soil test-based integrated nutrient management and streamlining soil-plant-water diagnostic services; for example, none of the laboratories in the Vidarbha region is equipped to analyse 'B' in soil.

Table 5: Climatic zones, rainfall and crops yields - Vidarbha

Climatic zone as per Dept. of Agriculture, Maharashtra	Districts	Annual average rainfall (mm)*	Major crops**	Area** ('000 ha)	Yield** (t/ha)
Assured Rainfall Zone	Buldhana, Akola and Amravati	770-940	Soybean	817	1.07
			Cotton	577	1.83
			Pigeonpea	237	0.77
			Sorghum	106	1.43
			Chickpea	232	0.85
			Wheat	115	1.58
Moderate Rainfall Zone	Wardha, Washim, Nagpur and Yavatmal	890–1,130	Soybean	916	0.82
			Cotton	773	1.49
			Pigeonpea	289	0.64
			Sorghum	78	0.76
			Rice	76	1.03
			Chickpea	211	0.86
			Wheat	163	1.38
Eastern Vidarbha Zone	Bhandara, Gondia, Gadchiroli and Chandrapur	1,300–1,430	Rice	668	1.53
			Soybean	152	0.78
			Cotton	114	1.75
			Pigeonpea	57	0.77
			Chickpea	49	0.56
			Wheat	38	1.04

Mono-cropping to Sustainable Cropping Systems

In the Vidarbha region, over the last 10 years, cotton is the major crop and there has been a shift towards soybean (70 percent) and wheat (90 percent) cultivation along with pigeon-pea (17 percent), rice (11 percent) and maize (31 percent), which are grown as monocrops. The ignorance towards inclusion of pulses, sorghum (67 percent decline), pearl millet (77 percent decline) and oilseeds into cropping system, has resulted in decline in the factor productivity, often coupled with more probability of crop failures. Introduction of vertical or horizontal integration in existing cotton and soybean crops with suitable pulses (e.g. pigeon-pea, green gram, black gram, cowpea etc.) and oilseeds (e.g. soybean, sunflower and groundnut) will result in a shift from a traditional, but risky, 'mono-cropping' system to a less-risky 'multiple cropping' system, and help to stabilise the system and potentially increase the farmers' incomes as a result.

Climate Resilient Crop Cultivars, Robust Seed Systems

The need of the hour is to undertake participatory evaluation of high-yielding, climate resilient, crop cultivars and establish robust seed systems. Cotton, soybean, pigeon-pea, sorghum and maize are the predominant rain-fed crops in the Vidarbha region. Lack of availability of high-yielding varieties and hybrid seeds in pulses and sorghum, and the seed replacement ratio (SRR) of 15 to 20 percent, are responsible for low crop productivity.

Cultivation of High-value Crops and Drought Proofing

In water scarce areas, harvesting runoff by constructing farm ponds and providing supplemental irrigation in a selected area with proper protection (poly-house/shade-net) growing high-value crops will increase the income levels of farmers. The remaining area can be utilised for growing less-water requiring, drought-tolerant crops along with fodder. In the Vidarbha region, agricultural diversification towards high-value products, such as fruits and protected cultivation of vegetables and flowers, organic crops and medicinal plants, can potentially increase farmers' incomes in select areas.

Improving Livestock Productivity

In Vidarbha, livestock is not a major income-generation activity, whereas small ruminants and poultry holders are in large proportion in some clusters. Income generation from the sale of animals (greater than 50 percent) and milk production (less than 40 percent) has been observed to be more profitable than other livestock income sources. At present, the country faces a net deficit of 60 percent green fodder, 22 percent dry crop residues and 64 percent feeds. So the proposed strategy is to provide fodder seed as well as facilitate quality fodder production at farmer's field, which will promote dual purpose maize along with multi-cut sorghum and pearl millet on limited farm area.

Value-addition and Marketing

Collectivisation of producers to harness synergies through market linkages, value addition and procurement of inputs will potentially increase the profitability for the farmers.

ICT and Extension System

In Vidarbha region, ICT is a promising option to strengthen the capacity of local extension agents by providing easy access to required information. In addition, ICT is the most effective solution for monitoring and evaluating day-to-day activities.

Work by ICRISAT teams, Doubling Farmer's Income

Identification of Representative Pilot Sites

The ICRISAT team identified pilot sites along with the district officials in Vidarbha. During this visit, the team had discussion with different stakeholders, including JDAs, DSAOs, SDAOs, AOs and farmers, in all districts. The team identified representative pilot villages/blocks in consultation with DSAOs and other officials, as shown in Table 6.

Table 6. Representative pilot sites across 11 districts in Vidarbha

District	Pilot Block	Selected Villages	Cropping pattern
Amravati	Chandur bazar	Belora Hirapur, Dabha, Pala, Durgapur and Shendani	Cotton, pigeon-pea, and soybean–Kharif (K); Chickpea–Rabi (R)
	Nandgaon	Kharwadi, Talvel and Wadura	
Akola	Murtajapur	Lakhapuri and Durgawada	Soybean, cotton, red-gram and sorghum (K); Wheat and chickpea (R)
	Akot	Khaparwadi, khurd, Khaparwadi Budruk, Jaulka, Lothkhed	
Buldhana	Nandura	Kokalwadi, Pimpriadhav	Pigeon-pea, soybean, maize, black-gram, green-gram, cotton, sorghum (K); Chickpea and wheat (R)
	Mehkar	Dongaon	
Bhandara	Sakoli	Jambli, Bodra, Gudhari, Girola, Baradkinhi, Mundipar, Kitali, Sarati	Paddy, soybean, pigeon-pea (K); Wheat, chickpea (R)
	Lakhni	Pimpalgaon, Kairi, Manegaon, Samewada	
	Mohadi	Usarla, Salai Budruk, Katebramhi.	
	Tumsar	Khapa, Hasara, Hingana	

Chandrapur	Mul	Bembal and Chuck Bemba	Paddy, soybean, cotton (K) Chickpea, wheat and rabi sorghum (R)
	Pomb-hurna	Ghosari, Phutana Mokasa, Chuck Phutana	
Gadchiroli	Gadchiroli	Markabodi, Shivani, Murmadi, Aambetola and Sawargaon	Paddy, cotton (K); Paddy, chickpea (R)
	Chamorshi	Kunghada re., Vaghdhara, Khopardi, Bhendla, Jairapur and Talodhi mo.	
Gondia	Morgaon Arjuni	Parastola, Dhamtitola, Arattondi, Ilda, Bhar-noli, Rajoli, Sappgaon, Kanhalgaon, Khadki, Keshori, Kanheri, Kelvad, Tukumna-rayan, Dongargaon, Amarpayali, Varnahi, Ambhora, Gardenpur, Garvara	Paddy, pigeon-pea (K); Wheat, chickpea (R)
	Sadak Arjuni	Chikhli, Baki, Ma-neri, Kanheri, Kokana, Khoda, Chingi, Raka Palasgaon, Pimpri.	
Nagpur	Katol	Therladhote, wandali, Digras B., Wadvihira, Khangaon, Kolabi, Chinchala, Naygaon, Dahirwadi	Cotton, soybean intercropped with pigeon-pea (K) Chickpea and wheat (R)
	Savner	Khubala, Risala, Hingna, Kocchi, Pipla (Ritha), Sonpur	
Yavatmal	Pusad	Kondai, Dahlwad Bk., Khadakdari, Ye-hala, WeniKh., Harshi, Pokhari, Balawadi	Cotton, pigeon-pea, and soybean (K) Chickpea (R)
Wardha	Seloo	Manabala Janglapur, Kolhi, Kolgaon, Ghorad, Kinhi, and Sukali station	Paddy, soybean, cotton (K) Chickpea, wheat and sorghum (R)
	Samudra-pur	Gual, Bhosa, Umra, Nandpur, Derda, Lavangi and Mangaon	
Washim	Malegaon	Tiwali, Ghata, Mirzapur	Soybean, cotton, pigeon-pea (K) Gram (R)
	Karanja	Gaiwal, Sohol, Wai, Murambi	

Soil Sampling and Analysis

All the districts in Vidarbha show wide-spread deficiency in major nutrients as well as deficiency in secondary and micro nutrients. The laboratory test results have indicated nutrient deficiencies in the order of 93-100 percent in Nitrogen; 34-100 percent in Phosphorus; up to 35 percent in Potassium; 10-85 percent in Sulphur; 19-71 percent in Zinc; 16-17 percent in Boron; and 1-48 percent in iron. Between 6 and

Photo 6: Participatory soil sampling demonstration

58 percent of the fields have indicated low levels of soil organic Carbon. Therefore, during the DFI team visit, farmers and department officials were trained in stratified soil sampling (Photo 6). Samples were then collected from some fields in pilot sites—located in Pimpri Adhav village, Nandura Taluk, Buldhana, Dongaon Village, Mehkar Taluk, and Buldhana–for understanding the soil health in the region.

Partnerships with Regional Stakeholders

In order to harness the synergies of regional and national partners (NGOs, research institutes), the ICRISAT team mapped and reached out for potential partnerships with identified NGO partners in consultation with the district agricultural officials. The ICRISAT team also met officials of *Panjabrao Deshmukh Krishi Vidyapeeth*, at Akola, and requested them to be associated with this consortium and join the initiative, which they agreed.

Growth Engines

Based on the discussions with department officials and farmers, the following growth engines have been identified across all pilots in Vidarbha.

Table 7: Growth engine identified for pilot sites-Vidarbha

Growth engines	INM	Soil and water management	Mechanization	FPO	Protected cultivation
Cotton*/ Paddy*	Y	Y	Y	Y	
Pigeon-pea	Y	Y		Y	
Chickpea	Y	Y	Y	Y	
Milk	-	Y	-	Y	-
Vegetables	Y	Y	Y	Y	Y

Table 7 provides the details of the crops and the management plan. A number of important things that are required to be implemented for various crops as part of the growth engines are listed below.

Cotton

Aerobic composting of cotton waste: Besides obtaining good quality compost, farmers can avoid a carry-over of Pink boll worm which has become of late a very serious pest in many parts of India.

Raising cotton nursery and going for transplanting: This can be practiced by farmers who have some off-season irrigation facility. They can transplant the plants in the main field with the onset of monsoon season.

Using only compost in soil and applying fertilisers through foliar application only: This has been successfully used by some knowledgeable farmers.

Encouraging farmers/groups to produce local pest-control recipes and bio-pesticides: On the basis that several pest-control practices are locally known, training can be imparted to village youths in bio-pesticide production through NIPHM, Hyderabad.

One time manual picking of cotton: This can be tried by using chemical desiccants, besides encouraging some companies (e.g. Bayer) to come forward to cotton purchase agreement with machine harvesting.

Paddy

The possible interventions in paddy as growth engines are listed below:

- Machine transplanting in low-land;
- Direct seeded rice;

- INM;
- *Azolla* production;
- Rice-Fish production; and
- Tapping into the export potential of brown (unpolished rice) and *chinor* (fragrant) rice.

Pigeon-pea

The activities planned for increasing the pigeon-pea production are listed below:

- Enhance production of pigeon-pea-based cropping system using high-yielding hybrids/varieties along with improved land, water and crop management practices;
- Soil test-based nutrient management;
- Cultivation of early maturing high-yielding pigeon-pea hybrids in Alfisols and medium-duration hybrids in Vertisols;
- Develop village-level seed systems to achieve self-sufficiency in seeds of farmer-preferred improved varieties of pigeon-pea;
- Build capacity of farmers and Self Help Groups (SHGs) in sustainable pigeon-pea production technology; and
- Provide technical back-stopping for refinement of pigeon-pea production technologies, including transplanted pigeon-pea.

Vegetable Cultivation

One and off field trainings and demonstrations will be given to the farmers on the following interventions:

- Plant production of vegetable crops through nursery raising;

- Use of low-cost plant support systems for cucurbitaceous and solanaceous crops;
- Use of low-cost protected structures, such as shade-net and poly-tunnels;
- Grafting for higher productivity and profitability of vegetable crops;
- Deploying pollinisers and pollinators in enhancing the crop productivity, especially in cucurbits;
- Efficient use of water and nutrient using micro-irrigation systems; and
- Processing of vegetables (e.g. wafers, pickles, ketchup etc.) at village level by women SHGs.

Livestock

The key interventions to enhance the production of milk, meat and eggs are listed below:

- Breed improvement through large-scale cross-breeding, upgradation of local buffaloes with improved ones and selective breeding in indigenous cattle;
- Fulfilling fodder demand and developing wasteland as fodder ground. Hybrid seeds of multi-cut forage crops will be useful for fodder availability;
- Nutrition improvement, improved fodder availability and ample drinking water for livestock will result in substantial increase in the milk production;
- Introduction of semen of superior bulls in selected animals to increase in the cattle production;
- Formulation and supplying of balance ration for dairy animals;
- Feeding of probiotics to buffalo calves to enhance the growth rate and increased weight, reduce mortality rate

and improve health status of calves, resulting into high milk production;

- Rearing of *Desi* poultry breeds for meat and eggs production;
- Promote backyard poultry for the benefit of farmers; and
- Comprehensive livestock health care activities, including disease surveillance programme for quick response and control of diseases, such as a vaccination campaign, large number of animal health camps etc.

Trials and Demonstrations during *Rabi* 2017-18

A team of scientists along with the department officials visited the districts, between 21 September 2017 and 1 October 2017, and oriented department staffs about the protocols of participatory trials and demonstrations. Table 8 provides the details.

Table 8. Details of participatory trials initiated in pilots across 11 districts in Vidarbha

District	Location	No of trials
Akola	Murtajapur taluk and Akot taluk	120
Amravati	Chandur bazar and Nandgoan Khandeshwar taluks	24
Bhandara	Sakoli-Lakhani taluks and Tumsar-Mohadi taluks	45
Buldhana	Mehkar and Nandura Taluks	48
Chandrapur	Mul and Pombhurna taluks	90
Gadchiroli	Gadchiroli and Chamorshi taluks	10
Gondia	Sadak Arjuni and Arjuni Morgaon taluks	45
Nagpur	Katol and Savner taluks	110
Wardha	Seloo and Samudrapur taluks	90
Washim	Malegaon and Karanja taluks	90
Yavatmal	Pusad taluk	16

As entry point interventions, the ICRISAT-led consortium has provided drought-tolerant chickpea (JG 11) seeds, machine harvestable chickpea (NBeG 47) seeds, deficient secondary and micronutrients (Zinc, Sulphate, Borax), PGP-cum-nutrients (Aquasap) and aerobic composting culture for participatory demonstrations in the pilot sites.

Zero till multi-crop planter and shredder to help in preparing the material for composting are being demonstrated in each district.

Conclusion

More trials are being implemented and the progress is being monitored on a regular basis. Undoubtedly, the initiative has a significant potential to economically uplift the country's farmers, besides improving the economic prospects of the nation as a whole.

Research and Development A Tool for Transformation

DP Srivastava

Low R&D expenditure perpetuates technology dependence, reduces profit margin and affects competitiveness of Indian companies in global market place. The Economic Survey for FY 2018-19 notes that India's spending on R&D (0.6 percent of GDP) is well below than that in developed nations and major economies. India needs to make more use of top-down approach, where targets and resources are provided for R&D in mission mode. There is also a need to allow contract research. The US government funds contract research in foreign laboratories even in the sensitive defence sector. China has outpaced India in terms of the number of patents secured by it. It has been more successful in using market access and corporate acquisition overseas, as tools to gain cutting edge technologies. The Indian corporate sector contributes much lesser than its counterparts in western countries and China. There has to be fairer burden sharing. The need for indigenous R&D effort in India is reinforced by the past sanctions that the country experienced following its nuclear tests in 1974 and 1998.

Make in India

THE Government has announced the '*Make in India*' policy to build up India's manufacturing sector, and generate employment. Its success in the long run will depend upon its Research & Development (R&D) efforts. The *Make in India* programme should be complemented with another programme, *Design in India*. India has to leap-frog through transfer of technology, which should not only include the 'know-how', but also 'know-why'. This involves the Government policies, private sector initiatives and building up of human resources.

No nation has succeeded in building up industrial and technological capacity through a policy of self-reliance alone. The industrial revolution spread from Europe to the United States (US). Japan, during the Meiji Restoration, imported the western technology. China, in the post-revolution period, relied upon the Soviet help to build up its industrial base. During Deng Xiaoping's period, it switched to western markets and technology. It has been very successful in leveraging access to the Chinese market to obtain technology. It has also followed a policy of overseas acquisition of companies, with cutting edge technologies, to access sensitive technologies. Despite a back-lash, and attempts by the US and the European Union (EU) governments to impose regulatory controls, China continues to move ahead on this path. The US remains the world leader in technology. It still taps foreign brains to maintain its technological lead. This is not only manifested in immigration, but also through the Defense Advanced Research Projects Agency (DARPA) programme, which is based on contract research by foreign laboratories and individuals. The US companies have R&D centres in India, China and Europe.

Technology transfer has emerged as a key parameter for development. This takes place through government as well as private channels. The barrier to such transfer also includes government and private sector restrictions. The government controls include both bilateral and multi-lateral regimes, like the Nuclear Supplier Group (NSG), Missile Technology Control Regime (MTCR), and WASSENAAR Arrangement. China has blocked India's accession to NSG regime. The Chinese position is unlikely to change in foreseeable future. India's option is, therefore, to build up its indigenous R&D and technological development capacity, while leveraging market access to induce technology transfer, as China has done.

Flow of technology through commercial channels is no less important than government-to-government agreements. Most of the R&D expenditure and technology incubation in the Organisation for Economic Co-operation and Development (OECD) countries takes place in the private sector. The private sector restrictions, driven by commercial considerations, are represented by the *Intellectual Property Rights* (IPR) protection. Sharp increase in patents granted shows stress on innovation in the *Information Age*, as well as an increasing trend towards restriction. With or without India's integration in the NSG, the IPR protection will remain a commercial barrier to technology transfer.

Effective technology transfer not only means lowering the barriers at source, but strengthening the recipient's absorption capacity. This entails *capacity building*. The stepping-up of indigenous R&D capability minimises the need for technology transfers. Strong domestic base will erode technology denial regime, and help in India's integration in the mainstream.

Patents Granted

India lags behind IPR generation. Grant of patents is an index of success of a country's R&D efforts. India ranks behind Japan, the US, Germany, France, Switzerland, China and Israel in terms of international (Non-Residence) patents granted. This is, of course, an approximation, and there are exceptions. According to the World Intellectual Property Organisation (WIPO) figures for 2015, the patents figures are presented in Table 1.

Table 1: Patents owned by major countries (WIPO, 2015)

Country	Resident	Rank	Non-Resident	Rank	Abroad	Rank
UK	4,934	9	2,626	18	16,569	7
US	140,969	3	157,438	1	116,139	2
Germany	24,530	5	4,384	13	62,319	3
Japan	1,46,749	2	42,609	3	1,24,389	1
China	2,63,436	1	95,880	2	16,065	8
India	822	25	5,200	12	4,998	16
Russia	22,753	6	12,146	8	2,245	23
France	16,468	7	1,656		27,454	5
Israel	723	26	3,769	16	5,673	13
Czech	650	28	173	45	454	26
Switzerland	3,446	10	278	37	18,702	6

Source: WIPO Statistics, 2015.

Patent is a market mechanism; socialist countries did not have this tradition and they are yet to catch up. China grants a large number of domestic patents to its companies, to protect them from patent infringement suits (after they have successfully reverse engineered foreign product). Patents granted abroad are truer measure of a country's R&D efforts than domestic patents, as countries like China follow a lax patent regime at home, to essentially protect patent infringement by their companies. Going by this measure, Chinese companies and laboratories obtained 16,065 patents abroad and ranked 8th, as shown in Table 1. In comparison, Indian companies and laboratories obtained only 4,998 patents, and ranked 16th.

Not only does India lag behind China in the international patent ownership, but the gap is also increasing with time, as shown in Table 2.

Table 2: Patent Ownership–India versus China (WIPO, 2015)

	2001	2015
India	228 (27th rank)	4,998 (16th rank)
China	327 (25th rank)	16,065 (8th rank)

Source: WIPO Statistics.

As shown in Table 2, over a 15-year period, while the number of international patents won by Indian companies have increased by 2,192 percent (21.92 times), the number of international patents won by Chinese companies have gone up by 4,912 percent (49.12 times).

Foreign-owned laboratories may not patent their technology in their home countries. In such cases, these figures may not be reflected in the statistics of the country, where the laboratory is located. This may artificially depress figures in respect of countries like Czech Republic, where either the research institution is foreign owned, or it carries out contract research on behalf of a foreign country or entity. This also applies to some extent to India, which hosts number of foreign laboratories; for example, General Electric, Intel, Boeing, Microsoft and Google, all have research establishments in India.

It is true, of course, that in frontier areas of technology, especially in military or strategic sectors, countries/companies may not file for patents in view of confidentiality, as patent application involves disclosure. However, factoring this reality does not increase India's comfort level. China has mastered the '*stealth*' aircraft technology; is working on the '*Ram Jet*' technology; and has obtained major segment of world market in Unmanned Aerial Vehicle (UAV) research, all or some of which may have been done on the basis of reverse engineering, resulting in potential patent infringement. Nevertheless, China has made progress. India's continued arms imports reflect the country's failure to reverse engineer and master the technology developed overseas.

China has been making sustained efforts to move from manufacturing to generation of *intellectual property*. According to Economist magazine, much of China's push for patents comes from its government policy. The government incentives include cash bonuses, covering the substantial cost of filing for patent ownership in some cases and reducing corporate income-tax from 25 percent to 15 percent for firms that file many patents.[1]

R&D Expenditure

According to the UNESCO Institute for Statistics (UIS), top five R&D spenders in absolute terms are the largest economies: The US, China, Japan, Germany and the Republic of Korea. However, in terms of R&D expenditure, as a percentage of GDP, the Republic of Korea leads the group, followed by Israel, Japan, Finland and Sweden. There are six countries, which have exceeded 3 percent of GDP as R&D expenditure: South Korea, with 4.3 percent, is the world leader, followed by Israel (4.1 percent), Japan (3.6 percent), Denmark, Finland and Sweden. The US, Germany, Austria and Switzerland spend around 3 percent of GDP. Brazil is the highest spender in Latin America with 1.2 percent, while India spends 0.8 percent of GDP on R&D.[2] China's R&D expenditure was 2.1 percent of GDP in 2016.

According to R&D magazine, India's R&D spending in 2017 was expected to be USD 77.5 billion (in Purchase Power Parity, or PPP terms). This means India's share of world R&D spending will be 3.7 percent, an increase of 6.3 percent over the previous year. This is lower than China.[3]

China was expected to increase its R&D spending by 7.1 percent to USD 429.5 billion (PPP). Chinese spending is already higher than all other countries, except the US. China's R&D has also surpassed that of all 34 European countries combined in 2016.[4]

Role of Private Sector in R&D

Three principle sources of R&D funding are: (i) industry; (ii) government; and (iii) funds from abroad.

In the OECD countries, industry or private sector accounts for a major portion of spending in major countries like Germany (66 percent by industry: 30 percent by government); Israel (65 percent by industry: 25 percent by government); Japan (77 percent by industry: 16 percent by government); South Korea (75 percent by industry: 22 percent by government); Switzerland (70 percent by industry: 22 percent by government); and the UK (40 percent by industry: 33 percent by government). The proportion of government versus private sector spending is reverse in the former socialist economies. In case of Russia, the industry accounts for 29 percent, while as the government accounts for 63 percent of the total funding. In India, similar to the former socialist economies, the government accounts for 75 percent of R&D expenditure, while private sector accounts for balance 25 percent.

The role of governments, business and universities in R&D spending in different countries is summarisedin Table 3.

Table 3: Share of Government,Business and Academia Investments in R&D 2015: Share of Government Business and Academia

	USA	Israel	China	India
Total R&D spending (PPP Billion USD)	479	12.2	371	48.1
Share of contributions				
Business	341	10.3	286	17
Government	54	0.2	59	29
Universities	64	1.5	26	2
Private NP	20	0.1	--	--
R&D spending (percent of GDP)	2.8	4.3	2	0.8
Researchers per million population	4,231	8,255	1,113	156

Source: UNESCO, as quoted in Economic Survey 2017-18.

The EU's target for its Member States to invest 3 percent of their GDP in R&D by 2020 includes 2 percent from the private sector, whereas the governmental public funding is limited to only 1 percent only, i.e. a ratio of 66 percent by industry to 33 percent by governments.

Out of Chinese R&D expenditure of 1.54 trillion Yuan (USD 233 billion) in 2016, over 78 percent came from 'enterprises'.[5] The most striking is the case of Huawei. Different phases of growth of the company illustrates both sides of the coin–the cost of technology dependence, and the sustained effort put in by the company to build up its indigenous base for R&D. From 1987 to 2011, Huawei has invested at least 10 percent of its sales revenue into R&D each year.

"In 2010, Huawei paid USD 222 million in patent royalties to its western counterparts, while its total payout to Qualcomm has exceeded USD 600 million, which undoubtedly is the largest royalty any Chinese company has ever paid. As huge as these royalties are, they earned Huawei over USD 20 billion worth of contracts." However, its commercial success built on imported technology carries its own risks. As the Huawei owner Ren Zhengfei mentioned:

"Huawei has managed to carry its banner uphill and planted it on the top. But then it finds out that it has been surrounded by its enemies. Virtually all essential patents in the telecom industry belong to Western companies. After 10 years of technology accumulation, Huawei has been caught in an unpleasant situation: yes, it is on the top of the hill, but it has been barricaded by enemies who occupy the foot of the hill and the hill side."

Huawei has tried to deal with the dilemma through a combination of stepped up R&D expenditure, and partnership with the rivals. "In 2005, Ren Zhengfei emphasized partnership with competitors as a strategic priority of its future development." The company has built worldwide partnerships for technology and market development. It has set up joint labs with Texas Instruments, Motorola, IBM, Intel, and Lucent Technologies, and established research institutes in India, Switzerland and Russia."

Source: The Huawei Story by Tian Tao with Wu Chunbo, pages 67 and 69

Chinese companies have invested heavily in R&D. As shown in Table 4, the top four Chinese tech companies spent between 8 and 15 percent of their sale on R&D, as against the Indian government's norm of 2 percent of company's net profit.

L&T

In comparison to Chinese companies, Larsen & Toubro (L&T), India's premier engineering company, spent only 0.16 percent of sales on R&D. In terms of net profit, this amounted to 2.64 percent.

Table 4: Top Four Chinese Company's R&D Expenditure

Top Chinese companies							
Name	World rank 2014	World rank 2016	Industrial sector (ICB-3D)	Rank in their industrial sector	R&D spend 2015-16 (€ mns)	Growth in R&D spend, 2014-16	R&D to sales ratio
Huawei	26	8	Technology hardware & equipment	2	8357.9	26.3	15.0
ZTE	105	65	Technology hardware & equipment	12	1954,1	12.4	13.8
Baidu	203	93	Software & computer services	7	1444.5	63.3	15.4
Tencent	179	117	Software & computer services	9	1177.4	25.8	8.1

Source: Bruegel based on EU Industrial R&D Investment Scoreboard, 2500 largest R&D spenders worldwide, 2016 edition compared to 2014 edition, see http://iri.jrc.ec.europa.eu/scoreboard.html.

Table 5 presents the details of L&T's R&D expenditures between 2012 and 2017.

Table 5: L&T's Research & Development Expenditure (2012 to 2017)

L&T Consolidated as Group	2012-13	2013-14	2014-15	2015-16	2016-17
Royalty and technical know-how fees	49	26	22	49	16
Expenditure on research and development	107	133	165	187	178
R&D as percent of Sales	0.14%	0.15 %	0.18 %	0.18 %	0.16 %
R&D as percent of Net Profit	2.04 %	2.72 %	3.33 %	3.38 %	2.64 %
Consolidated Revenue	75,594	86,110	93,012	103,815	111,412
Consolidated Net profit	5,252	4,875	4,964	5,538	6,739

BHEL

According to BHEL's Annual Report, its R&D expenditure for the financial year 2015-16 was Rupees 893.07 Crore, which is 3.36 percent of the turnover.

Role of Government: Different Approaches to R&D

There are essentially two approaches followed by governments in running their R&D programmes.

(i) Top-down approach. In this case, the government lays down priority sectors, and provides funding.

(ii) Bottom-up approach. In this case, research proposals are received from individual scientists, screened and approved.

Major projects involve multi-sectoral research by large team of scientists, with considerable government funding. Examples could be aero-space, nuclear to pharma industry. The top-down approach is better suited for this purpose.

The US

The US government has two major programmes for encouraging R&D efforts–the DARPA (Defence Advanced Research Projects Agency) and National Science Foundation. DARPA sets strategic goals and provides funding. DARPA's projects include development of internet, which started as a military research program to ensure the survivability of the communication network in a nuclear war. National Science Foundation provides funding on a lower scale. It works on the basis of call for proposals from individual scientists, which are then screened and selected for funding. DARPA can be considered as a top-down approach, while National Science Foundation represents a bottom-up approach.

China

In April 1983, a group of Chinese scientists wrote a joint letter to Deng Xiaoping pointing out that China was lagging behind in the development of key technologies. The Chinese leader simply initialled on the representation,'Do it'. This was the beginning of 836 Program, as it was called after the year and the month when it was initiated (1983, June). The programme provided for funding for R&D and product development in key areas. An interesting feature of this programme was that it included funding of R&D efforts in private sector, which was just developing at the time. The Chinese government's funding programme was a key to its success. Private entrepreneurs could use government funding as the basis for attracting more money from banks for product development.

In order to get around the US export control restrictions, China had started acquiring the US companies, which may have low capital base, but had developed cutting edge technologies. This eventually forced the US Congress to pass an Act setting up a mechanism to scrutinise foreign acquisitions in the US–Committee on Foreign Investment in US (CFIUS). The Chinese have continued to acquire the US nuclear and defence secrets, sometimes possibly by espionage. This article does not go into these aspects, and is confined to what is available through open sources. The Chinese example suggests an excellent method–*own the equity and you own the IPR.* If a company has acquired another company, it will have the inside track whatever are the government restrictions.

The EU

The EU has provided Euro 80 billion funding for the 7-year research programme, *Horizon 2020*, for the period 2014-20. This is in addition to the funding by private sector and national governments. This combines all research and innovation funding in one integrated programme. The EU initiative,

Innovation Union, in co-operation with non-EU countries, focuses on major challenges, including energy, food security, climate change, and ageing population.[7]

India

In India, the Department of Atomic Energy (DAE) and Indian Space Research Organisation (ISRO) are examples of the top-down approach, where the government sets strategic goals and provides funding. The Council for Scientific and Industrial Research (CSIR) and the Department of Science and Technology (DST), which call for proposals and then select projects for funding, are examples of the bottom-up approach.

The DAE and Department of Space have had to work under a restrictive environment, after India was denied technology as a result of sanctions imposed on it following its nuclear tests in 1974 and 1998. Yet, they managed to maintain the momentum. They have also managed to create and sustain a vendor base.

The DAE, apart from maintaining strategic autonomy, has built up power generation programme through Pressurised Heavy Water Reactors (PHWR). India is one of the few countries to have an advanced Fast Breeder Reactor programme. For nuclear power programme, while equity came from the Government, 70 percent resources were raised in the form of debt from market.

The ISRO has recently carried out its 100th satellite launch. It was unique in the sense that satellites were placed in two orbits. The ISRO had earlier completed *Moon Mission* and *Mars Mission*. It maintained a balance between self-reliance and international co-operation. While the Polar Satellite Launch Vehicle (PSLV) remained the main work horse, heavier communication satellites for geo-stationary orbit were launched on board Ariane rockets. In turn, ISRO was accepted for launch of satellites from other countries, including the US. ANTRIX, its commercial arm, has been accepted as a cost effective, reliable launcher in a competitive international market.

Defence Research and Development Organisation (DRDO) has also carried out R&D in some critical areas. Its task is more difficult, as it has had to work under international sanctions regime longer than any other organisation. Given the sensitive nature of its programme, its successes often go unnoticed. DRDO has 308 patents to its credit.

CSIR

The Council for Scientific and Industrial Research (CSIR) generates 20 percent of its budget through contract research, and licensing fee. This is a healthy indicator, though the percentage could be improved. Yet, another index of excellence of CSIR's work is that CSIR licenses 13.3 percent of its patents, as against global average of 5 to 7 percent.

Table 6: Patent Ownership by Publicly Funded Organisations

Publicly Funded International R&D Organisations		Foreign Patents Granted During 2006-07 to 2015-16*	
		USPTO	PCT
CSIR, India		714	818
CNRS, France		1628	3813
RIKEN, Japan		484	741
Max Planck, Germany		361	614
CSIRO, Australia		265	515
CAS, China		605	2424
CSIR, South Africa		39	81

Table 7: World's R&D Laboratories and Institutions

Organisation	World Rank	Publications (2014)	Patents (Unique Published PCT Application /US Granted), 2014	Scientific Manpower	R&D Expenditure (Federal + Institutional Funding)
CSIR, India	84	5745	79/124	3,793	$465.42 mn
Massachu- setts Institute of Technology, USA	40	6171	320/303	3,750	$2.06 bn
Mayo Clinic, USA	68	5648	71/49	2,873	$912.00 mn
California Institute of Technology, USA	117	3280	180/158	3,900 (all employees)	$580.00 mn
Oak Ridge National Laboratory, USA	329	1915	29/0	4400 (all employees)	$1.4 bn
Fudan University, China	87	5313	12/21	2,700	NA
National Institute of Advanced Industrial Science & Technology, Japan	171	2208	76/153	2,337	$765.75 mn

CSIR ranked first amongst Indian research laboratories and companies in terms of patents. However, India ranked 81st globally amongst 141 countries in 2015. About 10,615 patents have been granted to Indians over the past 10 years. The CSIR is the only Indian organisation amongst the top 100 global institutions.

Table 8: India's Main Innovators

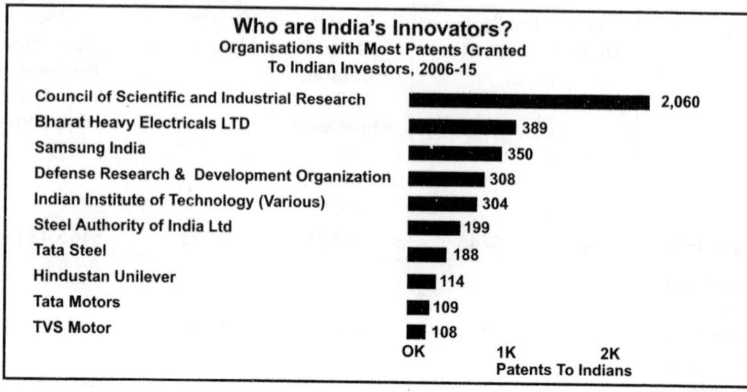

Table 9: Rate of Growth of Publications in SCI Journals

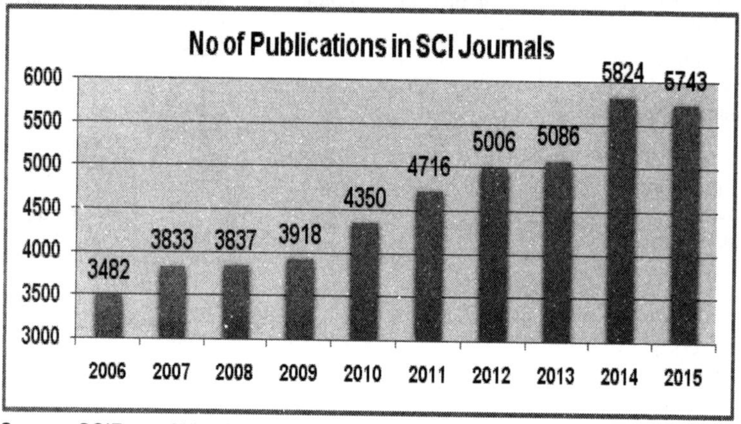

Source: CSIR as of March 26, 2016.

Science and Technology under 12th Five Year Plan

There have been positive achievements in the field of science and technology. 'Relative position of India with respect to scientific publications has improved from 15th in 2003 to 9th in 2010.[8]' The target under the 12th Five Year Plan was to take it to the 6th position, which has been successfully achieved. However, the Plan document notes '...the current rate of improvement is slow and falls short of global standards in many areas. This is indicated by the fact that India's share of top one percent publications is only 0.5 percent, as of 2006, less than those of other Asian countries like China and South Korea. Inventiveness in our basic science is low and India's innovation system ranking varies between 50 and 60 among the nations."[9]

The Plan documents stated further: 'The country needs to move up from investing one percent of gross domestic product (GDP) in the R&D sector to two percent of GDP and more, as has been the case with several developed and emerging economies for quite some time. This must be achieved through an additional government effort, but also a much increased private sector effort.'[10]

The Scientific Advisory Committee (SAC) to PM under *National Vision for Science* has suggested the development of a new, expansive personnel policy for R&D sector, based on the best global practices. The committee has also suggested that the audit discipline need to be modified from procedure–or process based to performance–objective based system.[11]

NITI Ayog: Innovation Policy

The Government has set up the Atal Innovation Mission (AIM) at the NITI Ayog. The objective is to promote a culture of innovation and entrepreneurship in India. Under this initiative, ten *Atal Incubation Centres* have been set up. These will provide suitable physical infrastructure, as well as mentoring to start-ups, provide seed capital and training.[12]

Licensed Production

Historically, Indian industry has followed the model of licensed production, where foreign company transfers 'know-how' against the payment of licensed fee. This creates technology dependence, where the R&D is done by the foreign company.

The financial cost is not limited to outgo of licensing fee alone, but also results in increase in the project cost. The licensor insists on purchase of its own equipment or purchase from suppliers approved by it, as a condition for process guarantee. The licensed production model means that indigenous content remains low and design capability does not grow.

The private sector controls on technology transfer flow from the desire to maintain a competitive edge and maximise commercial gains. In recent years, these terms have become harsher. The scope of licensing agreements has become narrower, licensing fees and royalty have gone up. Many of the foreign partners sensing opportunities and India's growing market are no longer satisfied with licensing fee, and instead demand equity participation.

Continued technology dependence means that Indian companies remain behind the product cycle. Multi-National Companies (MNC) allow licensed production only when the technology has become outdated. This places Indian companies at a disadvantage in competing with the global market place.

Charges for Use of Intellectual Property Rights

Table 10: Rate of Growth in Licensing Fee–India

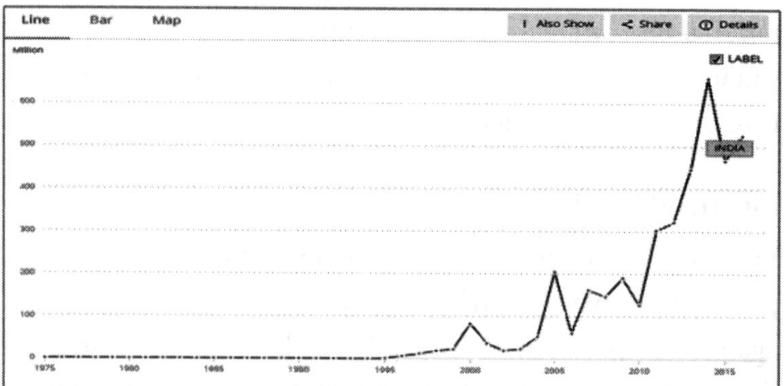

Table 11: Rate of Growth in Licensing Fee - China

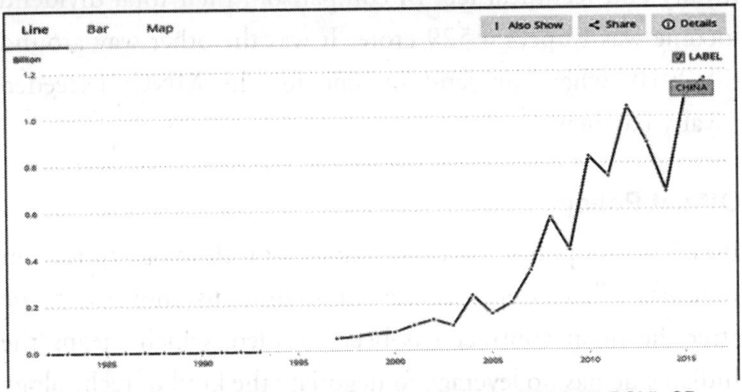

Source: World Bank, https://data.worldbank.org/indicator/BX.GSR.ROYL.CD

Dependence on imported technology means increasing outgo of charges for use of IPR.

According to the World Bank figures, payment of royalty and license fee amounted to USD 524.879 million in 2016. There is a steep upward curve since 2010. Tables 10 and 11 indicate the trending curves of India and China, respectively.

China paid USD 1.161 billion in the year 2016 according to the World Bank data. Though this is double than India's spending (USD 524.879 million), taken as a proportion of the Chinese GDP, or exports, this is much smaller outgo in relative terms.

According to the Government data, royalty payment has risen from 13 percent of FDI flows in 2009-10 to 18 percent in 2012-13. The outflow on account of royalty and fee for technical services, taken together, accounted for 16 to 33 percent of the Foreign Direct Investment (FDI) inflows between 2009-10 and 2012-13.[13]

Royalty payment exceeded dividend income for MNCs in India. In 2012-13, 71 MNCs earned a combined sum of Rupees 4,836 crore from the Indian subsidiaries in the form of royalty and technical fee. In comparison, their total dividend income was Rupees 4,529 crore. It was the other way around till 2010, when dividend income for the MNCs exceeded royalty payment.[14]

Off-set Policy

India's off-set policy leaves the choice of technology to foreign vendors. What is even more important, this choice is made after the main contract has been decided, which means the Indian side has no leverage to negotiate the kind of technology it wants. Besides, there is price manipulation by foreign vendors. The cost of components to be locally produced is hyped up to show that the target of local production has been met. Conversely, price manipulation is resorted to argue that local production of a key component, or technology, would not be cost competitive, and can best be supplied by the foreign vendor, perpetuating our technology dependence.

Foreign Direct Investment (FDI) in R&D

India has been very successful in attracting foreign R&D investment in a number of categories, including electronics and information technologies. India attracted about a third of nearly 200 Engineering R&D (ER&D) centres created in 2015.

This included centres established by Rolls-Royce, Ericsson, BASF, Bosch, Michelin, Foxconn and LeEco. India has more than 1,000 ER&D centres.[15]

Indian Academia in a Globalised World

According to the Times Higher Education World University Rankings 2018, Indian institutes continued to perform poorly in global university rankings (Mint 6.9.2017). The Indian Institute of Sciences, Bangalore, considered as the top University in India, was placed in the 251-300 groupings of the best universities. This represented a fall from 201-250 band in the previous year's ranking. The Indian Institute of Technology (IIT) Bombay continued to be in the 351-400 band. But, IIT Delhi and IIT Kanpur have dropped from 401-500 band to 501-600 band. This may not entirely reflect quality. The Indian institutions suffer on account of 'internationalisation' criteria, as there is restriction on attracting foreign students and faculty. In case of IITs, their core strength is their BTech courses, while less attention is paid to the MTech and PhD programmes.

The Economic Survey of Government of India for 2017-18 notes that there are fewer Indian students pursuing PhD courses in the US universities in Sciences, Technology, Engineering and Mathematics (STEM) than Chinese students. However, there is an increase in PhD enrolments in India.[16] The comparison is relevant. However, to understand the complete picture, we need to know the percentage of students, who returned to contribute to growth of science and technology in their home country.

According to an Economist report, more Chinese PhD students return to China in comparison to the Indian students who continue to stay overseas. This is critical in terms of absorbing the benefit of advanced studies. The Chinese model is based on government sponsorship for studies abroad, and persuading them to return through a combination of legal stipulation and jobs. The last part is especially important. While we need not restrict the number of Indian students going abroad on their own, the Government could sponsor more scientists from government organisations for PhD courses abroad with a legal bond to return.

In 2015-16, 126,451 students were enrolled in PhD programmes in India, of which 62 percent were in the STEM fields. This survey may be more relevant if the figures of students, who complete the PhD programme is given, as well as their absorption in their areas of study

Interaction between the Academia and the Industry

IITs have set up *Incubation Centres* to encourage innovation. For instance, IIT Delhi is running an incubation centre, which provides help to industry on fee basis, apart from providing support to students. There are 60 start-ups. IIT takes up to five percent equity share in such start-ups. IIT Delhi has also set up a *Technology Park* with 100 companies. One hundred patents were registered in 2017. IITs have attracted research funding up to Rupees 350 crore with 15 percent contribution from the industry. This is an example of interaction between academia and industry, but more needs to be done. IITs have also received a grant of Rupees 300 crore from DRDO for setting up a Joint Advanced Technology Centre.

Department of Science and Technology

The Department of Science and Technology (DST), under its Science and Technology Fund, encourages Industrial R&D and Technology Development. Earlier, the stress was on basic research. The DST has launched *Global Innovation Technology Alliance* (GITA), which is an investment vehicle where DST has 49 percent share and industry contributes 51 percent share. GITA finances industry-led projects with participation of academia. The DST also manages the US-India Endowment Fund for Innovation.

The research proposals are pursued jointly by both sides. Out of 27 projects, 13 have been commercialised.

The Indo-German Science and Technology Centre is managed on the basis of 2+2 model, where the academia and the industry participates with the academia in the lead. The DST, under its '*Giving is Gaining*' model, channels co-operation with neighbouring countries and Africa. This covers twining of African Centres of Excellence (ACEs).

Frontier Areas of S&T: AI, Big Data and Privacy

The US remains the world leader in Artificial Intelligence (AI) in terms of patents according to a WIPO Report. But China is fast catching up. A Chinese AI start-up, Yitu Tech, won a contest sponsored by the US intelligence community to create algorithms that could identify surveillance image out of data base of millions of photographs. The success of the Chinese company is attributed to access to big data of millions of people compiled by Chinese security services to refine its algorithms. Yitu, the AI contest winner, works on behalf of multiple security agencies in China.[17]

The Chinese advantage in terms of access to large database will increase over time, as the western countries are increasingly adopting laws on data privacy. China has no such constraints. More than 120 countries have adopted data privacy laws on European model so far. In case of India, there is a need to hasten gradually. Dr Devi Shetty, in a recent seminar on Health and Law, explained that Indian software companies can develop software for medical diagnosis based on patient database, which could be much larger than that of the West.

China is trying to close the gap with the US companies by stepping up funding for R&D in AI.

Way Forward: Indian Private Sector needs to Do More

The target of the 12th Five Year Plan was to increase the R&D spending from less than 1.0 percent of GDP to 2.0 percent, with additional 1.0 percent contributed by the private sector.

The R&D spending actually stands at 0.6 percent of GDP according to recently released Economic Survey. The Indian private sector should contribute more to R&D. Currently, they contribute 25 percent of total R&D spending as against global average of 75 percent. Without building up the R&D base, Indian companies will lose competitiveness in the international market, and lag behind in product development.

Contract R&D

Contract R&D by Indian public and private sector laboratories, and academic institutions may be used as a tool to develop technology on the most competitive basis. Contract R&D in foreign laboratories, where indigenous capabilities do not exist, must be allowed.

The Indian scientists may be associated with the technology development phase. India permits foreign MNSCs including Intel, GE, Microsoft, and Google to set-up research laboratories in India to tap Indian brains. The benefit, in terms of IPR generated, goes to the parent company. However, the reverse is not allowed with perhaps few exceptions.

China has extensively used this method to access technology by setting up research laboratories abroad. Huawei has a research laboratory in India. Apart from the US companies, the US government has a specific programme, DARPA, which is based on contract research overseas. If the US, which is the world leader in technology, does not hesitate in tapping foreign expertise through contract research, there needs to be no hesitation to do likewise by India. Contract research in foreign laboratories is a cheaper option than import of technology or the product.

Market Access as Leverage to Acquire Technology

Access to Indian market should be used to leverage more technology transfer by foreign vendors, who should be encouraged to set up Joint Ventures in hi-tech areas.

Acquisition of Cutting Edge Technology

Indian companies have invested overseas. This is driven in large part by desire to increase market share. Hence, the investment has flowed into auto, steel, commodities, oil and gas sectors. However, India has also missed many opportunities. Technology acquisition has not played a major part in the decision-making. To encourage PSUs, this should be built into their charter.

Conclusion: Top-down Approach or Mission Mode

For large programmes, a top-down approach, rather than a bottom-up approach is more suitable. DAE, ISRO or DRDO are some of the successful examples of the top-down approach. Mission mode may be needed not only in strategic areas, but also in water, energy and other areas.

R&D is a tool for transformation of the economy. No country can aspire to be a leading power in the *Information Age* without the capacity to design and innovate. It is critical to success of the *Make in India* programme.

References

1 Economist, 16 October 2010.

2 UNESCO Institute for Statistics, at http://uis.unesco.org/apps/visualisations/research-and-development-spending/ (accessed 13 February 2018).

3 R&D Magazine athttp://digital.rdmag.com/researchanddevelopment/2017_global_r_d_funding_forecast?pg=24#pg24

4 R&D Magazine athttp://digital.rdmag.com/researchanddevelopment/2017_global_r_d_funding_forecast?pg=22#pg22

5 Chinese Academy of Sciences at http://english.cas.cn/newsroom/china_research/201710/t20171020_184378.shtml

6 Reinhilde Veugelers,'The Challenge of China's Rise As a Science and Technology Powerhouse', Policy Contribution, Issue No. 19 July 2017.

7 European Union web-site https://europa.eu/european-union/topics/research-innovation_en

8 12th Five Year Plan Document, Page 235, http://planningcommission.gov.in/plans/planrel/12thplan/pdf/12fyp_vol1.pdf

9 Ibid.

10 Ibid.

11 Ibid.

12 NITIAyog, http://niti.gov.in/content/atal-innovation-mission-aim

13 Rahul Varman, "Royalty Payments: The Royal Treatment of Foreign Companies in India," at www.rupindiaa.wordpress.com, 9 March 2014.

14 Ibid.

15 R&D magazine, WINTER 2017.

16 Economics Survey of India, FY 2017-18.

17 Financial Times, 18 January 2018.

Can Healthcare be Affordable for All in India?

Col Dr DPK Pillay

India's overburdened health system remains plagued with multiple issues. According to the latest UN reports, India figures amongst the poorest in several health indices, even below sub–Saharan Africa. The top ten causes of death in India are chronic diseases, such as cardiovascular and respiratory diseases. There is an urgent need to create more healthcare facilities and professionals in India, including specialists, general physicians, nursing staff and technicians. The country needs a healthcare system that is multi-layered, has multi-skilled workforce, and is well equipped with medical assets that are well dispersed and easily accessible geographically. There is an urgent need for more resources to be allocated for public healthcare. Expenditure on healthcare has been on the decline from 4.4 percent of GDP in 2000 to about 1.2 percent in 2017-2018. The National Health Policy 2017, however, aims to increase the healthcare expenditure by the Government as a percentage of GDP from the existing 1.15 percent to 2.5 percent by 2025.

In regard to the medical education, admittedly, the number of medical colleges has increased from 20, at the time of the independence in 1947, with a capacity of 1,500 MBBS seats, to 476 colleges at the present, offering 61140 seats in the MBBS course. The Government plans to establish about 200 more medical colleges in the next 10 years to meet the projected shortage of several lakh doctors in the country. Going forward, the post-graduate seats also need to be drastically increased. Importantly, the capitation-fees system needs to be abolished. In addition, the 300-bed hospitals at district levels, especially in disturbed areas, could be turned into medical schools as well as post-graduate training institutions.

Even though the Government has intensified its efforts to overhaul the public healthcare system by (a) capping prices of several medical devices and medicines, (b) schemes launched for screening of non-communicable diseases and (c) raising the central healthcare budget by more than a quarter, an affordable healthcare for all still remains elusive. In this context, the launch of Ayushman Bharat holds some promise.

This article attempts to focus on the factors that potentially ail the current healthcare sector. His article also identifies possible remedial measures to make the healthcare available and affordable for the general public.

Aspiring for Good Health

EVERY person aspires for good health, which by it self is a valued achievement, as almost all other human accomplishments and achievements depend on one's good health. Mahatma Gandhi said, '*It is health that is real wealth and not pieces of gold and silver.*' In the Budget of 2018, the Finance Minister said, 'Only '*Swasth Bharat* can be a *Samriddha Bharat*. India cannot realise its demographic dividend without its citizens being healthy.' Maintaining good health definitely imparts some direct and indirect benefits to individuals and, thus, to the society as a whole. It also frees one of the burden that otherwise would be spent on the treatment of ill health at the personal and the national levels in public provisioning of healthcare services. Indirectly, such expenditure also influences the distribution of resources. People's good health contributes directly to the economic growth of a country. It clearly reduces production losses and also contributes in terms of higher work productivity by healthy workers. Therefore, health with its own intrinsic value helps in the attainment of other valued goals for enhancing personal and social well-being. This well-being and security from diseases, debilitation, and death is translated at the level of societies, communities, regions, and the nation. If a country can, from a high rate incidence of morbidity and mortality, achieve a state where people generally enjoy long and disease-free lives, it is considered an important social change. This is something that every nation must aspire to achieve.

The Right to Health is recognised as a Fundamental Right in India and enshrined under Articles 39 (e)[1], 39 (f)[2], 42[3], and 47[4] of the Constitution. Article 47, in particular, states that the State shall regard the raising of the level of nutrition and standard of living of its people, and the improvement of public health as among its primary duties. The United Nations Committee on Economic, Social, and Cultural Rights has observed that the Right to Health must be understood as the 'right to enjoyment of a variety of facilities, goods, services, and conditions necessary for the realisation of the highest attainable standards of health'.[5] Despite the foregoing, it is also a fact that health does not receive the attention it deserves even though the deaths from ill health and diseases far outweigh those due to war and violence. Not many recall that the Spanish Flu killed over a 50–100 million people between January 1918 and December 1920.[6] Compare this to the worldwide attention and memorial services dedicated a century later to the victims of World War I, which happened concurrently. War and conflict are riveting, while grief and suffering are mundane and boring. There has been growing recognition worldwide among political leaders that individuals place great importance on health and overall well-being. This is true even in India where earlier people passed on their conditions on their *karma*.[7]

Efficient healthcare systems in the country should, as a minimum, aim to guarantee protection against diseases, as well as against the effects of an unhealthy lifestyle. Even today, in many developing countries, the causes of death are generally infectious and parasitic diseases; while in developed countries, many deaths are caused due to life-style chronic diseases, as per the World Health Organisation Report,[8] which lists non-communicable diseases, like cardiovascular diseases, cancer, diabetes, and chronic respiratory diseases as major killers. The number of people who die before attaining the age of 60, i.e. in the productive age group, continues to rise, particularly in low- and middle-income countries. According to the UN, threats are greater for poorer people, particularly due to lack of access to healthcare service and malnutrition, compounded by poor accessibility to basic necessities, like clean drinking water and basic hygiene. Disparities in healthcare security have been found in both, developing and industrial countries, with diseases like HIV/AIDS being cited as a global epidemic. Incompatible understanding of the concept between various countries, and the associated costs involved, has led to the creation of the stage for breakdown in global cooperation. The failure to address health issues has a significant impact on food and economic securities, as well as environmental security. New epidemic health threats, such as the avian flu, Ebola, and the SARS crisis, show the vulnerabilities of the world and its inhabitants. These epidemics establish the necessity of a well-coordinated response that spans the continents and incorporates global humanitarian and public health action teams. Infectious diseases, such as HIV/AIDS, tuberculosis, and malaria, have seen 150 million deaths since 1945, as compared to 23 million deaths from various political and military conflicts. The AIDS epidemic has caused over 26 million deaths, 95 percent of which are in developing and extremely poor countries. Thus, even the state of health and loss of lives impact political stability, economic productivity, social cohesion, as well as the agricultural productivity and food security. Poor healthcare measures are indicated by the following indices:

(1) High rate of spread of infectious diseases;
(2) High malnutrition rates;
(3) 'Under 5' mortality rates;
(4) Low life expectancy;
(5) High mortality and disease prevalence; and
(6) Spread of waterborne diseases.

The role of the Government in looking after the general health of citizens is not only limited to the health related initiatives, but also related directly to the quality of drinking water, sanitation, hygiene, general living conditions, healthy and balanced nutrition, the quality and level of education of the masses and social awareness programmes, early child development and several other social-security measures, such as population control, gender equality and women empowerment, and mitigation of the effects of an ongoing global climatic change and natural disasters on the people's health, community participation and many others. Making public health a shared value across the sectors is a political challenge that demands a strategy where collective action is crucial. Health related initiatives have to come from the Government but the individual citizens, community and private enterprises play a vital role in promoting good health in people. Every country needs a health system that is multi-layered, with a multi-skilled workforce. However, it must also be understood that the State alone cannot ensure good health or provide protection against every cause of illnesses. The individuals and communities also play a vital role in maintaining healthy societies, particularly, where community practices are involved, such as female genital mutilation, gender inequality, and abortion of female foetuses amongst many others.

Status of Health Sector and Indices in India

Of late, diseases and health issues have become matters of greater political and legal sensitivity. Frequent crisis has brought healthcare matters to a level of prominence that it had not previously witnessed in India. The Government has acknowledged public demands for greater accountability, accessibility and greater control on the healthcare sector.

The deaths of children in Gorakhpur[9] due to disruption of oxygen supply; the cases of excessive billing and negligence in big corporate hospitals;[10] and many other such instances across the spectrum have highlighted the systemic failures in public health provision. The medical negligence in Fortis hospital, at Gurugram, which is a super-specialty hospital, has also showed that the unregulated private sector is no solution to India's healthcare problems. The protests against the National Eligibility cum Entrance Test (NEET) examination[11] have brought forth the complexities involved in ensuring a fair and inclusive system of medical education. The resistance to the Karnataka Private Medical Establishments Act (KPME) has demonstrated the difficulty in regulating the private sector and the influence of doctors working in the private sector. The list is long and endless. All these issues indicate the health sector in India needs much greater attention and possibly a serious overhaul.

As per the data released by the Government, the infant mortality rate (IMR) has declined from 37 per 1,000 live births in 2015 to 34 per 1,000 live births in 2016. This is still a long way off the 2019 target of IMR 28 per 1,000 live births.[12] Every eighth reported medically certified death has been of the infants (age less than 1 year). Chart 1 lists the causes of death in 2015 as per the statistics released by the Registrar General and Census Commissioner.[13]

The top ten causes of death in India are reported to be due to chronic diseases, cardiovascular and respiratory diseases being the two major killers. The magnitude of those dying before the age of 50, whilst still being in the productive age, has continued to rise over time. The cause for death for poorer people,

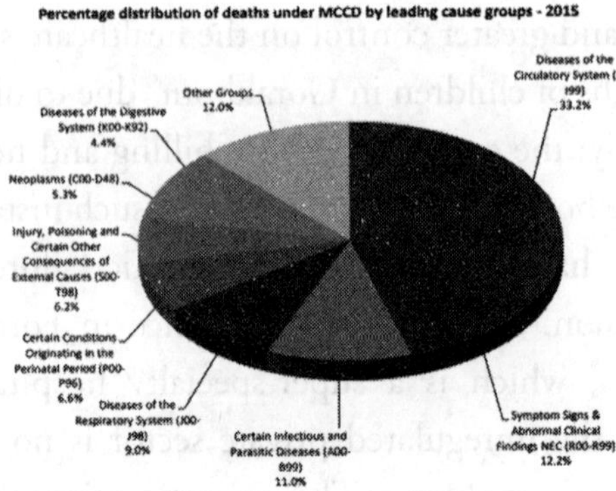

Chart 1: Percentage of distribution of deaths in India–2015[14]

particularly, due to lack of access to healthcare services and malnutrition, is compounded by the lack of basic necessities–clean drinking water and basic hygiene. Mental illness is also amongst the top ten killers in the country, followed by liver and road accidents. India compares with sub-Saharan Africa on several parameters and lags behind many of its neighbours. According to an analysis of the Healthcare Access and Quality (HAQ) Index published in *The Lancet*, a British medical journal,[15] India performed better than only Pakistan over a period of 15 years (2001–2015) among 19 countries in South Asia and Southeast Asia (including China) by potential and actual healthcare access and quality. The failure to provide basic healthcare services adds to the financial burden and also increases the indebtedness of the working or jobless poor. Studies show that only 5 percent of hospital expenditure was covered through insurance schemes with the poorest of the poor (47% of rural and 37% of urban population) meeting the expenses out of their own pocket. There is a serious need and attention required in dissociating healthcare from affluence. Currently, a mere MBBS degree is insufficient to practice and doctors need to do specialisation. India is short of 2 million doctors, according to a PWC Report. Not only are the number of Post-Graduate seats low, but also the subject-wise distribution of the 61 specialities is lopsided. For example, there are instances where a state has more than 100 Post-Graduate seats for anaesthesia. Some states have less than 10 seats for Paediatrics which, given the number of infant related deaths, is the need of the hour. The US has 21,000 Under-Graduate seats and 39,000 Post-Graduate seats while India has 52,000 Under-Graduate seats with a corresponding 14,500 Post-Graduate seats in clinical subjects.[16] Health policies implemented over the last few decades have caused this unfortunate situation. As a result, there is an acute shortage of doctors, specialists, medical teachers and nurses. There is an acute shortage of doctors in the PHC and CHC.

The shortage of doctors for various diseases is illustrated in Table 1.[17]

Public health facilities suffer from poor infrastructure and human resources availability. For instance, according to the Rural Health Statistics 2017, 13% of the sanctioned health

Table 1: Current available and actual requirement of doctors

Discipline	Current number of practicing specialists / Required number	Current PG seats / Required PG seats
Cardiology	4,000 / 88,000	268 / 3,200
Paediatric	23,000 / 225,000	1,200 / 10,500
Chest Medicine	1,200 / 23,000	329 / 2,000
Neurologist	1,100 / 52,000	171 / 2,800
Gastroenterology	2,000 / 54,000	102 / 1,800
Orthopaedic Surgeon	9,000 /77,000	978 /3,300
General Surgeon	18,000 /100,000	2,124/10,000
Neuro Surgeon	1,400 /20,600	204 /800

worker (female) posts and 37% of the health worker (male) posts remain vacant.[18] Overall, only 11% of sub-centres and about 13% of primary health centres (PHCs) are functioning as per the Indian Public Health Standards (IPHS). There is, therefore, an urgent need for more resources to be allocated for public healthcare along with all necessary measures required to strengthen the delivery of all basic and standard healthcare services.

The Government expenditure on healthcare was 4.4 percent of GDP in 2000, which was reduced to 4.0 percent of GDP in 2010. In 2015, the expenditure on health was only about 1.2 percent of GDP, which is amongst the lowest in the world.[19] In this year's budget, the Finance Minister of India has assured an increase to 2.5 percent and an allocation of Rupees 56,226 crore, which is an increase of 12 percent over the previous year. He has also announced several major initiatives, including a proposal for one of the largest public-funded Rupees 5 Lakh insurance scheme that will cover nearly 10 crore families.

India's Achievements in the Health Sector

Factually, India has covered a significant ground in the past. The milestones in the history of public health have made a great impact on millions of lives in the country.

In 1947, at the time of the country's independence, the total number of physicians was 47,524, with 'doctor to population' ratio of 1:63,007. According to the Medical Council of India (MCI), at present there are around 9.29 lakh doctors registered in the Indian Medical Register, which makes a 'doctor to patient' ratio of 1:1,674, which is significantly much higher than the 1947 ratio. However, the current ratio is still less than the WHO norm of 1:1,000.[20]

The Parliamentary Committee in its report on functioning of the MCI said that the register of the MCI[21] may not be updated given that large number of doctors have migrated to overseas destinations or may not be available due to death or other reasons.

Around 55,000 doctors and 25,000 PG doctors graduate in India every year, thanks to a rapid growth of medical colleges in India, particularly those that are run privately. In 1947, there were only 20 medical colleges, with a total intake capacity of 1,500 MBBS seats. Today, there are 476 colleges, offering 61,140 MBBS seats. The Government plans to establish around 200 new medical colleges in the next 10 years to meet the projected shortage of several lakh doctors. Several other indicators have also shown an improvement since 1947, for example, the *infant mortality rate* (IMR), the *maternal mortality ratio* (MMR), as well as *life expectancy* at birth.

Primary Health Centres (PHCs) are the cornerstone of rural healthcare delivery system in India and even those have increased from 77 in the first plan that was rolled out in 1955. As on 31 March 2015, there were 25,308 Primary Health Centres (PHCs) and 5,396 Community Health Centres (CHCs) functioning in the country.[22]

Opportunities in Healthcare as a Revenue Industry

Contrary to a popular belief, the biggest industries are not Oil and Gas and Automobile industry. Healthcare is a sector that will drive the 21st century economy with a current valuation of US$ 8 trillion competed closely by the agricultural sector.[23] In India, a report prepared by ASSOCHAM says the value of the healthcare sector in 2016, which stood at US $110 billon, will see a compounded annual growth rate (CAGR) of

22 percent and a three-fold jump to US $372 billion by 2022. The medical-devices market in India, valued at US $4 billion in 2016, is likely to cross US $11 billion by 2022 because of the growing geriatric population, increase in medical tourism and a gradual decrease in the cost of medical services[24]. Moreover, the healthcare sector allows a range of levels of skills–unskilled to highly skilled–which generates employment for all strata of society. The healthcare sector encompasses activities in hospitals, general and specialist medical practices, health clinics, medical laboratories, as well as dentistry. It comprises workers primarily delivering healthcare services, such as healthcare professionals (doctors, nurses, midwives, paramedics, pharmacists and dentists), associate healthcare professionals, public health professionals, health management, and administrative and support staff.

The requirement for health services will also need to ensure the availability of affordable medicines and essential lifesaving drugs. This requires a fine balance between the *intellectual property rights* and affordability. There is also a need for good regulatory systems, with reliable health forecasting and warning systems, and the willing participation of the people. Where good health practices are taboo or dangerous practices, such as female genital mutilation, exist, an aggressive awareness and education campaign as well as the empowerment of communities are urgently required, as earnest measures in keeping up with the fast changing times.

Initiatives by the Government

While there is an overall improvement in the healthcare parameters, there still exists a huge gap and several deficiencies in the delivery of desirable healthcare security to general masses in India. The allocation of the Government funding has lately been falling. Unfortunately, the private sector has been unable to make the basic healthcare accessible and affordable to the general masses, in particular, the people belonging to the lower socio-economic strata. Issues, such as availability of clean drinking water, sanitation and hygiene, further compound the situation. The poor health statistics in India is a cumulative effect of a poor health and sanitation infrastructure, overburdened health systems, a poor 'doctor to people' ratio, non-availability of medicines and lifesaving drugs, poor neo-natal and pre-natal care, non-availability of midwife and pregnancy care, and nutrition for children and expectant mothers.

Some of the necessary measures that can be considered to meet the basic healthcare security requirements are as under:

(1) Guaranteed access to healthcare and health services;
(2) Community-based disease prevention;
(3) Health promotion;
(4) Nutrition promotion;
(5) Epidemic preparedness;
(6) Disease surveillance and control;
(7) Risk-sharing arrangements that pool membership funds and promote community-based insurance schemes;
(8) Improved water and sanitation facilities; and
(9) Specific focus on people living in rural areas from the lower socio-economic strata, in particular, the women and children.

It must be emphasised that India is home to a third of the world's poor, numbering millions, approximately equal to the combined populations of Europe and Africa. Measures to ensure the equality amongst the people, and alleviation of their healthcare insecurity, must be linked to governance measures and must form part of the human developmental governance. Several Indian programmes have been lauded by the world and many international organisations for their ambition in scale, scope, as well as execution. In India, due to a massive population in the country, many welfare programmes floated by the Government are unique in nature, and their execution is equally challenging and gigantic; for example, the recent initiative by the Prime Minister in mobilising the banks for opening accounts for every poor Indian has been a massive exercise. It has led to opening of a record number of bank accounts, which is unique in itself and, practically, a very difficult, if not unattainable, achievement in any other part of the world. So is the *Rashtriya Swasthya Bima Yojana*, or the MNREGA, or even the conduct of the Indian election process, all of which have triggered debates across the country in so far as the coverage and targets of these programmes is concerned. There are criticisms that these programmes exist more on paper rather than in actual fact, and that they do not actually change the lives of the people for the better. Some of the unique measures adopted by the Government in India for accomplishing health security are discussed below.

- *Rashtriya Swasthya Bima Yojana*[25] *to Ayushman Bharat*
  The Rashtriya Swasthya Bima Yojana (RSBY) was launched in 2007. This is essentially an insurance scheme, where the government covers insurance payments for the poor and financially vulnerable families. The scheme intends to provide cashless insurance for hospitalisation in both public and private hospitals. The scheme started in 2008 and was implemented across 25 states of India. A total of 36 million families were enrolled by February 2014.

The RSBY is a project under the Ministry of Labour and Employment. The scheme has earned recognition from the International Labour Organization (ILO) and the World Bank as the best health insurance scheme for the poor in the world. In the 2018 budget, the Finance Minister announced that he intends to implement the New Health Assurance Mission (NHAM) that will assure health insurance for all citizens to cover 10 crore poor families, with an allocation of Rupees 5 lakh per family. This programme is the fourth iteration of the RSBY.

In 2016-2017, RSBY was renamed as the *Rashtriya Swasthya Suraksha Yojana* (RSSY). Subsequently, in 2017-2018, this was renamed as NHPS.

There are two ways in which the new scheme differs in its scale. Firstly, the amount of Rupees 5 lakh per family is a fivefold hike from the initial Rupees 1 lakh per family. Secondly, it differs in its reach of providing cover for 10 crore families and, therefore, covers about 40 percent of India's population. The huge allocation may also attract the entry of the private sector into health delivery for the poorest, which was so far reluctant to enter into the programme due to low profit margins. However, the proof of the pudding will be when it is actually translated to true healthcare in reach and scope.

- *Aam Aadmi Bima Yojana*[26]

  The scheme gives life insurance coverage and also covers partial and permanent disability to the head of the family or to the sole earning member of the family. This is for the rural landless households. As an extended benefit, this scheme also gives educational assistance to the children of landless, who are students in 9th and 12th standard.

- *Deendayal Disabled Rehabilitation Scheme*[27]
  This scheme aims to ensure equal opportunities, equity, social justice, and empowerment of persons with disabilities.
- *Central Government Health Scheme*[28] *and Ex Servicemen Contributory Health Scheme*
  It is entitled for all categories of government employees and defence veterans.
- *Integrated Child Development Services*[29]
  These services were introduced to prevent malnutrition, as well as related health issues in mothers and infants, and children below the age of 6 years.
- *Janani Suraksha Yojana*[30]
  Instituted in 2005, and executed by the Ministry of Family Welfare, this scheme gives a one-time cash grant to pregnant women for paying for institutional/home births, as well as skilled assistance for aided deliveries. There is also a scheme called *Udisha*, which is an initiative aimed at quality improvement of early childhood care for survival, growth, and development.
- *Revised National Tuberculosis Control Programme*[31]
  The programme provides, free of cost, quality anti-tubercular drugs across the country. This is distributed through the numerous PHCs. There is now a tie-up with the private-sector Directly Observed Treatment-short Course (DOTS), which is the global tuberculosis control strategy of the World Health Organisation (WHO). In this year's budget, an allocation of Rupees

600 crore has been set aside towards nutritional support for TB patients, which aims to provide Rupees 500 in cash per month for the newly detected TB cases for a period of up to six months. A re-treatment patient would receive Rupees 4,000 for eight months (Rupees 500 per month); and a drug-resistant patient would get Rupees 12,000 for the duration of treatment that could last for up to two years.

Recent Initiatives by the Government

- *Recognition of Diploma from College of Physicians & Surgeons (CPS) Mumbai*

  The Government has enacted some important bills in the recent past. Of those, there is one notable bill that overturned the decision of the Medical Council of India (MCI) in 2009, which de-recognised the Diploma given by CPS Mumbai, a professional body in existence since 1913. This effectively releases a large number of specialists and overcomes the artificially created shortages in the country by regulation of post-graduate seats.

  However, possibly due to a fear of litigation, the Government, as a U-turn, now only recognises three diplomas and six fellowships granted by the CPS as approved by the MCI.[32]
- *Additional Post Graduate Vacancies*

  The MCI, at the behest of the Government, has revised the 'teacher to student' ratio to increase post-graduate seats in clinical subjects. As per a notification, dated 31 January 2017, issued by the MCI under its Post-Graduate Regulations, the 'teacher to student' ratio shall be 1:3 for Professor and 1:2 for Associate Professor. This will yield about 5,000 additional Post-Graduate seats in clinical subjects. The increased availability of seats, along with a centralised entrance exam–NEET (PG)–is a major step in reforming the medical education in the country.[33]

- *National Medical Commission (NMC) Bill 2017*

  The Parliamentary Standing Committee on health and family welfare has made valid recommendations in its report released in March 2016, which was followed by NITI Ayog, placing a draft Medical Council Bill placed for public comments, incorporating many of the standing committee recommendations. The draft Bill was a reaction to many criticisms of the functioning of the MCI from all quarters, including the Supreme Court of India. The Indian Medical Association (IMA), which has over 2.77 lakh members, strongly objected to the draft National Medical Commission (NMC) Bill 2017, which was presented in the Lok Sabha on 29 December 2017.

  The IMA called for a strike and the major issues raised were that the new National Medical Commission (NMC) Bill 2017 will make the system prone to corruption and wanted some provisions reviewed, asserting the draft NMC is an anti-poor bill, with pro-private management clauses. The IMA alleged that it will 'cripple' the functioning of medical professionals by making them 'completely answerable to the bureaucracy and non-medical administrators'.

  The IMA is concerned that the new bill takes away the voting right of every doctor in India to elect their medical council, as the NMC has a provision to induct non-medical persons into the new body of medical governance. The NMC proposes to do away with permissions needed to start a medical college, allowing private medical colleges to increase undergraduate and postgraduate seats on their own.

According to Section 26(1)(b) of the Bill, permission to start medical colleges, conduct post-graduate or super-speciality courses or increase seats in MBBS, post-graduate course and/or super-speciality courses will be directly granted by the Medical Assessment and Rating Board, which will have three members nominated by the Government. It is a fact that the groundwork for the Bill arose after several complaints were filed against the MCI, and its top officials, for using its sweeping powers to derecognise medical colleges and manipulating admissions to rake in money in garb of inspections and permissions.

India suffers from a peculiar situation each year, where 1.5 lakh doctors sit at home and study for post-graduate examinations. This number is a conservative estimate, and it occurs because of the huge discrepancy between the number of under-graduate and post-graduate seats. It takes an average of 2 to 3 years for a student to obtain a post-graduate seat. This situation is also a hotbed for corruption, with capitation becoming a normal part.

Medical education is expensive in India. The capitation fee for MBBS seats was Rupees 65 lakh in 2015, increasing to Rupees 1.75 crore in 2016. Around the same time, the capitation fee for post-graduate seats was between Rupees 1.5 crore and 4 crore.

The present-day fees for MBBS / post-graduate courses are in the range of Rupees 15 to 50 lakh per annum (plus the capitation fee). There are over 7 lakh aspirants for 52,000 MBBS seats and over 1.5 lakh aspirants for 14,500 post-graduate seats. This explains why thousands of Indian medical students prefer to study in China, Russia and Ukraine whose MBBS degrees have recognition problems in India.

Medicine, as a profession, is losing its sheen as a noble profession. The capitation fee makes the students to look at it in terms of a 'return on investment', rather than as a calling. Hundreds of mission hospitals (the second largest provider of healthcare in India after the Government) have had to close down due to shortage of doctors and medical specialists.

The top ten causes of death in India cannot be treated by a doctor without a PG degree. As per Section 33(1)(d), the NMC can permit a medical professional to perform surgery or practise medicine without qualifying the *National Licentiate Examination*, but only in circumstances that may be specified in the regulations. The Section 15.II (b) of the MCI Act ensures that that the basic qualification to practise modern medicine is MBBS and this clause has been removed in the new Bill. As per the NMC Section 55(2)(zl) of the NMC Bill, the *Ethics and Medical Registration Board* can maintain a separate national register that would have the names of the licensed AYUSH practitioners. The NMC Bill also has provisions to allow *Ayurveda* as well as *homeopathic* doctors to undergo a six-month bridging course to practice allopathy. There are several beneficiaries of the traditional health systems in the country, which need a regulation for safer medical practice, as bringing all medical practitioners under one ambit may be easier to regulate for the patient safety purposes. The MCI and the IMA may have managed to delay the passage of an important Bill, but with health issues having moved up the political agenda, this is not a dead end for reforms. The Government has enacted several important legislative measures and, hopefully, intends to follow through with the reforms in this vital sector.

- *National Health Policy 2017*
  The National Health Policy of 1983 and the National Health Policy of 2002 served in guiding the healthcare sector in the Government Five-Year Plans. The National Health Policy 2017 aims to 'increase health expenditure by Government as a percentage of GDP–from the existing 1.15 percent to the proposed 2.5 percent by 2025'.
- *Price Capping of Essential Drugs and Devices*
  Early last year, the Government capped prices of medical devices, such as knee implants, heart stents and sixty-nine essential medicines by up to 75 percent to make them more affordable. However, this has not been without concern from the manufacturers who have cited commercial unsustainability of the sale of their products at the slashed prices, which are not competitive enough in India. There are concerns that some manufacturers may exit the field, causing shortages of these medical devices and essential medicines at hospitals. In 1995, when the *Drug Price Control Order* (DPCO) and later its successor, the DPCO 2013, were

issued, many drug producers left the Indian market and, from being a market-leader in pharmaceuticals, India became dependent on China for the supply of main ingredients in many commonly used drugs and the front-line medications. Any disruption to the supply chain from China, as witnessed in the run up to the Beijing Olympics, could affect the manufacture of critical drugs in India. Thus, there is a flip side to the price cap proposed by the Government.

Sanitation and Hygiene

As per the WHO estimates, about 10 percent of all deaths in India are caused by poor sanitation and hygiene. Diarrhoea alone accounts for above 5 percent of all deaths in India. Inadequate sanitation also leads to significant economic losses. As per a *Water and Sanitation Programme* study carried out in 2010, the economic losses in India amounted to about 6.4 percent of India's GDP in 2006 (approximately US $53.8 billion), mainly due to poor sanitation. Lack of toilet facilities is also the leading cause of several crimes against women in India, as they are compelled to leave their homes to relieve themselves in open and bushy areas away from their dwellings, becoming vulnerable to sexual violence.[34] Poor sanitation has also been linked to malnutrition. Open defecation, for example, exposes children to bacteria that sickens them and results in stunting of body growth and of intelligence, impacts that are often permanent.[35] The World Bank report, *Nutrition in India*, notes that India loses over US $12 billion due to vitamin and mineral deficiencies.[36]

As per the UNICEF[37] reports, it is estimated that:

(1) Only about 31 percent of India's overall population has access to improved sanitation and, in rural India, only 21 percent people use improved sanitation facilities.

(2) Over 594 million people in India defecate in the open, which comprises nearly 50 percent of the population. In relatively poorer Bangladesh, only 7 percent of the population practices open defecation. Comparatively, in China, which has more population than India, only 4 percent of the population defecates in the open.

The Prime Minister announced the *Swachh Bharat Abhiyan* on the birth anniversary of Mahatma Gandhi in 2014, drawing on the revered leader's lifelong insistence on good hygiene and sanitation. Gandhi was the first political leader in India to tell the Indian people that poor sanitation was a public hazard and that there was dignity in cleaning one's own toilet. It is a matter of concern that standards of hygiene are abysmally low in India. *Swachh Bharat* campaign triggered a competition between cities. It has spurred many NGOs and some popular Bollywood stars to exhort the people, on the mass media, to defecate behind the closed doors of toilets. As a consequence of their sustained campaign, the results are showing in the form of a record number of sustainable toilets, open defecation-free towns, schools with gender-specific toilets and a decrease in water-borne diseases in 'open-defecation-free' (ODF) villages and towns. A survey by QCI conducted last year has found that only less than three in 10 urban households (26.75 percent) were without a toilet as against 50 percent as per the 2011 census. In rural households, it has reduced to 32.5 percent from 69 percent. That is, the toilet coverage has more than doubled in rural India during the last three years.

Key Health Expenditure Estimates for India

India spends relatively much lesser on healthcare as compared to China (3 percent of GDP) and the US[38] (about 9 percent of GDP).

In December 2014, the Government ordered a further cut of nearly Rupees 60 billion in the healthcare funding due to fiscal strains.[39] While progress is visible on various health outcomes, India still records some of the world's poorest health statistics. The state-wise data shows that the states with the largest number of health-related fatalities are the ones with poorer levels of infrastructure for healthcare. It is in such places that the people from the lower socio-economic strata take recourse to quacks, fake-medicine men and other miracle cures, which further deteriorate the health and financial condition of the family.

According to *National Health Systems Resource Centre*, the *Total Health Expenditure* (THE) for India is estimated at Rupees 4,83,259 crore (3.89 percent of GDP and Rupees 3,826 per capita) for the financial year 2014-15, which constitutes the current and capital expenditures incurred by the Government and private sources, including external/donor funds.

The *Current Health Expenditure* (CHE) was Rupees 4,51,286 crore (93.4 percent of THE) and capital expenditures was Rupees 31,973 crore (6.6 percent of THE).

The *Government Health Expenditure* (GHE), including capital expenditure was Rupees 1, 39,949 crore (29 percent of THE, 1.13 percent of GDP and Rupees 1,108 per capita) for the financial year 2014-15, which amounted to about 3.94 percent of General Government Expenditure in 2014-15.

According to *National Health Accounts,*[40] 63 percent of total health spending in India in 2014-15 was *out of pocket expenditure* (OoPE).

The failure to provide basic healthcare services adds to the financial burden and also increases the indebtedness of the working or jobless poor. As a share of private spending, OoPE is almost 90 percent. Healthcare expenditure can be catastrophic, with one estimate suggesting that OoPE on healthcare accounts for an addition of around seven percentage points to India's poverty figures. The reports show that only 5 percent of hospital expenditure was covered through insurance schemes. Financing of health-related initiatives in a country like India has to come from the Government. In the organised sector, the workforce comes under some employer-provided insurance schemes.

In India, there are a large number of people in the unorganised sector and very few people can afford to procure private health insurance. Even if they are able to buy some insurance, many health conditions are not covered.

For effective healthcare of general public, the following three dimensions should be covered:

(a) Well-equipped health services infrastructure;

(b) Preventive measure and timely monitoring of diseases; and

(c) Financial allocations to reduce the OoPE of the poor.

Therefore, the country needs a health system that is multi-layered, and has multi-skilled workforce and is well-equipped, reinforced with medical assets that are well dispersed across the length and breadth of the country and easily accessible to all. The need and availability of affordable medicines and essential drugs is a must; this is where the battle between *intellectual property rights* and affordable drugs comes in. There is also a need for good regulatory systems, with reliable health forecasting and warning systems and willing participation of the people. There are some areas where good health practices are taboos, which require a good awareness campaign, as well as empowerment of the relevant communities to earnestly take the necessary measures.

Suggestions to Improve Reach, Quality of Healthcare

For effective healthcare of entire Indian population, a multi-pronged approach is required.

- Firstly, there has to be complete breadth of coverage across the country, not just confined to cities and towns but also the small villages and hinterland.
- Secondly, the country needs a healthcare system–multi-layered, multi-skilled workforce, well-equipped and accessible–one that covers the full spectrum–medical doctors, nurses, pharmacists, laboratory assistants and technicians, support staff etc. All these vocations are high as well as low-skill employment generators.
- Thirdly, the availability of affordable medicines, diagnostic equipment and essential drugs is a must.
- Fourthly, there is a need for good regulatory systems, which is transparent, reliable and corruption free.
- Lastly, good health practices require a good awareness campaign, as well as empowerment of communities to take earnest measures. People must be made to understand that, the key to good health are day-to-day (inexpensive) preventive measures and not the (expensive) medical cure.

In addition to the above approach, the following suggestions are made:

(i) *Create more healthcare professionals*

The need of the hour is to create more healthcare

professionals by recognising this sector as a vital sector for national growth and security. This also demands easing of norms and bureaucratic control exerted by bodies like the MCI etc. Easing of norms by these professional bodies can help in creating more healthcare sector professionals; thereby, creating more jobs for the young population, which can prove to be a valuable demographic dividend for the economy, instead of becoming a burden on the country in case they do not get employment. The recent agitations by *Jats* and *Patels* prove this point. To be effective, the ratio of 'doctors to nurses' and 'doctors to technicians' should be 1:4 and 1: 4, respectively. It is currently in the range of 1:1.6; thus, having a huge scope for employment.

(ii) *Reduce the costs of medical education*

There should be a drastic reduction in the costs of medical education and, most importantly, the capitation-fee system must be abolished to restore some dignity to the medical profession–one of 'service' instead of 'business or profit'. The costs of education are keeping away many aspirants. The track record of doctors from deprived and poorer backgrounds indicates a sense of purpose and commitment to service. Currently, the high fees and a stiff competition don't allow many candidates from this background to make it to medical colleges. This needs correction and some curtailment of the MCI powers.

(iii) *District Hospitals should be medical colleges*

A good medical practitioner is the product of practice and not by education and, therefore, a good doctor is a by-product of a hospital and not a medical college. The district level 300-bed hospitals, especially in disturbed areas, could be turned into medical schools, as well as post-graduate training institutions. The initial annual student intake could be around 50. Therefore, possibly up to about 664 new medical colleges can come into existence in the country, with a minimal investment from the Government. Norms for teaching faculty can be reasonably relaxed from the current stringent norms enforced by the MCI. It would be desirable that seats are offered to the local students in the regions, which will make the dreams of the poorer sections of the community, to become doctors, come true. The fees should be minimal and the selection on merit alone.

(iv) *Self-financing post-graduate seats*

The PG programme should be self-financing and not require any payment of capitation fees. There should be roughly equal number of PG seats as UG seats and even these could be offered in the district hospitals. This will also make medical students move compulsorily to rural areas. The PG education is free in developed countries.

(v) *Nursing sector*

As the nursing sector is generally an ignored sector, it is also in a state of crisis; in a few years, there will be a serious shortage of nurses. In other countries, nurses can progress within various specialties (e.g. they can become nurse anaesthetists in the US, excluding the requirement of a doctor anaesthetist), but not in India. The *Health Sector Skills Council* (HSSC) courses provide for career growth of nurses and also other allied health skills, which as an excellent initiative needs to be more widely utilised. The nursing demand is not just in hospitals but also as homecare nurses, which requires basic nursing skills in elderly people's homes. Given the availability of the youth in the country, this is an opportunity waiting to be tapped. This initiative will relieve some burden from the healthcare centres as well as from those relatives of the elderly who would be willing to pay for the services being rendered by homecare nurses. The Government is losing out on this sector; it can help to provide employment to many youth through better management controls. The *Nursing and Medical Council Authorities* charter needs a re-look and necessary amendments, where required.

(vi) *Norms for practice of medicine*

Currently, a basic (MBBS) medical degree is considered to be insufficient to practice and the doctor needs to be specialised. The *Parliamentary Standing Committee* has made valid recommendations in its report released in March 2016. The major step will be to increase the number of post-graduate seats in order to combat the great shortage of specialists. The *National Board of Examinations* (NBE), which was set up in 1975 by the Government, to improve the quality of medical education in the country, by establishing standards for post-graduate examinations in modern medicine, has taken the first step by instituting the post-graduate degree, called the *Diplomate of National Board* (DNB). The DNB has been deemed equivalent to the MD/MS degree vide a public notice issued by the Ministry of *Health and Family Welfare*. The NBE qualification requires no donation. It costs about Rupees 80,000 per year and trains about 6,000 post-graduate students every year. These students are selected through a transparent common entrance test based on merit. The DNB is well-recognised, especially internationally. However, the NBE has been without a Governing Council since October 2014, causing hardship to students and restricting the body from adding more seats or starting new courses.

(vii) *Statutory status to the NBE*

There is a need for provisioning of statutory status to the NBE, which is pending for last 22 years. The NBE has trained 30,000 specialists in 40 years, from 1976 to 2015. The NBE is currently training a third of the Indian post-graduate students where all seats are allocated on merit, with no management quota, no capitation fees and a salary is paid to the students. Fourteen Indian states use the NBE rankings to allot seats from the state quota. The Supreme Court of India has directed that the NBE conduct tests for foreign students and the NEET.

(viii) *Creation of infrastructure overseas and medical diplomacy*

Creation of infrastructure to train foreign students may be considered, as the goodwill generated for the host country is immense. India gets a large number of requests for medical seats, particularly from poorer countries in Asia and Africa. India should also explore a possibility of medical diplomacy, by setting up hospitals and medical colleges in Africa and other Asian countries. The experiment in Kabul and other places, where India set up hospitals, has worked out well.

Conclusion

The attention paid to the healthcare-related deaths in India is in complete contrast to the deaths caused due to violence, even though the numbers of people dying or suffering from health related disorders are significantly much higher.

Despite all measures listed in this article, statistics reveal that a third of the world's poorest people live in India despite the country's economic growth and a rising GDP. This poverty results in corresponding deficiencies in health, schooling and living conditions, which is a great source of insecurity.

Mahatma Gandhi recognised that violence was inextricably linked to poverty. He said, '*Poverty is the worst form of violence.*' The progress of a nation is not measured in terms of GDP or per capita income, because they fail to capture the actual income available in the hands of individuals. A GDP is not an indicator of the human development objectives and the well-being of people, which include health, education, and a sense of security–at home or at work place or in the overall environment.

Attainment of human development objectives are adversely affected by poor educational levels, health status, and insecurity at thc individual and community levels.

A sense of security is not measured on how a country defends its territories and frontiers, but how it helps in the daily struggles that people face in homes, in the areas where people live together as communities, where they can plan individually and collectively, and decide the future they want for themselves and their families.

Gandhiji's advice during the pre-independence struggle is

still relevant today: '*Recall the face of the poorest and weakest man you have seen, and ask yourself if this step you contemplate is going to be any use to him.*' The government has a lot of promises to keep and hopes to fulfil.

(Inputs and details of the paper have come from concepts propounded by the doyen of medical profession, Dr Devi Shetty, and reviewed by Dr Giridhar Giani)

References

1 Article 39(e) in The Constitution Of India: 'That the health and strength of workers, men and women, and the tender age of children are not abused and that citizens are not forced by economic necessity to enter avocations unsuited to their age or strength.'

2 Article 39(f) in The Constitution Of India: 'That children are given opportunities and facilities to develop in a healthy manner and in conditions of freedom and dignity and that childhood and youth are protected against exploitation and against moral and material abandonment.'

3 Article 42: Provision of just and human conditions of work and maternity relief.

4 Article 47: Duty of the State to raise the level of nutrition and the standard of living and to improve public health The State shall regard the raising of the level of nutrition and the standard of living of its people and the improvement of public health as among its primary duties and, in particular, the State shall endeavour to bring about prohibition of the consumption except for medicinal purposes of intoxicating drinks and of drugs which are injurious to health.

5 UN Committee on Economic, Social and Cultural Rights, General Comment No. 14, The Right to the Highest Standard of Health (Article 12 of the Convention on Economic, Social and Cultural Rights, 2000 (Doc. E/C.12/2000/4., Para 4. See also, Nirmal, B.C., "The Human

Rights to Health, Access to Drugs and Global Medical Patents", Indian Journal of International Law, 49(3), Indian Society of International Law, New Delhi, July-September 2009.

6 Taubenberger, Morens, 1918 Influenza: The Mother of All Pandemics, Emerging Infectious Diseases 2006 Jan; 12(1): 15–22, Available at https://www.ncbi.nlm.nih.gov/pmc/articles/PMC3291398/ accessed on 17 April 2018.

7 The karmic principle that generally Indians and Hindus, in particular, believe that one is repaid by the same amount of pleasure or pain that one caused to others with one's original action. Thus, any misfortune passed on to one's Karma (action or deeds).

8 50 Facts: Global Health Situation and Trends 1955-2025, World Health Report, available at http://www.who.int/whr/1998/media_centre/50facts/en/ accessed on 23 December 2017.

9 The 2017 deaths attracted media attention in the week of 7-13 August 2017, when the vendor for liquid oxygen cut off supplies to the State run Baba Raghav Das Medical College hospital allegedly due to unpaid dues of several lakh rupees. 30 children died within 48 hours: 17 children in the neo-natal ward, five in the AES (acute encephalitis syndrome) ward and eight in the general ward leading to an uproar as the hospital was in the State Chief Minister, Shri Yogi Adityanand constituency.

10 The case relates to a billing of Rupees 16 Lakh, including 660 syringes used on a seven-year old girl who died due to dengue in FMCI in Gurugramin a super-speciality hospital in September 2017.

11 NEET is conducted for admission to MBBS/BDS courses in India in medical/dental colleges run with the approval of Medical Council of India/Dental Council of India under the Ministry of Health and Family Welfare, except for AIIMS and JIPMER Puducherry, which are institutions established through an Act of Parliament. The Tamil Nadu government introduced a bill to circumvent NEET and the stringent measures to prevent cheating and malpractices received adverse media attention as some girls were asked to change their clothes and other issues like the degree of difficulty of the paper in different languages.

12 For further details, refer to the statistics on causes of death obtained through the Civil Registration System released by the Registrar General & Census Commissioner, India, available at http://www.censusindia.gov.in/2011-Documents/mccd_Report1/MCCD_Report-2015.pdf accessed on 15 March 2018 .

13 Ibid

14 Civil Registration System released by the Registrar General & Census

Commissioner, India, available at http://www.censusindia.gov.in/2011-Documents/mccd_Report1/MCCD_Report-2015.pdf, as accessed on 15 March 2018.

15 Healthcare Access and Quality Index based on mortality from causes amenable to personal healthcare in 195 countries and territories, 1990–2015: a novel analysis from the Global Burden of Disease Study 2015available at http://www.thelancet.com/pdfs/journals/lancet/PIIS0140-6736(17)30818-8.pdf accessed on 17 April 2018.

16 Civil Registration System released by the Registrar General & Census Commissioner, India, available at http://www.censusindia.gov.in/2011-Documents/mccd_Report1/MCCD_Report-2015.pdf, as accessed on 15 March 2018.

17 Healthcare Access and Quality Index based on mortality from causes amenable to personal healthcare in 195 countries and territories, 1990–2015: a novel analysis from the Global Burden of Disease Study 2015available at http://www.thelancet.com/pdfs/journals/lancet/PIIS0140-6736(17)30818-8.pdf accessed on 17 April 2018.

18 https://nrhm-mis.nic.in/Pages/RHS2017.aspx?RootFolder=%2FRURAL%20HEALTH%20STATISTICS%2F%28A%29RHS%20-%202017&FolderCTID=0x01200057278FD1EC909F429B03E86C7A7C3F31&View=%7b9029EB52-8EA2-4991-9611-FDF53C824827%7d accessed on 17 April 2018.

19 Divya Rajagopal India's disproportionately tiny health budget: A national security concern? Economic Times available at https://economictimes.indiatimes.com/industry/healthcare/biotech/healthcare/indias-disproportionately-tiny-health-budget-a-national-security-concern/articleshow/49603121.cms accessed on 17 April 2018.

20 S Bala Bhaskar, The Mandatory Regulations from the Medical Council of India: Facts, Opinions and Prejudices, November 2016, available at https://www.ncbi.nlm.nih.gov/pmc/articles/PMC5125180/ accessed on 18 April 2018

21 Page 11 of the 92nd Report of Parliamentary Standing Committee on Health and Family Welfare on the Functioning of Medical Council of India available at http://164.100.47.5/newcommittee/reports/EnglishCommittees/Committee%20on%20Health%20and%20Family%20Welfare/92.pdf accessed on 18 April 2018.

22 Rural Health Statistics 2014-15 released by Ministry of Health and Family Welfare Statistics Division, Government of India, available at http://wcd.nic.in/sites/default/files/RHS_1.pdf accessed on 18 April 2018

23 Extracted from the presentation made by Dr Devi Shetty of Narayana Hrudalaya Hospitals at the Vivekananda International Foundation on Tuesday, 19 December 2017

24 Indian healthcare market to hit $372 billion by 2022,PTI available at //economictimes.indiatimes.com/articleshow/61903998.cms?utm_source=contentofinterest&utm_medium=text&utm_campaign=cppst accessed on 17 April 2018

25 Available at http://www.rsby.gov.in/

26 Available at https://aaby.mahaonline.gov.in/HOME/index.aspx; as accessed on 28 January 2015

27 More details available at http://socialjustice.nic.in/ddrsmain.php; as accessed on 28 January 2015

28 More details available at http://msotransparent.nic.in/cghsnew/index.asp; as accessed on 28 January 2015.

29 More details available at http://wcd.nic.in/icds.htm; accessed on 28 January 2015

30 More details available at http://nrhm.gov.in/nrhm-components/rmnch-a/maternal-health/janani-suraksha-yojana/background.html; accessed on 28 January 2015.

31 More details available at http://www.tbcindia.nic.in/rntcp.html; accessed on 28 January 2015

32 Alka Dhupkar, 36 Diplomas Derecognised After U-turn by Centre, 22 February 2018, available at https://mumbaimirror.indiatimes.com/mumbai/other/36-diplomas-derecognised-after-u-turn-by-centre/articleshow/63021727.cms, as accessed on 17 April 2018.

33 Press Release titled 5000 Additional PG seats in clinical subjects in the coming years by Press Information Bureau released on 1 February 2017, available at pib.nic.in/newsite/PrintRelease.aspx?relid=157892, as accessed on 17 April 2018.

34 'Inadequate sanitation costs India Rs. 2.4 trillion (US$53.8 billion)', The Economic Impacts of Inadequate Sanitation in India, Water and Sanitation Program (World Bank), 2011,available at http://www.wsp.org/sites/wsp.org/files/publications/WSP-esi-india.pdf; as accessed on 26 January 2015.

35 'India's Poor Sanitation Linked to Malnutrition', Times of India, New Delhi, 18 July 2014.

36 Ibid

37 'Water Sanitation and Hygiene', UNICEF; available at http://www.

unicef.org/india/ wes.html, as accessed on 24 January 2015.

38 Kalra, Aditya, 'India Slashes Health Budget, Already one of the World's Lowest', Reuters News Agency, 23 December 2014; available at http://in.reuters.com/article/2014/12/23/india-health-budget-idINKBN0K10Y020141223; as accessed on 5 February 2017.

39 Ibid

40 National Health Systems Resource Centre (2017), National Health Accounts Estimates for India (2014-15). New Delhi, Ministry of Health and Family Welfare, Government of India, available at https://mohfw.gov.in/sites/default/files/National%20Health%20Accounts%20Estimates%20Report%202014-15.pdf, as accessed on 17 April 2018.

Equitable Use of River Basin Water

Dhirendra Singh, Avinash C Tyagi, Harish Kumar Varma and Vikas Khitha

Management of Water Resources has always been a challenge and this has assumed greater significance in the context of global warming which is leading to lesser availability of this resource. The problem gets further aggravated because of rising populations and environmental degradation. The Constitution sets out the basic legal framework under which the hierarchical needs of water for various purposes needs to be managed by the Union, the States, local bodies various other Non-government bodies, families and individuals. Out of the total utilisable water availability, nearly eighty-eight percent is from the rivers.

The Water Resources Atlas of India has identified 23 river basins out of which 13 are major basins. Thus, the proper management of these basins, which invariably cut across the state boundaries, assumes great significance. The two-day conclave

at the Vivekananda International Foundation (VIF), on 29 and 30 November 2017, came up with various suggestions on the equitable use of water for national development, especially to make the use of the Constitutional provisions relating to the River Basin Boards, to set them up and to manage them through cooperative efforts of all stake holders.

Towards Sustainable Water Usage

WATER Management in India has always been a challenge because of large temporal and spatial variations in its availability. The task is becoming more challenging due to global warming having significant impact on water availability, both in space and time. The challenge is accentuated by an ever-increasing population pressure and a rising demand for its use, resulting in water scarcity in many areas. Moreover, the challenge is further compounded due to matters concerning environmental degradation and the deleterious effects of climate change in the minds of both individuals and governments. The common person is concerned with health issues of polluted water and air, as well as water scarcity for daily needs; the agriculturist suffers crop losses; and the industrialist from power deficiency and absenteeism, as a result of unhealthy environment-related diseases. The concentration of natural resources, such as water, coal, iron, and other minerals, and their careless/unregulated exploitation cause local environmental degradation. In addition, the export and use of these resources elsewhere, with jobs and value-addition taking place away from home, have also given rise to local resentment.

As we all know, defence from external threats is very important for safety, security and development of a nation. Similarly, defence from internal threats emanating from water and food insecurity is also very much essential for overall development of the country. A fast growing population, increasing urbanisation and industrialisation, competition for water from different sectors, accentuated by the climate variability and change, are putting immense pressure on the availability of usable and potable water for different sectors. Water allocations to agriculture will fall owing to the combined impacts of climate change, environmental needs and competition from higher value economic sectors, posing a great challenge to ensure food security[1] for our rapidly growing population. So there will be a growing pressure on farmers to produce more with lesser water, and to spread the benefits of judicious use of water more widely and wisely. This task will be even more challenging because higher atmospheric temperatures, due to climate change, will reduce potential land and water productivity. Further, to improve energy security, growing bio-energy crops in an irrigated agriculture scheme has added another new and complex dimension to sustainable food production, due to increased water withdrawals for bio-crops, leading to enhanced risks to food security. Thus, it is important to understand the synergies and the trade-offs to ensure the sustainability of the environment. In the future, food security strategies will become more complex.

In view of the above, sustainable and equitable use of the natural resources, especially clean drinkable water is vital for the well-being of individuals and the community as well as for a secured nation. Number of initiatives have been launched by the Government, such as doubling farmers' income, rural drinking water to all, smart cities, *Swachh Bharat Abhiyan*, the *Make in India* campaign, development of inland waterways, rural health programme, etc. The success of these initiatives will depend on a sustainable and efficient use of the scarce water resources, with integrated and holistic water management, preferably at the river basin levels. As a first step to equitable allocation, it is necessary to identify a hierarchical set of requirements, with basic needs of drinking, washing and cooking as the first priority, as stipulated in the *National Water Policy 2012*, followed by its use for agriculture and industry purposes, and finally for use in leisure and sporting activities etc. In addition, use of water in electric-power generation is another significant area, which needs attention and is required to be factored in the overall development of basins. Apart from the human needs, the environment too needs water to preserve the aquatic eco-system and its rejuvenation. Therefore, the scope to include recycling of natural resources as far as practically possible in all such cases assumes significance.

A core challenge before India is, thus, about proper management and use of water in all major river systems, which can come about only by proper and effective governance and by undertaking associated institutional reforms.

Based on a high level conclave organised by Vivekananda International Foundation and International Commission on Irrigation and Drainage on the subject, this article presents an analysis of the present situation of water resources development in India and proposes a number of necessary and urgent steps required to be taken.

Water Resources in India and their Development

Broadly, the Water Resources Atlas of India has identified 23 river basins, out of which 13 are major river basins, namely *Indus, Ganga-Brahmaputra-Barak, Subernarekha, Brahamani-Baitarni, Mahanadi, Godavari, Krishna, Pennar, Cauvery, Tapi,*

Narmada, Mahi, and *Sabarmati*. These basins cover an area of about 2.6 million square km out of a total area of about 3.18 million square km.

Out of the total estimated 1,869 BCM of annual average flows, these major basins carry about 85 percent (1,583 BCM) of water. It is also seen that, out of the total utilisable water available (690 BCM) in the country, 88 percent (609 BCM) is available in these basins. In addition, the total annual replenishable groundwater potential of the country is 433 BCM. Thus, the total utilisable annual water availability of the country is assessed at 1,123 BCM.

So far, out of 690 BCM utilisable surface water, storage capacity of about 255 BCM has been created and another 51 BCM is under construction through major and medium sized projects. Maximum storage probabilities lie in the Himalayas. These include quite a few in the *Ganga* basin in Nepal, and in the *Brahmaputra* basin (in India and Bhutan). The peninsular rivers like *Mahanadi, Godavari* and *Narmada* also offer some scope for harnessing available flows during floods.

Out of an ultimate irrigation potential of about 140 million hectares (MHa), about 109 MHa (45 MHa from major and medium sized irrigation projects and 64 MHa from minor irrigation projects, both from surface and groundwater) has been created. Of this, about 87 MHa has been already utilised.

As per an assessment by the *Central Electricity Authority*, the economically exploitable and viable hydro-electric potential is estimated to be about 1,48,701 MW, which is about 84,044 MW at 60 percent load factor, out of which about 44,960 MW (53 percent) has been harnessed so far. In addition, 56 sites for *Pumped Storage Schemes* with probable total installation of about 94,000 MW have also been identified, of which about 4,800 MW of hydro-electric power generation have been developed and about 1,080 MW is under development.

In terms of water supply, as per the census data of 2011, 43.5 percent of households (HHs)–that is 70.6 percent in urban and 30.8 percent in rural areas–have access to piped-water sources, whereas 53.0 percent HHs (i.e. 26.9 percent in urban and 65.2 percent in rural areas) depend upon non-piped improved sources, such as well, hand-pump, tube-well/bore-well, while the remaining 3.50 percent HHs (i.e. 2.5 percent in urban and 4.0 percent in rural areas) depend upon unimproved sources, such as spring, rivers, canals, tanks, ponds, lakes and other sources.

On the other hand, in respect of sanitation, 44.0 percent households (i.e. 79 percent in urban and 27.6 percent in rural areas) have sanitary toilets, whereas 2.9 percent HHs (i.e. 2.4 percent in urban and 3.10 percent in rural areas) have insanitary latrines, while the remaining 53.1 percent of households (i.e. 18.6 percent in urban and 69.30 percent in rural areas) do not have toilets.

It is estimated that almost 80 percent of water supply for these uses get back into the eco-system as wastewater. An estimated 38,354 million litres per day (MLD) sewage is generated in major cities, but the sewage treatment capacity is only 11,786 MLD (about 31 percent). Similarly, only 60 percent of industrial waste water, mostly large scale industries, is treated. Currently, about 37 percent of waste water (22,963 million litres out of a daily sewage generation of about 61,754 million litres) is being treated, as per the 2015 report of the *Central Pollution Control Board*.

International best practice suggests that a better management of water resources and a more rational allocation of water to those sectors that add most value to GDP is best pursued through *River Basin Organisations* (RBOs). A River Basin, considered as a geographical area determined by the watershed limits, is recognised as an appropriate unit of water development due to its hydrological characteristics of upstream–downstream influences. Any land-use change in the watershed has its impact on the characteristics of its flows. However, its management is difficult and, many a time, leads to problems besides conflicts, as political boundaries cut across those mandated by nature. These organisations have, as a mandate, to safeguard the finite and vulnerable nature of water, pursue water development and management in a participatory fashion at the river basin level. RBOs promote the role of women in the provision, management and safeguarding of water, and promote the fact that water has an economic value. RBOs also help serve as the custodians of water resources that ensures the best possible allocation of water across sectors in an impartial and judicious manner. Dynamic master plans for the *River Basin Management* are often prepared to guide RBOs and these are implemented by consensus amongst the stakeholders at River Basin Level. Integrated Water Resources Management (IWRM) is kept in view in all such decisions by the RBOs.

Majority of the water resources development planning in India is carried out in isolation for specific sites. No doubt, there are multipurpose projects but even in case of such individual projects, the concept of integrated plan for utilisation of available resources is missing. It is a common scenario that most of the river basins in India are experiencing 'moderate to severe' water shortages, brought on by the simultaneous effects of agricultural growth, industrialisation and urbanisation, all of which have steadily placed a growing demand on fresh water.

Thus, we have a complex system dealing with a scarce but vital national resource involving a large number of stakeholders. The management of this complex eco-system is one of the major challenges for India to transform into a New India. This can come about only by proper and effective governance of water and undertaking the associated institutional reforms.

Legal processes can play a crucial role in undertaking such institutional reforms, which can be accomplished within the concept of basins and catchment areas.

Constitutional and Institutional Framework in India

A brief yet adequate indication of the Constitutional provisions, and other policies related to planning, development and management of water resources, is dealt within the following sections.

Specific Provisions

The three most referred to provisions in the Constitution related to water are:

- Entry 17 of List II (State List) of the Seventh Schedule;
- Entry 56 of List I (Union List) of the Seventh Schedule; and
- Article 262 of the Constitution.

These provisions are discussed as under:

Entry 17 of List II (State List) of the 7th Schedule

Water, that is to say, water supplies, irrigation and canals, drainage and embankments, water storage and water power are subject to provisions of Entry 56 of List I.

Entry 56 of List I (Union List) of the 7th Schedule

Regulation and development of inter-state rivers and river valleys to the extent such regulation and development is under the control of the Union is declared by Parliament by law to be expedient in the public interest.

Article 262

Disputes relating to Water–adjudication of disputes relating to waters of inter-State rivers or river valleys:

- Parliament may, by law, provide for the adjudication of any dispute or complaint with respect to the use, distribution or control of the waters of, or in, any inter-State river or river valley.
- Notwithstanding anything in this Constitution, Parliament may, by law, provide that neither the Supreme Court nor any other court shall exercise jurisdiction in respect of any such dispute or complaint as is referred to in clause (1).

Other Related Provisions

Apart from the aforementioned provisions in the Constitution about water resources, the issues related to water and water uses also appear in several Articles and/or Schedules of the Constitution as under:

- Article 243ZD in respect of Committee for district planning, which, inter-alia, provides that every District Planning Committee shall, in preparing the draft development plan, have regard to matters of common interest between the *Panchayats* and Municipalities, including spatial planning, sharing of water, other physical and natural resources, the integrated development of infrastructure, environmental conservation, and the extent and type of available resources, both financial or otherwise.
- Similar provisions exist in respect of Committee for

Metropolitan planning under Article 243ZE.

- Additional powers of the Bodoland Territorial Council to make laws Article 244(2)–Sixth Schedule–Entry 3B (vii) flood control for protection of village, paddy fields, markets and towns (not of technical nature) and Entry 3B (xiii) irrigation.

The following Entries of List I (Union List) of Seventh Schedule:

- Entry 24: Shipping and navigation on inland waterways, declared by Parliament, by law, to be national waterways, as regards mechanically propelled vessels; and the rule of the road on such waterways;
- Entry 25: Maritime shipping and navigation, including shipping and navigation on tidal waters; provision of education and training for the mercantile marine and regulation of such education and training provided by States and other agencies;
- Entry 30: Carriage of passengers and goods by railway, sea or air, or by national waterways in mechanically propelled vessels; and
- Entry 57: Fishing and fisheries beyond territorial waters.

The following Entries of List III (Concurrent List) of Seventh Schedule:

- Entry 20: Economic and Social Planning, and
- Entry 32: Shipping and navigation on inland waterways as regards mechanically propelled vessels, and the rule of the road on such waterways, and the carriage of passengers and goods on inland waterways subject to the provisions of List I with

respect to national waterways.

The following Entries of Eleventh Schedule:

- Entry 3: Minor irrigation, water management and watershed development;
- Drinking water; and
- Roads, culverts, bridges, ferries, waterways and other means of communication.

Although there is no specific mention of 'water', in the Entry 20 of the List III (Concurrent List) of Seventh Schedule, this entry undoubtedly covers the matter related to planning of water resources–a resource which is not only lifeline of the social system but also an essential input for economic development.

Other Administrative Instruments

Apart from the legislation, administrative actions like formulating a Water Policy or setting coordinating Councils have been taking place from time to time in the Centre and States. Many States have enacted legislation to regulate surface and ground water. However, most such legislations are biased towards the use and exploitation of surface water. A welcome development has been the emphasis on people-oriented and managed water management systems. The *National Water Policy* also encourages the participation of the private sector, which is expected to bring in innovative ideas, financial resources, service efficiency and better management on corporate lines.

Thus, we have a complex system dealing with a scarce but vital national resource, involving a large number of parties. The management of this eco-system is one of the major challenges for governance.

- The *National Water Policy of India* (2012), inter-alia, requires that the planning, development and management of water resources be based on considering the river basin/sub-basin as a unit.

- The *National Environment Policy* 2006 promotes an integrated approach to the management of river basins by considering upstream and downstream inflows and withdrawals by season, interface between land and water, pollution loads and natural regeneration capacities, to ensure maintenance of adequate flows, in particular, for the maintenance of in-stream ecological values, and adherence to water quality standards throughout their course in all seasons.
- The *Guidelines for Preparation of River Basin Master Plan* issued by the CWC stipulate that even though river basin organisations are proposed for integrated planning and development of river basins, States need to prepare *master plans* for portion of river basins falling in their State, which could later be consolidated by the *Central Agency*. The *National Water Mission* is actively engaged in obtaining the *State Master Plans* under the '*Climate Change Adaptation Strategy*', presently with some guidelines for the purpose.

Challenges in Implementing IWRM

As indicated above, the IWRM and the river basin management approach are the need of the hour for equitable and efficient management and sustainable use of scarce water resources to meet the challenges of water and food security, recognising that water is an integral part of the eco-system. The IWRM is a process which promotes the co-ordinated development and management of water, land and related resources, in order to maximise the resultant economic and social welfare in an equitable manner without compromising the sustainability of vital eco-systems. Thus, the IWRM is about integrating all sources of water, all water using sectors, temporal and spatial integration, all stakeholders, relevant policy framework, legal and institutional framework, human and environmental needs, etc.

As most of the river basins in India encompass areas from more than one State, the Union Government has to play an important role of coordination to ensure that the practices are sustainable. However, given the existing constitutional provisions and cross-cutting nature of water management as per the Constitutional provision, the Union Government is finding itself in a fix to ensure a sound integrated holistic basin plan on its own and ensure the implementation without taking the concerned States into confidence. It also remains a fact that the idea of establishment of effective river basin entities for the holistic development of water resources has indeed not materialised in real terms, despite the existence of the *River Board Act* since 1956. This is because of the fact that States are generally not interested to bring in other players like the Centre, perceiving some loss of power as a consequence.

The above has led to a situation wherein the river basin management in India has confined to solutions of very specific problems till date. All the river basin organisations established as of now, function as an *Advisory Committee/Board*, with the exceptions of *Cauvery River Authority* and *Narmada Control Authority*, which are formed under the directions of Tribunals. The only example where the objective was integrated planning was in the establishment of *Damodar Valley Corporation*, which resulted in the preparation of '*Preliminary Memorandum on Unified Development of Damodar River*' by ML Voorduin (August 1944). Based on that plan, the basin development works were taken up after the independence. However, all the components included in the Plan have not yet been fully implemented because of various reasons.

The *Bhakra Management Board*, often cited as a successful example, was constituted under the *Punjab Reorganisation Act* 1966 under which a master plan was drawn to harness the potential of three eastern rivers, namely the *Sutlej*, the *Beas* and the *Ravi,* under the *Indus Water Treaty* provisions. The *Bhakra* and *Beas* Projects form a major part of the Plan, and were established as a joint-venture of the erstwhile States of Punjab and Rajasthan. Pursuant to this, *Bhakra Management Board* was renamed as *Bhakra Beas Management Board* (BBMB) with effect from 15 May 1976. Since then, the *Bhakra Beas Management Board* is engaged in the regulation of the supply of Water and Power from *Bhakra Nangal* and *Beas* Projects to the States of Punjab, Haryana, Rajasthan, Himachal Pradesh, Delhi and Chandigarh.

Similarly, *Tungbhadra Board, Brahmaputra Board, Bansagar Board, Rajghat Board, Narmada Control Authority, Godavari River Management Board, Krishna River Basin Management Board, National Ganga River Basin Authority* etc. have been set up with specific purpose or issues in mind. As such, they are also not catering to integrated and holistic planning, development and management at basin level. It is now essential to move forward, without any further delay, wherein the management of the river basins could be taken up based truly on the principles of equity and justice, working in a participative, consultative and collaborative manner for sustainable development of the basin resources.

Invoking the Constitutional provision under *Entry 20 of List-III (Concurrent List) of the Seventh Schedule*, which provides for social and economic planning could also be considered.

Undoubtedly, a question whether such exercise will be acceptable to the concerned parties, i.e. the State governments is quite pertinent. However, a professional approach will definitely help the stakeholders in appreciating the issues and selecting a better option, thus, achieving the objective of improved management of the resource.

In contrast, China adopted the '*Water Law of the People's Republic of China*' in January 1988, which was subsequently revised in August 2002 and further revised recently in July 2016. The law was formulated in order to rationally develop, utilise, conserve and protect water resources, prevent and control water damage, realise the sustainable utilisation of water resources and meet the needs of the national economy and social development. The Water Law is China's key water legislation that provides a comprehensive framework for integrated water management. The law includes provisions on water resources ownership, water abstraction rights, water resource planning, water resources development and utilisation, the conservation of water resources and dispute settlement. It defines river basin commissions and their responsibilities, and strengthens the administrative authority of those bodies. Between the planning systems, the water abstraction permit system and the system of water function zones, the framework comprehensively addresses the key aspects of water resources management. As a result of efforts undertaken for implementation of water law, while the annual GDP has grown at an annual rate of about 10 percent over the last 30 years, water utilisation has only increased by one percent annually. The national crop output has increased by 50 percent while agricultural water usage has remained the same.

The planning, development and management of water resources on the IWRM principles with basin/sub-basin as a unit is yet to gain momentum in our country as most of the river basins are inter-State and there is lack of collaborative spirit between them. The key areas of concern and challenge in implementing IWRM in the country are as follows:

- *Constitutional Provisions and Limitations*: The Centre has exercised its jurisdiction in the matter of inter-State rivers by enacting the *River Boards Act* of 1956. The Constitution provides for the management of an inter-State river basin by legislation or by setting up of a Board under the Act. However, till now no effective Board has been set up by the Centre taking recourse to this legislation.
- *Political Will*: In effective management of river basins, one of the major issues has been the equitable distribution and optimum use of surface water resources as, generally, river basins involve more than one State as well as a number of stakeholders. Inter-State water disputes have turned out to be a vexing issue in respect of water sharing. And this has resulted in the conflicts amongst States who are neighbours to each other. It is a volatile mixture of politics, law and rights, affecting livelihood and peaceful coexistence of people.
- *Project Oriented Approach*: Basins are not being developed in an integrated manner for the optimum utilisation of resources. The existing projects are getting adversely affected by harnessing of the water in the upstream reaches through many programmes like the watershed programmes, which was unforeseen when water was getting allocated earlier by judicial

interventions like Tribunals for water allocations with identified projects at that time.

- *Complexities of the system*: Due to growing economy and an accelerated GDP, the 'per capita income' is increasing fast; this has led to fast changing lifestyle and dietary patterns, resulting into greater water demands, which, in turn, has enhanced the competition among sectors for water use. Further, demand from large number of stakeholders for scarce but vital national resource adds strain to the eco-system.

In the past, greater stress was laid on the use of those provisions of the Constitution that deal with dispute resolution through setting up of *Water Dispute Tribunals* (WDT). These were not true to the spirit of participative and collaborative approach and invoking available provisions in *River Board Act* 1956. This was in contrast with other international experience of river basin management and settlement of differences through negotiations and cooperative and collaborative efforts, as indicated in Section 5 below.

Appreciation of these areas, and resulting equitable distribution between consumers, would provide satisfaction to large members and yet return adequate quantities back to the eco-system. Such an attitude of give and take towards the problem would eliminate the adversarial relations, which have now become the norm between basin States, and induce them to work together for the benefit of all and, therefore, will be a win-win situation for all. And amongst these efforts, the most important is the setting up of *River Basin Organisation* (RBO), comprising representatives of all the riparian States, Central agencies, and all other stakeholders, which will be the most effective instrument for equitable exploitation of the resource.

No dispute should be entertained till the matter has been taken up for resolution at the level of RBO.

Although there are number of very good examples and successful pilots of integrated management of water resources at micro-watershed level, both with Government taking lead as well as initiated by the NGOs and the communities, but their scaling up at wider scale has been very sluggish and difficult because others are not in sync with the development leading to sub-optimal utilisation of the natural resource. Accordingly, focused attention will be needed to scale up successful models.

River Basin Organisations (RBO)

There are many international examples of different river basin management models/approaches/organisations around the world, with river basins facing different challenges. River basins are at varying stages of development, with different learnings and experiences. Some of these, such as the *Murray-Darling Basin Authority* (MDBA, Australia), *Tennessee Valley Authority* (TVA, US), *Nigerian River Basin Development Authorities* (RBDA), the *Orange-Senqu River Commission* (ORASECOM), the *International Commission* for the *Protection of the Danube River* (ICPDR), the *Mekong River Commission* (MRC), the *Nile Basin Initiative* (NBI), and *Senegal River Basin Development Organisation* (OMVS) to name a few, are briefly mentioned. Brief details of the river basin management approach adopted is given below.

i. **Tennessee Valley Authority (TVA):** TVA was created by the US Congress in 1933 and entrusted with a unique mission–to improve the quality of life in the Valley through the integrated management of the region's resources. The TVA mandate included a comprehensive approach to natural resource utilisation and watershed management, with objectives ranging from reclamation of land, conservation of soil, improvement in the productivity of the crop, promotion of crop cooperatives, flood-control, generation of hydroelectric power, control of malarial mosquitoes and improving navigation. TVA was viewed as a model for integrated watershed management in economic development and is known as '*Temple of Development*'.

ii. **Murray-Darling Basin Authority:** The process of evolution of Murray Darling Basin, food bowl of Australia, consists of three phases:
   - Pioneering Phase (1900-1920);
   - Development Phase (1920-1967); and
   - Management Phase (from 1968 onward).

The RBO management approach has been evolving for over 100 years, with three different institutional models:

- River Murray Commission, 1917;
- Murray Darling Basin Commission, 1989; and
- Murray Darling Basin Authority, 2004.

With the enactment of the Water Act 2007, the MDBA was established as an independent expertise-based statutory agency. The basin plan was introduced in 2012 to provide a coordinated approach to water-use across four Australian states, with an objective to achieve a balance between environmental, economic and social objectives. The sustainable management of the Murray–Darling Basin river system is a collective endeavour of the basin-states and the Australian Government, with river-dependent industries and communities.

iii. **International Commission for the Protection of the Danube River (ICPDR):** The ICPDR is a transnational body, which has been established to implement the Danube River Protection Convention, the major legal instrument for cooperation and trans-boundary water management in the Danube River Basin flowing across 19 countries in Europe. The ICPDR works to ensure the sustainable and equitable use of waters and freshwater resources in the Danube River Basin. The ICPDR was formally comprised by the delegations of all Contracting Parties to the Danube River Protection Convention. However, it has also established a framework for other organisations to join. Since its creation in 1998, the ICPDR has promoted policy agreements and the setting of joint priorities and strategies for improving the state of the Danube and its tributaries.

iv. **Nigerian River Basin Development Authorities (RBDA):** Eleven River Basin Development Authorities were set up through River Basin Development Authorities Act (1976), as a strategy for Nigerian rural development, to develop and manage surface and ground water resources within the basin, and provide access to safe and adequate water for domestic, industrial, flood control and agricultural purposes to enhance the quality of life of the people and promote the socio-economic development of the country. These were multi-disciplinary in nature and were governed by a two-tier administration, involving the political set up as well as an executive limb in each one of the authorities. The numbers of RBO increased to twelve during the turn of the century. Later, the numbers reverted to eleven. These have successfully remained in existence for water governance involving stakeholders, notwithstanding certain identified drawbacks in achieving as much as was conceived during their inception. The country is reconciled to continue with the RBOs and aiming IWRM through the available set up, that encompasses the state and federal governments, and the local agencies.

Orange-Senqu River Commission (ORASECOM): The ORASECOM was established by the governments of Botswana, Lesotho, Namibia and South Africa, in November 2000, to promote the equitable and sustainable development of the resources of Orange-Senqu River. The ORASECOM provides a forum for consultation and coordination between the riparian states to promote integrated water resources management and development within the basin.

v. **Nile Basin Initiative (NBI):** The Nile Basin Initiative, established in February 1999, is an inter-governmental partnership of ten Nile Basin countries–Burundi, DR Congo, Egypt, Ethiopia, Kenya, Rwanda, South Sudan, The Sudan, Tanzania and Uganda–to provide a forum for consultation and coordination among the basin states for the sustainable management and development of the shared Nile Basin water and related resources for win-win benefits. Eritrea participates as an observer.

vi. **Senegal River Basin Development Organisation (OMVS):** The OMVS was created in 1972 as a regional cooperative management body of the Senegal River, which currently includes Guinea, Mali, Mauritania, and Senegal and others. The OMVS creation comes in the context of serious climatic deterioration, marked by a persistent and severe drought that devastates the entire valley. The OMVS assigned common mission to achieve food self-sufficiency, secure and improve the incomes of the populations, preserve the balance of eco-systems in the basin, to reduce the vulnerability to climate hazards and external factors, accelerate the economic development, which cemented by the ideals of solidarity, sharing, equity and culture of peace.

vii. **Mekong River Commission (MRC):** The MRC was established through the April 1995 Agreement on Cooperation for Sustainable Development of the Mekong River Basin (the Mekong Agreement) by the governments of Cambodia, Lao PDR, Thailand and Vietnam. The People's Republic of China and Myanmar are dialogue partners. The objective of cooperation among member countries is to promote optimal and well-balanced development of the basin, while ensuring the equitable sharing of benefits among all users of basin water and related resources. The objective also aims to prevent any harmful effects that may hinder the continued functioning of the Mekong River systems to ensure the continuation of the multi-generational benefits that the Mekong River Basin brings to all its people. In 2010, the MRC approved an IWRM-based Basin Development Strategy, which was updated in 2015 and endorsed in early 2016. It provides a framework for trans-boundary governance of this development process, including alignment of national plans and projects, basin management processes and the identification of strategic analyses to address current knowledge gaps.

The Conclave on River Basin Management

The Vivekananda International Foundation (VIF) in collaboration with the *International Commission on Irrigation and Drainage* (ICID) organised a conclave on '*River Basin Management*' for equitable use of water on 29 and 30 November 2017. Through this conclave, the following questions were addressed:

(1) Does the legal framework facilitate cooperative, collaborative and equitable water development among inter-state river basins?

(2) Why do the disputes arise? Has enough been done to avoid differences becoming disputes? And have the Water Dispute Tribunals served the desired objectives successfully; if not, why? What are the main reasons for delay in awards?

(3) Are we ready with the data, science and tools required for holistic river basin planning, development and management?

(4) Are mechanisms for conflict management in place? Do we have platform(s) for social engineering to facilitate collaboration and cooperation among various stakeholders? And, do we have the mechanism for confidence building among stakeholders?

(5) Do the existing policies and approaches within the major sectors–hydropower development, food security and wastewater disposal–address the issues related to equitable river basin needs and do the river basin

management practices support these policies and environmental needs?

The conclave was inaugurated by Chief Minister of Uttarakhand, Trivendra Singh Rawat. The conclave was attended by more than 50 experts from various sectors, which amongst others, included the representatives of the *Ministry of Agriculture, Water and Power*, and a number of experts, including former Secretaries of the *Ministry of Water Resources* (MoWR), former Chairmen of *Central Water Commission* (CWC), former Chairman *Brahmaputra Board*, Chairman of *Krishna River Management Board*, representatives of *Asian Development Bank* (ADB), Government of Uttrakhand, Maharashtra and Telangana, *Indian Agricultural Research Institute* (IARI), *International Crops Research Institute* for the Semi-Arid Tropics (ICRISAT), the *Energy and Resources Institute* (TERI), *Council on Energy, Environment and Water* (CEEW), *Central Board of Irrigation and Power* (CBIP) and *International Commission on Irrigation and Drainage* (ICID).

The Chief Minister highlighted that River Ganga, originating in Uttarakhand, provided water for irrigation to about 40 percent of the irrigated area, leading to food security of a large population of the country. In addition, faith in the divinity of the river is also linked to livelihoods. He further highlighted the need for taking strong actions to conserve each drop of water in view of (a) diminishing per capita water availability, (b) increasing population and (c) urbanisation, and stressed upon the need for an integrated and holistic river basin management. In order to meet the challenge, Rawat stressed on the need for creation of storage projects, recycling and reuse of waste/poor quality water, recharging of groundwater, rejuvenation of rivers and making water conservation a mass movement. He also stressed on the importance of harnessing abundant hydropower in the region (as only about 4,000 MW have been developed out of 25,000 MW potential) for economic prosperity of the state as well as the nation.

There are many issues and sectors that need to be considered while undertaking an integrated and holistic river basin planning. However, the conclave discussions were focussed only on three major issues - hydropower development, food security and waste water management.

The outcome of the conclave and the recommendations emerging from the discussions, that spread over two days, are as summarised in the following sub-sections.

Legal Context

Governments, whether federal, state or local, have to address the challenges associated with equitable use of water through river basin development in the present circumstances in a variety of ways. These matters were not of such great concern when the Constitution was being framed, so the subject of '*environment*' as such does not appear in any of the Lists in the Seventh Schedule. On the other hand, the Constitution makers gave priority to the working of a federal polity where the primary aim was to provide social, economic and political justice to its citizens and mandated the judiciary to be the protector of the rights of the individual and arbiter of disputes between the Union and States, and between the States.

However, complacency has given way to concerted action, both nationally and internationally. The United Nations Conference on Environment, held at Stockholm in 1972, placed the protection of the biosphere at the centre of international policy. Several Constitutional Amendments have been made since then. The most significant amendments have been the insertions of (a) the Article 48A in the *Directive Principles of State Policy*, (b) the Article 51-A(g) in the part on *Fundamental Duties* and specific changes to the Seventh, Eleventh and Twelfth Schedules of the Constitution, all of which cast responsibilities on the Union and State governments, as well as rural and urban local bodies. However, surprisingly, substantive legislation is still done by taking recourse to Act 253 that gives the powers to the Union to legislate for giving effect to international agreements, which is a very indirect way to go about addressing a matter of such great importance. It is high time that the Constitution is amended and a specific item be introduced in the Seventh Schedule, preferably in List 1, which is the Union List. There are many reasons for putting it in the Union List, as it is difficult to segregate air, water, wind and the eco-system into geographical boundaries. In fact, it is a global phenomenon, let alone a national one. What happens to El Nino in the South-Pacific affects the Indian monsoon and agricultural production.

The *National Environmental Policy* of 2006 characterises India's freshwater resources, comprising river systems, groundwater and wet lands as its single most important natural endowment. Equitable use of this invaluable natural resource is vital for the wellbeing of individuals and the community. The term 'equity' is extremely important, as undue importance is given to legal rights and the legal system, in spite of the country's robust legal structure whilst resolving some issues, can create complications elsewhere, especially if it leads to an imperfect management of the eco-system.

The Constitution provides a role for all three tiers of the

government–the Centre, the States and the local bodies–in the management of water. It would be apparent that primacy in this matter has been given to the States, with the Union given a role in regulation and development of inter-State rivers and river valleys to the extent to which such regulation and development under the control of the Union is declared by Parliament, by law, to be expedient in the public interest. The Centre has exercised its jurisdiction in the matter of inter-State rivers by enacting the River Basin Act of 1956. Thus, the Constitution provides for central management of an inter-State river basin by legislation or by setting up of a Board under the Act. However, till now, no River Board in a true sense has been set up by the Centre taking recourse to this legislation.

It emerged from the discussions that the Constitutional Provisions are well thought out and hence, perhaps there is need no change. However, what is required is to put greater reliance on those provisions that encourage cooperative efforts at all levels to find optimal solutions satisfying all stakeholders (Article 263) and that the dispute resolution measures through Tribunals (Article 262) should be resorted to as a last resort only. In this regard, suggestions made by the Commission on Centre-State Relations–chaired by the former Chief Justice of India, Justice MM Punchhi–in its Report of 2010 (Ref. Chapter 2 of Volume VI, Paragraphs 6.2.01 to 6.2.04) need to be actively considered.

The issue has also been looked into by the Justice Doabia Committee in 2012, which after examining the present provisions of the River Boards Act of 1956, and noting its deficiencies, has recommended a revised *River Basin Management* (RBM) Act. This revised RBM Act needs to be enacted and implemented without any further delay.

In respect of coordinated planning at various levels, both the Punchhi Commission on Centre-State Relations and the Second Administrative Reforms Commission have emphasised the need to implement the Constitutional Provisions relating to District Planning (Article 243ZD) and Metropolitan Planning (Article 243ZE). In the latter case, no such body has been constituted as yet. The plans drawn up by these bodies need to be integrated with the plans of the *Basin Management Organisations*, especially for surface irrigation, groundwater exploitation, drinking water, sanitation, industrial use and wastewater treatment.

Since river basin management involves holistic development of river basins, with a national perspective that there has to be a set of common principles to be adopted by all stakeholders. The states have to enforce water-use efficiency, appropriate cropping patterns, recycling of water, control of pollution, river water quality management, environmental flow and a host of other requirements. It is seen that most states do not address these issues. Recognising this, and with a view to evolving a set of national principles, the Draft *National Water Framework Law* was drafted by an expert committee. This is proposed as legislation by the Central government under Article 252 of the Constitution. This matter, which is currently under examination, needs to be expedited.

Governance of River Basins

As stated earlier, as a first step to equitable allocation, it is necessary to identify a hierarchical set of requirements, with basic needs of drinking, washing and cooking as first priority and then proceeding to uses for agriculture and industry, and later meeting the leisure and sporting requirements. But apart from meeting the human needs, the environment too needs recycling of natural resources for maintenance of the eco-system and its rejuvenation.

If one were to consider the usage of the usable water, agriculture receives the greatest share of the total water allocation of nearly 92 percent, of which nearly 60 percent of comes from the surface water. This surface water is in thirteen major river systems, which drain the sub-continent from a catchment area of about 260 million hectares. Over 70 percent of the rivers drain into the Bay of Bengal and 20 percent into the Arabian Sea. The remaining water drains into interior basins and lakes. Whereas this resource is not increasing, the population is steadily increasing which, in turn, is increasing the water-demand steadily. And to add to this distress, there is an alarming deterioration in the quality of water because of contamination by biological, toxic, organic and inorganic pollutants. There is also the phenomenon of silting of reservoirs and drying up of lakes and ponds. The core challenge before India is, therefore, the proper management and use of water, especially the surface water. And this can come about only by proper and effective governance, in which legal processes can play a crucial but not a dominant role.

Governance must have a geographical focus if coordination has to result in meaningful results. In the case of water, this can be accomplished within the concept of basins and catchment areas, but becomes difficult when political boundaries cut across those mandated by nature. Without going into the complexities of water systems cutting across international boundaries, for our purpose, we need to concentrate on national river basins.

For the purpose of good governance, an integrated approach, with defined watersheds as the geographical area of attention for planning and implementation needs to be adopted. Within this area, attention would need to be given to the study of precipitation, water bodies, groundwater and its recharge (including subterranean rivulets), flowing surface water, soil management and cropping practices etc. At the micro-watershed level, perhaps political boundaries may not be an issue but, as the area increases, they are bound to appear, considering the number of river basins and the number of States. Matters are getting more complex because of population increase, more investment in dams and canals, rising expectations, clamour for more exploitation–because of economic benefits on one hand–and the various factors against its exploitation, such as environmental degradation, pollution, loss of lands, resettlement issues and diminishing payback to the eco-system. The positive developments are scientific advances in water use for agriculture and industry, knowledge leading to pollution control, general awakening amongst the populace and civil society movements and community participation.

A major issue has been the shared use of the surface water resources involving more than one State and the management of river basins. Inter-State water disputes have turned out to be one of the most intractable problems faced by the nation. It is a volatile mixture of politics, law and rights affecting the livelihood of people. In recent times, it has also got intermingled with cultural identities, as witnessed during the recent demands for revival of the sport of Jallikattu in Tamil Nadu, where proponents mixed it with other grievances, including the sharing of Cauveri waters with Karnataka.

The stress has been on resolving these disputes through the Constitutional mechanism of taking recourse to Article 262 of the Constitution. Parliament under this provision has enacted the Inter-State Water Disputes Act of 1956. However, the functioning of Tribunals under this Act have been beset with several issues, such as (a) long delays, with cases lingering for decades; (b) lack of final power with Tribunals; and (c) resistance to accept awards by aggrieved parties. Moreover, contesting parties have other disputes, with water sharing being only one of them. The Tribunals have no say in the important issues, which have been listed earlier, especially the environmental concerns. Tribunals go by legal principles established over time, which can give primacy access to any of the riparian States or those who have prior appropriation or even follow the principles of equitable apportionment or lately of commonality of interests based on the principles, such as the Helsinki Rules. It is argued that the composition of the Tribunals and their procedures are not conducive to proper and scientific appreciation of the issues and dispensation of justice. Claimants always demand a major share of the resource, and present their data accordingly, to support their claims.

There is an unhealthy tendency to use water indiscriminately during the years of surplus. On the other hand, scientists are engaged in developing agricultural practices that (a) conserve water, (b) use only the required quantity of water, and (c) develop seeds and practices that increase yields with lesser quantities of water. An appreciation of these developments and equitable distribution between consumers would provide satisfaction to more number of people and yet return adequate quantities of usable water back to the eco-system. Such an attitude towards the problem would eliminate the adversarial relations, which have now become the norm between the basin States and induce them to work together for the benefit of all. There is a view that such Tribunals can do better justice to this complex task by broad-basing the Tribunal with members from concerned professions and by changing procedures which will make discussions and arguments more participative.

There is also a growing feeling that recourse to such Tribunals should be resorted to only when other efforts, such as mediation, negotiation etc., have failed. And amongst these efforts, the most important is the setting up of *River Boards*, comprising representatives of all the riparian States, Central agencies, and all other stakeholders, which will be the most effective instrument for equitable exploitation of this precious natural resource. No dispute should be entertained till the matter has been taken up for resolution at the Board. Thus, in India, the first and immediate step should be the constitution of appropriate authorities for all the river basins and their effective management, which should be on the principles of equity and justice, and by taking in account the existing and developing scientific knowledge available for an optimum utilisation of water, and with coordinated efforts from all stakeholders– individuals, communities, civil society organisations, and supported by the local, State and Central governments– working in a participative and collaborative manner.

Hydropower

With a growing concern about global warming and climate change, it is necessary to shift to non-fossil fuel based 'low-carbon' energy sources. Also, with stress on 'sustainable development', country is moving towards renewable energy. Hydropower plays a major role in the river basin development and needs a more coherent, coordinated and comprehensive approach for its generation and shared responsible use. Storages-based hydropower needs to be recognised as an overall water security strategy and adopted to make multi-purpose development possible, as power can potentially plays a major role in earning revenue.

Solar and wind energy, being only partially available during a day, were earlier not considered as suitable for absorption in the power grid, and their cost was also relatively very high. But recent developments in technology have brought down the cost of solar energy, and have enabled consideration of solar and wind energy sources also as eligible grid contributors. Hydropower, despite being renewable, and with least carbon emission, does not get the required support from the government as a renewable resource. Therefore, in the next decade or so, hydro (all sizes), wind, and solar should all form the preferred options for renewable sources of energy.

The fossil fuel based thermal plants and the nuclear plants are unable to respond quickly to the load changes; therefore, these plants are run to supply the base load. Hydropower plants and gas turbines on the other hand supply power to meet the peak load. Most hydro-power dams serve multiple purposes–flood control and water storage for irrigation - and hence impart flexibility in energy generation and the utilisation to suit the needs according to the variability in rainfall and the economic activities in the areas being served.

Unfortunately, despite all its advantages and importance, and the stability that hydropower plants provide in an admirable manner, hydropower generation is more and more relegated or even neglected in sharing the desirable Grid Mix; it seems to be losing the battle to the sector's opponents. The arguments against hydropower are all known and there is a need for a clear policy decision to decide, once and for all, whether hydropower is required, or not required. At the same time, hydropower needs to be made more attractive for private sector, which has, in the recent past, by and large, exited the sector.

Food Security

Agriculture must transform itself if it is to feed a growing global population and provide the basis for economic growth and poverty reduction. Climate change is likely to make this task increasingly difficult. To achieve food security and agricultural development goals, adaptation to climate change and lower emission intensities per output will be absolutely warranted. This transformation must be accomplished without depletion of the natural resource base.

Many small farmers in India are already coping with a degraded natural resource base. They often lack knowledge about potential options for adapting their production systems and have limited assets and risk-taking capacity to access and use technologies and financial services. More productive and more resilient agriculture requires a major shift in the way land, water, soil nutrients and genetic resources are managed to ensure that these resources are used more efficiently.

Water is the prime channel through which the impacts of climate change on the world's eco-systems and on the livelihoods of societies will be felt. Agriculture will be affected by increased evaporation demand, changes in the amount of rainfall and variations in river runoff and groundwater recharge, the two sources of water for irrigation. The distribution of precipitation, with longer periods between rainfall events and more intense precipitation, are expected to increase frequency of dry spells during the cropping season, and will directly affect soil moisture and the productivity of rain-fed crops. Crop selection and changes in crop calendars will help farmers adapt to new temperatures and rainfall patterns. The use of crops or varieties with better resilience to dry spells will be preferred. At the same time, watershed development works through rainwater harvesting would have to retain the soil-moisture for longer durations. However, watershed development has to be considered in tandem with the existing downstream projects, considering the river basin as one unit.

In order to encourage *Climate Smart Agriculture*, efforts are needed both on the supply side and on the demand side. Enhancing supply includes: increased access to and improved management of conventional water resources; habitat rehabilitation; dam operations; re-use of drainage water and wastewater; transfer of water between river basins; desalination; and pollution control. Demand management is defined as a set of actions that control water demand, either by raising the overall economic efficiency of its use as a natural resource, or operating intra- and inter-sectoral reallocation of water resources.

Farmers will favour more efficient irrigation technologies that reduce evaporation losses, such as drip irrigation and mechanised/sprinkler irrigation. These actions can be combined with deficit irrigation approaches to maximise productivity per volume of water applied rather than per area of land, reuse of waste water with appropriate precautions and mixing treated waste water with fresh water to reduce a high fresh water demand in agriculture. Existing large irrigation systems require to be modernised for better water allocation mechanisms, the clear transmission of alerts about water scarcity to farmers, and the adaptation of both infrastructure and management for more flexible and reliable delivery of water. Intermediate storage within the irrigation scheme and, where possible, access to groundwater are part of the options for building the resilience and reliability of water supply and must be considered in adaptation plans for irrigation schemes. In order to bring latest technologies, including micro-irrigation, satellite, drone and ICT in daily use for the benefit of farmers, extension services would require to be rejuvenated through private sector and civil society involvement.

Wastewater

The quality of both surface and groundwater is deteriorating due to pollution from wastewater discharge of large quantity of municipal and industrial untreated effluents into rivers as well as return flows from irrigated areas, which pollute water sources with residual fertilisers, pesticides, and herbicides. Groundwater is contaminated for geogenic and man-made reasons. Due to its high quantities of usage spread all over (about 56 percent of fresh water withdrawals), wastewater is to be considered as a resource, which can be put to agricultural, industrial, and domestic use, with varying degrees of treatment.

Thus, wastewater management is another critical and very important area, which needs attention in our attempt to increase the availability of water. A large part of wastewater is used in agriculture without any treatment or partial treatment, giving rise to extensive adverse health impacts. Wastewater is also a vast source of nutrients, which can be used in agriculture.

Recommendations

Management of river basins should be undertaken on the principles of equity and justice, and by taking account of all the existing and developing scientific knowledge available for an optimum utilisation of water and with the efforts of all stakeholders–individuals, communities, civil society organisations and the local, State and Central Governments–working in a participative and collaborative manner. Considering what China has done so far about its river basins, and with examples of other successful models (e.g. the Rhine river, the Mekong basin, the Murray-Darling basin), India should set about this task without further delay. Some of the areas that need immediate attention are listed below.

Water Resources Management: Legal Issues

1) Water resources development in the country needs to be guided by a long-term vision of future developments scenarios and emerging technologies.
2) While the basic framework of the Constitution for water management is in place, the necessary legal instruments that are required to put them in operation are lacking.
   a. A *National Water Framework Law*, as a legislation by the Central Government under Art 252 of the constitution needs to be finalised and adopted soon as an umbrella statement of general principles governing the exercise of legislative/executive powers by the Centre, the States and the local governing bodies.
   b. Bill seeking to amend the *Inter-State River Water Disputes Act* 1956 needs to be urgently passed to avoid undue delays in the resolution of inter-State water disputes.
   c. The *Draft River Basin Management Bill* that proposes establishment of separate *River Basin Authorities* for regulation and development of

waters for major inter-State river basins in the country, which is under consideration since 2013, requires urgent attention.

3) In a quasi-federal set up, negotiated settlements are more desirable, politically. With the presence of legislative route as a firm alternative, the negotiations may become easier. If the inter-basin transfers in consideration to the transfer of surplus water conflict with the existing settlements or awards, these existing instruments may need to be re-adjusted.
   a. There is a need to establish/empower a national agency for (i) quasi-judicial determination of basin surplus and deficit, (ii) finalisation of plans for inter-basin transfers, and (iii) to oversee their implementation.
   b. A detailed study in regard to the legal instruments, available and required, for water transfers from international basins, is required to be taken up.
4) As peninsular basin states do not agree to the availability of surplus water in the peninsular region, in order to ease inter-State issues, surplus water of Brahmaputra needs to be utilised, through the Himalayan links on priority. But this requires international cooperation of neighbours; enhancing the regional welfare as a part of the *Water Transfer Projects* with suitable instruments which can make the proposals attractive for neighbouring nations, addressing international legal issues could be explored since there are good examples of water cooperation in the international arena.

River Basin Management

1) Although basin has been identified as a unit of development in so far as the water resources management is concerned, the water resources development in India has been largely been centered around developing individual schemes and projects for the development of a particular region without any consideration to their downstream impacts. It is, therefore, imperative that planning, development and management of river basins needs to be done at basin level in an integrated and holistic manner.
2) Considering the new ambitious political goals of water to each farmer's field (*Har Khet ko Paani*) and doubling farmers' income, it becomes imperative that the watershed development activities under various schemes of the government (such as MNREGA), rainwater harvesting, implementation of the district irrigation plans, and other water development activities are coordinated under an empowered *River Basin Organisation.* It shall ensure a mechanism for coordination, collaboration and cooperation among all the authorities within a river basin at all levels of the administration.
3) In order to get grass-root level participation in the river basin planning, it is essential that quasi-formal organisations, such as Associations, Councils or Commissions, should be established initially based on the specific needs to bring various stakeholders at the same platform and create awareness among them

and the masses, in general, on the issues that the water sector faces and develop paths, which are flexible and based on scientific principles.

Hydropower Development

1) Hydropower, which is the cleanest form of renewable energy, has suffered a checkered past in the last two decades due to some ambiguity in the government policy and environmental activism. Its share in the total portfolio in the country suffers a steady decline and is presently about 13 percent, whereas it used to be about 40 percent in the seventies. With government's commitment to *Paris Agreement on Climate*, to increase the renewable energy for meeting its development needs, hydropower needs the focus to get back to its due share in the energy mix. In view of the decreasing interest in the hydropower sector, and the well-known arguments against it, there is an urgent need for a clear policy decision to decide, once and for all, whether hydropower is required, or not, and, if yes, then to announce new hydropower policy immediately.
2) Proposed storage projects, particularly in the country's NE region, should be undertaken as 'multi-purpose', 'multi-objective' projects. In any case, it should be ensured that the regional potential in hydropower is not converted to single-purpose run-of-the-river hydropower projects. In case of development of projects by the private developers, the government should fund the flood management and irrigation development components, utilising appropriate cost allocation principles, so that the hydropower is not burdened

with separable costs for other objectives. In order to make hydropower sector economically viable, proposal for suitable assistance for power component–in order to make tariff reasonable–may be moved considered by the government. In addition, long-term financing up to 20-25 years and interest subvention may also be considered.

3) Considering that the potential of hydropower largely lies in the Himalayan states, which suffer from gender specific migration of population due to lack of livelihood opportunities, hydropower development with potential to bring all round development in the project areas (having also the additional potential to provide accessibility and the multi-purpose development opportunities) should be considered as a strategic development option.

4) With a lack of awareness about life cycle costs and short-term environmental impacts, hydropower has been kept out of benefits of renewable energy sources. Hydropower needs to be given the status of renewable energy and all such investment incentives available to renewable energy related to GST, water tax or cess, inter-State and intra- State transmission charges etc. should also be extended to hydropower, irrespective of its size. In addition, cost of infrastructure may be considered for reimbursement through *National Clean Energy Fund* (NCEF).

5) There is an urgent need for taking the total review of the existing framework in implementing and developing the hydropower projects and improve the area '*Enforcing Contracts*' for ease of doing business,

with specific reference to incorporating balance risk sharing mechanism in contractual management. In addition, there is need for adopting standard format of the contract conditions, such as FIDIC etc., which provide balanced responsibilities for both client and contractor. This will avoid unnecessary disputes leading to time and cost overruns. To promote ease of doing business, single-window, online, time-bound approval and monitoring should be promoted.

6) Hydropower sector should take cognisance of environmental activism detrimentally impacting the national economy and should organise itself for awareness building among various stakeholders, including the executive, the legislature as well as the judiciary.
7) Significant disparities between policies applicable to hydropower vis-à-vis solar energy projects–in terms of PPAs, royalty energy, transmission, wheeling and waiver of cross subsidy charges for captive units, large capital outlays with high interest burden and issues associated with lack of power evacuation arrangements from remote project sites–need to be urgently corrected. The very large number of stalled hydropower projects both from the public and private sectors need a special redressal mechanism to free up locked capital contributing significantly to NPAs in the banking system.
8) A hydropower project life can easily be considered as more than 70 years, which will make average cost of power from the project less than Rupees 2.5 over life, although initial tariffs may be higher due to long gestation period and high interest cost.

Food Security

1) Major and medium irrigation projects contribute to assured food security in the country. They provide resilience to agriculture sector against climate variability through assured irrigation and will continue to play that role more in the changing scenario of *Global Climate Change* in the near future.
2) A number of new technologies and techniques are available for optimising the use of water in agriculture and improve the outputs for the farmers. However, such initiatives are required to be up-scaled in the field on a larger scale. Intermediary service layer are required to be strengthened and created where not existing, for integrating the new technologies into the routine agricultural practices.
3) Integration of processing, distribution and consumption promotion are required to improve the resilience of farmers against the price cycles created by shortages and surplus production.
4) Exclusive dependence on wheat-rice cycle based nutrition security is required to be curtailed and less water-consuming crops with higher nutrition value, which are more suited to local agro-climatology of the areas, should be promoted.
5) *Climate Smart Agriculture* practices, including drip and sprinkler irrigation have large potential in terms of using water more efficiently. These practices need to be promoted and extended further.
6) There is a greater need for intense farm level interventions for improving surface irrigation efficiency. These can be achieved through less-energy consuming

interventions based on simple technologies. But these would demand greater efforts and forming *Water Users Association* and *Participatory Irrigation Management.*

Wastewater Management

1) Wastewater from urban, industrial and agriculture need to be counted as a source of water, particularly in water-scarce regions of the country. Wastewater should, therefore, be factored into basin planning. Urban planning should address the issue of mixed wastewater from household and industry.
2) In view of increasing water scarcity, policy needs to be developed to (a) treat wastewater as a viable resource and (b) for safe use of wastewater or poor quality water after varying degree of treatment, for various applications-agriculture, industries etc.
3) While power intensive STPs are essential and have proven to be effective with limited efficiency, proven low-cost treatment of wastewater technologies also need to be encouraged.
4) Water users should be charged for water they use, by paying for three components: (a) volume of water supplied, (b) volume of water returned and (c) the pollution load that is discharged back into the water bodies.
5) There is need for building public awareness for welcoming the recycling and reuse of wastewater. Harmony, shared responsibility and coordinated efforts amongst the stakeholders are required.

References

1 The World Food Summit of 1996 defined food security as existing when all people, at all times, have physical, social and economic access to sufficient, safe and nutritious food to meet dietary needs for a productive and healthy life.

2 Damodar Valley Corporation, Preliminary Memorandum on Unified Development of the Damodar River submitted by M L Voorduin in August 1944.

3 http://szy.mwr.gov.cn/zcfg/fl/201405/t20140526_563987.html

4 Water Resources Management in the People's Republic of China, Bin Liu & Robert Speed, International Journal of Water Resources Development, ISSN: 0790-0627 (Print) 1360-0648 (Online), (http://www.tandfonline.com/doi/pdf/10.1080/07900620902868596).

5 https://www.tva.gov/

6 https://www.mdba.gov.au/

7 http://www.icpdr.org

8 http://www.waterresources.gov.ng/river-basin-operation-inspectorate/

9 http://orasecom.org/

10 http://www.nilebasin.org/

11 http://www.portail-omvs.org/

12 http://www.mrcmekong.org/

Towards Skills and Employment Strategy for India's Poor Districts

Partha Pratim Mitra

The focus of this study is to identify the reasons for India's poor districts remaining poor and backward, and designing a skills and employment strategy based on the ground conditions, as revealed by the census data. This study relies on the data published by the Registrar General of India (RGI) based on Census 2011 and released through the District Census Handbook Series (DCHS). The districts chosen for the study are have also been affected by the problem of left-wing extremism (LWE).

The first section of the paper brings up issues of natural resources in these districts and shows how these have not been instrumental in generating the necessary resources for the local development of the region. The second section discusses the problems of agriculture, education and health, leading to their poverty and backwardness. The third section focuses on devising a 'skills and employment strategy' given the local resources, and the need for human resource development and organizational interventions. The study concludes that for both wage increase and self-employment, there is a need to take into consideration the local resources and the infrastructure. More importantly, the human resource needs of the local inhabitants including their education and health facilities, needs to be given due priority for any effective skills and employment strategy.

Poor States in Development Ranking

THE focus of the study is to identify the reasons for India's Poor Districts remaining poor and backward, and designing a skills and employment strategy based on the ground conditions as revealed by the census data. This Study relies on the data published by the Registrar General of India (RGI) based on Census 2011 and released through the District Census Handbook Series (DCHS). The districts chosen for the Study are Adilabad (Telengana), Anantapur (Andhra Pradesh), Gaya (Bihar), Bastar (Chhattisgarh), Dumka (Jharkhand), Balaghat (Madhya Pradesh), Gadichiroli (Maharashtra), Koraput (Odisha), Mirzapur (Uttar Pradesh) and Bankura (West Bengal). These districts have also been affected by the problem of left-wing extremism (LWE).

This paper has three sections. The first section brings up issues of natural resources in these districts and shows how these have not been instrumental in generating the necessary resources for the local development of the region.

The second section discusses the problems of agriculture, education and health, leading to poverty and backwardness of people in poor districts.

The third section focuses on devising a 'skills and

employment strategy' given the local resources, and the need for human resource development and organisational interventions.

The study concludes that, for both wage increase and self-employment, there is a need to take into consideration the local resources and the infrastructure. More importantly, the human resource needs of the local inhabitants, including their education and health facilities, need to be given due priority for any effective skills and employment strategy.

The Official Discourse So Far

A brief review of the literature shows that the discourse for the development of the poor *left-wing extremism* (LWE) affected districts is divided. One school of thought treats it as a law and order issue, while the other treats it as a development deficit issue.[1] But, before we attempt to analyse the various socio-economic parameters of these districts, we would briefly review the existing discourse in the official circles on the problem of poverty and deprivation in the LWE-affected districts.

A Planning Commission report, while bringing out the reasons for deprivation of the local community, underscores the need to treat the problem of poverty in the LWE-affected districts not merely as law and order issue, but also as an issue to be brought out as congruence between policy and implementation. In its report, the committee focused on improving access to resources by the local population, particularly land and minor forest produce, strengthening of the *Panchayati Raj* System, activation of *Gram Sabhas* and participatory governance. Other important recommendations were:

- Improvement of educational infrastructure by providing fully qualified and trained teachers;
- Improvement in vocational training facilities that take

into consideration the local specific needs;

- Providing at least one residential school for boys and girls in these districts on the pattern of *Navodaya Vidyalayas*; and
- Bridging school facilities for slow learners and out-of-school children.

The committee suggested a structure with *ashram* and vocational schools in a cluster, *Eklavya* schools at the block and *Navodaya* schools at the district levels.

In its report, the committee also mentioned that the thinking in the government on the special problems of the LWE districts had started even earlier and went on to mention about a report of the policy planning division of the Ministry of Home Affairs (MHA) in the late 1960s, followed by the Manmohan Singh Committee on rural unrest in Bihar and Andhra Pradesh in mid-1980 sand then the committee of senior officials reporting on Naxalite violence chaired by VC Pandey in the late 1980s.[2]

In 2010, the government announced its decision to introduce a special scheme to address the development of 33 LWE-affected districts, later expanded to 34. These districts were a subset of the 83 LWE-affected districts identified by the MHA for coverage under *security related expenditure* (SRE) scheme. It was announced, in the budget for 2010-11, that the then Planning Commission would prepare an *integrated action plan* (IAP), which was formulated as an *additional central assistance* (ACA) scheme on an 100 percent grant basis. The scheme envisaged formation of a local committee with the Collector, SP and the Forest Officer, which would oversee the implementation by drawing up plans consisting of concrete proposals for school buildings, *Anganwadi* centres, primary health centres and directly receive block grants from the Centre.[3]

Subsequently, with the recommendations of the 14th Finance Commission being adopted, with the share of States in the net proceeds of Union taxes going up from 32 to 42 percent by the Central Government, the IAP, renamed as ACA for the LWE districts, has been transferred to the States, giving them sufficient flexibility to formulate and implement programmes suited to the local needs and aspirations.[4]

Present Focus on Most-backward Districts

In keeping with the vision to create a new India by 2022, a total of 115 districts have been identified for this purpose on the basis of objective criteria. Such criteria include education, health, nutrition, basic infrastructure–rural road connectivity, rural household electrification, access to potable water and individual toilets etc.–and are covered by the aspirational districts programme. These districts also include the 35 districts which are affected by LWE violence. Besides, while selecting these districts, it was ensured that Ministries of Government of India, implementing social sector schemes would select at least one most backward district in every State for extending the reach of the programmes in different parts of the country. Under this initiative, for all the 115 districts, senior level Government officers (Additional Secretary/ Joint Secretary) have been nominated as *Prabhari* officers. It has been envisaged that, using their experience, these officers would form a team with representatives of the State Governments and also act as a bridge between Centre and the State.[5]

Aspirational Districts Programme

The *Aspirational Districts Programme*, which covers the 115 backward districts, is a policy priority for the Government of India. The *NITI Aayog* would anchor the programme with support from Central Ministries and the State Governments. The objective of the programme is to monitor the real-time progress of aspirational districts based on 49 indicators (81 data-points) from the five identified thematic areas. While the *NITI Aayog* is steering the initiative in 30 districts, various central ministries oversee 50 districts besides the Ministry of Home Affairs, which focuses on the 35 LWE-affected districts, making a total of 115 backward districts.

An Empowered Committee, under the convenorship of the CEO of *NITI Aayog*, will help in the convergence of various government schemes and streamlining of efforts. To enable optimum utilisation of their potential, this programme focuses on improving people's ability to participate in the development programmes. Five thematic areas-Health and Nutrition, Education, Agriculture and Water Resources, Financial Inclusion and Skill Development, and Basic Infrastructure are this programme's core areas of focus.

Forty-nine key performance indicators have been chosen to measure the progress of the districts. These districts now aspire to draw level with the best district within their State and, subsequently, aspire to become one of the best in the country.[6]

Present Approach towards LWE-affected Districts

The present approach towards the LWE-affected districts consists of a combined strategy of security related and development initiatives in the form of an action plan. This strategy marks a change that has been witnessed earlier when the thrust was mostly on the security related measures and included support to States by the Centre for strengthening police infrastructure through SRE, deploying central armed forces, technical equipment etc. Development initiatives have also been taken for the LWE-affected districts, which focus on improving the road connectivity, mobile tower connectivity, financial inclusion, opening up of new ITIs skill development centres, *Kendriya Vidyalayas* and *Jawahar Navodaya Vidyalayas*, special central assistance to fill critical gaps related to public infrastructure and services for the 35 LWE-affected districts, bringing them under the 'Aspirational Districts' Programme where both Central and State Governments would work as a team to improve the socio-economic profile of the districts.[7]

Rich Mineral Resource Base of Poor Districts

It is important to understand the natural resource base of the LWE-affected districts. These districts are endowed with rich mineral and forest resources. Table 1 provides district-wise information on the major natural resources.

Most of the districts have valuable forest as well as mineral resources. However, very often, these resources are not accessed by the local population. The resources are in the control of outsiders who do the investment for business purposes, while the local inhabitants depend upon them for wage employment. This phenomenon, in effect, is the general situation in almost all the sectors of the poor districts, which have been affected by LWE. Therefore, there is the need to strengthen the local governance in *Panchayati Raj Institutions* (PRIs), so that democratic decentralisation takes place in letter and spirit. Next we discuss the socio-economic parameters of these districts.

Table 1: Major Natural Resources: LWE-affected Districts

Districts/State	Natural Resources
Adilabad, Telengana	Forest, limestone, manganese, coal, fire clay
Anantapur, AndhraPradesh	Clay, dolomite, iron ore, sterlite, shale, quartz
Gaya, Bihar	Forest, granite, slate
Bastar, Chhattisgarh	Forest, limestone, marble stone
Dumka, Jharkhand	Forest, coal, china clay, granite, stone
Balaghat, Madhya Pradesh	Forest, manganese, copper, bauxite, kainite, limestone
Gadichiroli, Maharashtra	Forest, iron ore, mica, clay, building stones
Koraput, Odisha	Forest, bauxite, limestone, quartz, quartzite, china clay.
Mirzapur, Uttar Pradesh	Stone, patiamoram
Bankura, West Bengal	Forest, coal, quartzite, china clay

Source: District Census Handbook, RGI, New Delhi

Poor Status of Education and Health Infrastructure

It is also important to understand the current state of education and health infrastructure for every 10,000 population in various towns of the districts.

The available information shows how difficult it is to access education and health infrastructure in towns of these districts.

The literacy rates are indicated to be very low in Adilabad (49.8 percent), Anantapur (63 percent), Gaya (63.7 percent), Bastar (54.4 percent), Dumka (71 percent), Balaghat (77 percent), Gadichiroli (74 percent), Kopraput (42 percent), Mirzapur (68 percent) and Bankura (70.3 percent).

In many cases, the literacy rates for the districts are below the literacy rates in various states and the national rate of 74 percent. The latest data available for various states shows that the literacy rate for Telengana is 66.46 percent, Andhra Pradeshis 67.6 percent, Biharis 65.8 percent, Chhattisgarh

Table 2: Education and Medical Infrastructure: LWE-affected Districts

Districts	No of Primary Schools	No of Middle Schools	No of Sec-ondary Schools	No of Senior Sec-ondary Schools	No of Col-leges	No of Hospital beds
Adilabad	8	6	5	1	0	17
Anantapur	5	3	2	1	0	14
Gaya	2	2	1	1	0	14
Bastar	9	5	2	2	0	41
Dumka	9	4	2	1	0	34
Balaghat	16	9	4	2	0	24
Gadichiroli	7	5	3	2	0	57
Koraput	8	2	2	1	0	24
Mirzapur	8	3	1	1	0	22
Bankura	8	1	1	1	0	16

Source: District Census HandBook, RGI, New Delhi

is 65.9 percent, Maharashtra is 82.3 percent, Odisha is 72.9 percent, and West Bengalis 77.1 percent. The states of Jharkhand (66.41 percent), Madhya Pradesh (70.6 percent) and Uttar Pradesh (57.2 percent) are the exceptions, with the districts having a higher literacy rate than the entire state.

While the literacy rate may not have a direct bearing on poverty and backwardness, a low literacy rate does create a barrier for any effective revival programme for the district in as much as skill formation and the employability of people become more challenging with low literacy rates.

The employment in the aforementioned ten LWE-affected districts, as depicted by the Census 2011 data, is presented in Table 3.

It would be observed that most districts have a very low percentage of 'main' workers, who have work for six months and more in a year, and 'marginal' workers, who have worked for

Table 3: Employment (as percent): LWE-affected Districts

Districts	Main Workers		Marginal Workers		Non workers	
	Rural	Urban	Rural	Urban	Rural	Urban
Adilabad	43	29	10.7	6.1	46.5	65.2
Anantapur	44	34	10.3	4.5	45.6	61.5
Gaya	23	22	15.9	8.4	61	69
Bastar	27	32	26.2	5.9	46.5	61.3
Dumka	17	23	31	6.8	51.5	69.6
Balaghat	31	29	23.6	7.4	44.9	63
Gadichiroli	37	29	19	8.2	43.4	62.6
Koraput	28	32	24.9	4.3	47	63.4
Mirzapur	21	23	14.6	9.2	64.2	67.6
Bankura	25	30	16.1	5.9	58.8	63.5

Source: District Census Hand Book

less than 6 months in a year, and a high percentage of 'non-workers', who are not in the workforce. This also implies that the dependency burden of households in these districts is very high. Primary lack of adequate employment opportunities have resulted in such a dire state of affairs.

Table 4 presents the occupational pattern in these ten LWE-affected districts, in terms of percentages, as cultivators, and agricultural labourers, engaged in household industries and in other occupations.

Table 4 indicates that the percentage of agricultural labour far exceeds cultivators in most districts, which only shows that landlessness is a major problem in these districts, forcing people to either work as unskilled labour or migrate to other districts or states. The percentage of workers engaged in household industries is also insignificant in most districts, except for Adilabad and Mirzapur. The two districts have local village industries in the household sector.

Table 5 presents the social demography of these ten districts

Table 4: Occupations (as percent): LWE-affected Districts

Districts	Cu (R)	Cu(U)	AL(R)	AL (U)	HHInd (R)	HHInd (U)	Oth (R)	Oth (U)
Adilabad	34	3	43	10	6.4	6.2	16	81
Anatapur	25	2	53	8	3	12	19	77
Gaya	24	4	52	9	5	9	20	77
Bastar	43	9	43	8	1	2	13	81
Dumka	32	4	50	8	4	5	14	82
Balaghat	31	7	55	16	2	3	7	73
Gadichiroli	41	4	44	17	2	4	12	74
Koraput	33	3	47	3	2	4	17	90
Mirzapur	23	3	42	7	8	17	27	73
Bankura	23	2	47	4	4	6	26	88

Legend: Cu-Cultivators, AL-Agriculture Labour, HHInd (R)-Household Industries Rural, HHind (U)-Household Industries Urban, Oth-Others, R- Rural, U- Urban
Source-District Census Handbook

Table 5: Social Demography (as percent): LWE-affected Districts

Districts	State		District SC		District ST	
	SC	ST	Rural	Urban	Rural	Urban
Adilabad	16.4	18.1	18.6	15.8	23.4	4.3
Anantapur	16.4	7	16.2	9.4	4.3	2.4
Gaya	16.0	1.3	33.2	11.9	0.1	0.1
Bastar	11.6	31.8	2.1	6.2	72.2	26.6
Dumka	11.8	26.3	5.8	8.8	45.9	6.0
Balaghat	15.2	20.3	6.8	10.5	23.8	14.9
Gadichiroli	11.8	9.4	10.7	16.0	16.0	14.4
Koraput	17.1	22.8	13.9	57.4	15.8	15.4
Mirzapur	20.7	0.6	23.0	12.7	0.6	0.2
Bankura	23.5	5.6	33.5	22.9	11.1	1.1

Source- District Census Handbook

in terms of the proportion of SC/ST population in the rural and urban areas along with the state percentage for this population.

The above table indicates that most of these ten districts have a large proportion of the tribal population in the rural areas, which is higher than the state percentage. Much of the tribal population is most vulnerable to social and economic deprivation and is often left out of the main stream development process.

Table 6 presents the land-use pattern in these districts to get an idea about the state of agriculture which is the main stay of these districts.

Table 6 indicates that in most districts, the percentage area under cultivation and irrigation is low. Therefore, agriculture has not been able to develop in these districts. As a result, the number of the job opportunities generated in this sector is also low, as the data presented in Table 3 on 'main' and 'marginal' workers shows the low percentages of these workers.

Table 6: Cultivable and Irrigated Areas: LWE-affected Districts

Districts	CultivableArea (Percentof Total Area)	Irrigated Area Percent of Total Cultivable Area
Adilabad	43	43.7
Anantapur	47	17.6
Gaya	63	68.5
Bastar	42.2	3.5
Dumka	48.7	33.3
Balaghat	2	-
Gadichiroli	22.5	42
Koraput	30.4	0.04
Mirzapur	56.7	63.2
Bankura	0.05	30.1

Source: Estimated from Land–use Data published in District Census Handbook

The next section discusses what can potentially be done to improve the skills and employment of inhabitants in these districts, given their difficulties as discussed earlier.

Developing Skill and Employment Strategy

The issue of skills and employment needs to be seen in a two-fold perspective; that is, wage employment and self-employment and in the context of sectors, which are local resource based and those which are foot-loose.

To understand the local resource base, Table 7 presents the important items available or produced locally in these districts.

Table 7: Items Available or Produced: LWE-affected Districts

Districts	Important items
Adilabad	Cement, mud bricks, cement pipes, toys, beedies, cotton yarn, Mughal tiles
Anantapur	Groundnut, textiles, soap, silk sarees, PVC pipes, groundnut oil, ready-made garments
Gaya	Agarbatti, stone statue, stone chips, furniture, sarees, long cloth, towels, bedsheets, dhoti
Bastar	Sponge iron, cement pipes, forest produce, bamboo, handicrafts, pottery, black smith, carpentry, leather tanning, weaving
Dumka	Leather, iron goods, irrigation equipment, furniture, earthen pots
Balaghat	Edible oil, bamboo products, English tiles, bricks
Gadichiroli	Bamboo, building stones, cotton
Koraput	Handicraft, handloom
Mirzapur	Carpet, brass utensils, textiles, agricultural tools
Bankura	Fishing hook, handicraft, handloom, silk weaving, pottery

Source- District Census Handbook

Table 7 indicates that the districts have the potential to produce goods based on natural resources and traditional skills that are locally available. Many of these districts are inhabited by tribal communities who have, over generations, inherited skills that are conducive for the growth of cottage and village industries based on the artisanal skills. The local industries that have the potential to develop are based on wood, bamboo, cotton, silk, leather, metal, pottery, minor forest produce, agro-based edible oil, cement and cement products.

The National Skill Development Corporation (NSDC) has carried out skill-gap studies for districts all over the country, including the present study, and made recommendations for skill development and employment, either locally or outside the district, as summarised in Table 8.

Table 8: Skill Development and Employment: LWE-affected Districts

Districts	Sectors Identified by NSDC
Adilabad	Mining, construction, tourism & hospitality, transportation and logistics
Anantapur	Mining, construction, tourism, textiles leather, auto &auto components, chemicals & pharma, metals &non-metals
Gaya	No study available
Bastar	No study available
Dumka	Agriculture&allied, leather, construction,food processing, handloom & handicrafts, textiles, engineering, banking& finance, warehousing & packaging
Balaghat	Sericulture, horticulture, animal husbandry, tourism, food processing banking & financial services, IT&ITIs
Gadichiroli	Bamboo, building& construction, health care, food processing, auto &autocomponents,leather,gems&jewellery,banking& financial services
Koraput	Agriculture, tourism, health care, IT&ITIs, banking & finance, construction material & hardware
Mirzapur	Cotton products, textile weaving & cloth, construction, real estate, health care & retail, transportation, security guards
Bankura	Pisciculture, forest produce, ferroalloys, ceramics, pottery, handicraft, fishing hook and fishing net, sericulture, animal husbandry, healthcare & retail, transportation & logistics

Source: NSDC District-Wise Skill-Gap Study 2012-2022

Table 8 indicates that certain sectors specific to the districts, and some other sectors foot-loose in nature, have been identified keeping the resource endowment of these districts wherever NSDC has carried out the skill-gap studies. It is, however, noticeable that certain sectors find a mention for many districts. These sectors are construction and tourism.

In recent years, construction has been a major employment provider after agriculture. However, what needs to be done in the construction sector is to create skilled manpower, for which the training facilities in these districts need to be improved. Many of these districts have places of historical importance and are also endowed with bountiful flora and fauna. These areas need to be opened up for tourism, for which the local youth needs to be given encouragement to become tourist guides and tour operators. This approach would also remove the isolation which many of these districts face and would, therefore, bring them into the main stream of development activities.

Table 7 lists the important items that are available or could be produced in these districts. While units could be setup to produce them or value added to them–wherever it is possible, through proper training, marketing and financial support–focus needs to be given towards the organisational issues, so that the local youth could be given an important stake in these organisations. Such importance is very often absent and, therefore, results in their de-motivation. For instance, there is a need to organise producers' cooperatives around important products or the local artisanal skills that are available in the districts. The state authorities will not only have to organise skill development training programmes, but also nurture formation of producer cooperatives, and provide them with the knowledge to start their businesses, by organising hand holding camps to make the local youth confident of managing the cooperatives.

The industry associations, chambers of commerce and local industries, both in the private and the public, will need to work with the district authorities to identify the skills that could be imparted to the local youth, to meet the industry's requirement and accordingly organise training activities. The local ITIs and polytechnics will also need to be integrated with these activities as part of a well-planned wage-employment plan, which results in the placement of the local youth. The youth will have the option to either get absorbed by the local industries or migrate, with adequate skills, to other districts for employment.

The various skill development programmes, as run by the central and state governments, need to be converged and integrated with the wage-employment plan for the district. A similar approach needs to be taken for formulation of a self-employment plan, which culminates in the formation of producers' cooperatives. All the central and state government programmes should converge and integrate with the self-employment plan for the district, with a tangible target of forming producers' cooperative and, where these cooperatives already exist, formulate a rejuvenation plan for them.

There is also a need to address the inadequacies in the education and health sectors. Many districts lack adequate facilities for education and health, which form the backbone of any skill-development and employability plan of a region for producing a healthy and educated workforce required for the development of the region. Lack of proper education and health facilities would imply that a workforce will not be able to meet the cognitive and physical challenges of a work schedule that involves both physical labour and learning skills required to improve the overall efficiency of the workforce and the overall domain of the working knowledge.

Each district will need to do a careful manpower planning, which begins with an assessment of the number of entrants in schools and the number of graduates at the primary, upper primary, secondary and higher secondary levels, and those that enter college, both in general and technical streams. Simultaneously, the industry associations, along with the local industries, will need to estimate the demand and the skills sets required by the industry. Such a careful and stage-wise analysis of the students will give an idea of the actual number of dropouts at every stage,so that career planning of children dropping out is carefully done for enhancing their employability and placement through vocational training opportunities. Such career planning of children will also make the vocationalisation of school education successful and the employability of students easier, as it will fit within the actual demand–supply position of jobs in the district.

Youth unable to get absorbed by the local industry could be prepared for self-employment through skill-development courses and, thereafter, taught how to start an enterprise or form producers' cooperatives, since it may be difficult for some of them to start individual enterprises. The entire education infrastructure of the district, including ITIs, polytechnics and degree colleges will need to be involved in the manpower planning exercise in consultation and coordination with the industry associations, local industries,training providers and PRIs.

An important source of funding district local plans is the *Pradhan Mantri Khanij Kshetra Kalyan Yojana* (PMKKKY), which has been launched by the Ministry of Mines. At least 60 percent of PMKKKY funds will be utilised for high priority areas, such as (i) drinking water supply; (ii) environment preservation and pollution control measures; (iii) health care; (iv) education; (v) welfare of women and children; (vi) welfare of aged and disabled people; (vii) skill development; and (viii) sanitation. The rest of the funds will be utilised for: (i) physical infrastructure; (ii) irrigation; (iii) energy and watershed development; and (iv) any other measures for enhancing the environmental quality in the mining sector within districts. The scheme could facilitate holistic development of the mineral-rich districts so that the benefits of development reach the local inhabitants.

Conclusion

Before concluding, it may be worthwhile to mention a documented experience of how to implement programmes in the LWE-affected districts under extremely difficult circumstances.

The authors have narrated a case study of Dantewada, one of the worst affected LWE districts in Chhattisgarh, where the education rights of children were ensured in extremely hostile ground conditions. The case study brings out the role of the local bureaucracy and its ability to work and deliver in hostile terrain, with support from the political leadership. The thrust of this local initiative was to utilise imaginatively the discretionary funds in the hands of the Collector and combining it with CSR funds. The strategy was to identify the implementation gaps visible in disaggregated data and accurately zero-in on the problem locally through innovative means. The focus of the education intervention programme has been on (a) setting up of residential schools in fringe locations, (b) setting up of a science museum, (c) a district library, (d) coaching facilities for children to gain admission in prestigious schools, (e) creation of important junctions in the district as education clusters, preparing students for admissions to professional courses, such as engineering, medical, polytechnics, nursing, etc. and (f) setting up of an education city-hub and livelihood-college for youth. The livelihood-college will focus on trades where there is a local skills gap. These trades include hospitality, plumbing, electrical works, masonry, solar panel maintenance, mobile repairing.[8]

To conclude, this paper has raised a number of issues that could go towards formulating a 'skills and employment' plan for poor LWE-affected districts. These issues are by no means exhaustive. While a lot has been said, a lot remains to be done. A systematic and focused approach, with tangible end-results, both for the wage workers and the self-employed, is required that considers the local resources and the infrastructure. More importantly, the human resources needs of the local inhabitants, including their education and health facilities, must be given due priority if an effective employment plan has to be formulated for uplifting those poor districts.

References

1 Satyajit Singh, Locals in Governance, Oxford University Press, New Delhi, 2016.
Study on Development Interventions in Naxalite Affected Areas in Chhattisgarh, Samarthan Centre for Development Support, Bhopal, 2014, available at www.samarthjan.org.
Concept Paper on Appropriate Development Strategies for Effective Implementation of Rural Development Schemes in IAP Districts,

Ministry of Rural Development, Government of India, 2011, ruraldiksha.nic.in

2 Development Challenges in the Extremist Affected Areas–Report of an Expert Group to Planning Commission, GOI, New Delhi, 2008, planningcommission.nic.in/reports

3 PIB Mumbai.gov.in, 10 January 2012.

4 Pib.nic.in, 24 February 2016.

5 Transforming 115 Districts Across the Country, pib.nic.in, 23 November 2017.

6 Transformation of Aspirational Districts–Baseline Ranking and Real Time Monitoring Dashboard, 2018, nitiaayog,niti.gov.in

7 Reply to starred question No 374 dated 21-3-18 in Lok Sabha by Minister for Planning.

8 Priyam Manisha, Sanjiv Chopra and Omprakash Chowdhary, Against the Odds: Education Initiatives in Dantewada, 20 May 2016, available at http://darpg.gov.in

'Paradise Lost' How to Regain it?

Jandhyala BG Tilak

Though the importance of values in education has been emphasised by many committees and commissions and the national policy statements on education in independent India, the education system has focused at best on examination scores and certificates/degrees, promoted competition, and rarely devoted adequate attention to the inculcation of human values to the young children. The rapid growth of profit seeking private education institutions associated with all kinds of corrupt and unfair practices has aggravated the problem. It is argued in this short article that value-based education is critically important for building a humane society; and this is also necessary for building a strong and high-quality education system.

We want that type of education by which character is formed, strength of mind is increased, and intellect is sharpened, as a result of which one can stand on one's own feet.

—Swami Vivekananda

Politics without principles, education without character, science without humanity, and commerce without morality are not only useless, but positively dangerous. 'Character is the most precious gift of education.'

—Sathya Sai Baba

Role of Education

THE role of education in social, economic and political development of societies is widely recognised for a long time. In India, the importance of education was recognised since the Vedic period, as the scriptures sing hymns in praise of education and knowledge. For example, it was stated, '*Na Gyanen Sadrusham Pavitram Iha Vidyate*' (Nothing is more sacred than the education), and:

> *Vidya naam narasya roopam-adhikam prachchanna gupta dhanam;*
> *Vidya bhogakari yasha sukhakari Vidya gurunam guru;*
> *Vidya bandhujano videshagamane Vidya para daivataa;*
> *Vidya rajashu poojitaa na tu dhanam Vidya vihina pashu.*
>
> (Education beautifies man; a hidden treasure of wealth; cause of fame, happiness and fulfilment of all worldly desires; master of all masters; appreciated among the family members as well as in foreign countries, a cause of highest bliss; honoured by the King where wealth is not honoured. A person without education is an animal indeed.)

After independence, many national leaders and philosophers, including Mahatma Gandhi, Zakir Hussain, Rabindranath Tagore, Sri Aurobindo, Madan Mohan Malaviya, Sarvepalli Radhakrishnan, Jiddu Krishnamurthy, and Sri Sathya Sai Baba realised the critical role of education in individual character building and national reconstruction; and even established a few specific model institutions at school and university levels as well.

Education seen as an Individual Investment

Education is nowadays recognised as an individual and social investment. This thought emanated in the 1960s, when the '*human investment revolution in economic thought*' was initiated by Theodore W Schultz, although this thought process is believed to have originally occurred since the days of Adam Smith. In India, among others, VKRV Rao highlighted the role of education in human resource development and, thereby, in socio-economic transformation of India. Recently, the human development specialists have reminded us again that education is not only for economic development but, more importantly, education itself is development, besides being a human right. The recognition of education as an instrument for development, and also as development in itself and a human right, led to massive expansion of education in many countries of the world, including India.

During the post-independence period, the educational system in India experienced an impressive rate of expansion, making the Indian education system one of the largest in the world in terms of the number of students, teachers, schools, colleges and universities. Today, the education system in India includes about 15 million schools, more than

800 universities, about 40 thousand colleges; approximately 260 million students in schools; about 34 million students in higher education institutions; and nearly 10 million teachers (2015-16). The student population in India is larger than population of many countries in the world. It is larger than the combined population of the United Kingdom, France, Germany, Italy, Sweden and Switzerland. While quantitative expansion has, thus, been remarkable, quality of education has become an important issue of serious concern. Inadequate infrastructure, congested classrooms, effectively very high pupil-teacher ratios, increasing number of under-qualified and under-paid contract/para teachers, lack of electricity, drinking water and functioning toilets etc. are the hallmarks of a majority of the schools in the country. Further, the *National Achievement Survey* reports of the *National Council of Educational Research and Training* (NCERT) and the *Annual Survey of Education Reports* of the *Pratham Foundation* often remind us how poor our school children are in terms of their levels of learning outcomes–the basic three 'Rs', which broadly but partially reflect a severe degree of under achievement of children in the scholastic dimensions of education.

Current Education System and the Erosion of Values

It is widely admitted that the examination or test scores are poor in reflecting the quality of education. The intrinsic quality of education refers to the values received and internalised by the students, the character that was built and the overall personality nurtured and developed by the education process. This is, indeed, the true quality of human capital produced by the education system. These intrinsic non-cognitive contributions of education are not tangible and quantifiable. But, of late, they are being realised as more important, as the schools and the society at large are experiencing rapid degeneration of moral and ethical values. Bullying, ragging, guns, shooting, violence, drugs, rapes, murder, terror, and other kinds of violence have become regular features of schools in many countries. These crimes are committed on young children, not necessarily by outsiders, but also by the insiders–the teachers, the managers, other staff, and fellow students. Schools have hardly any more been safe places for young children. There has been a virtual collapse of ethics and human values in the society. The sudden decay in values in the society has been alarming, with weakened or broken inter-personal relationships, and intra-family bonds–between husbands and wives, between parents and children and grandchildren, and between brothers and sisters. Human life, human dignity and ethos are rarely respected. Greed and selfishness has outplayed compassion and consideration for others; fierce competition has replaced cooperation; considerations of social welfare, wellbeing of the larger society and common good has given in to individual rights and narrow considerations of personal prosperity. The frequent reports in media–both electronic and print–on growing violence, crime, rape, intolerance, insensitivity, and related social maladies, affecting young children, adolescents and youth and covering adult population–represent a morally degenerated society. These reflect the poor character and degenerating values of the society today. Thus, an urgent need for inculcation of a heavy dose of human, moral and ethical values in education is paramount.

Education and National Development

The education system and the society are so intricately related that it is difficult to pin point where the source of the disease lies and where the cure should be attempted. There are two alternative schools of thought in this regard.

Some feel that school reforms may not help at all, unless the larger society is reformed, as schools are, after all, a part of the larger social system. The values inculcated in schools may conflict with those prevailing in the society and, hence, school reforms would fail. Thus, it is not the schools, but the society outside the schools that needs to be reformed first, before attempting to reform the school system.

The alternative thought is that schools are a better place to begin with the reforms, as it is in schools that young minds can be moulded to inculcate new values. Unless the seeds of reform are sown in the young minds in schools, the youth and the rest of the society cannot do anything. Reforms in the schools would be more effective, having ever-lasting effects on the development of a society with moral and ethical values.

Realising the immense role of schools in inculcating values and building character of the world's future citizens, many scholars, committees, commissions and governments have argued for reforming the schools. It is argued that it is the education system that requires major overhaul in this regard, which would rewrite the future of the country. However, the wider degeneration–rather degradation of values and morality in larger society–poses a major obstacle for schools to focus on ethics and moral values. After all, it is the schools that prepare the future citizens of the society. As the *Indian Education Commission* (1966) stated in its voluminous report, *Education and National Development*, 'The destiny of India is now being shaped in her class room.' The Commission also stated, 'If this "change on a grand scale" is to be achieved without any revolution (and even for that it would be necessary), there is one instrument, and one instrument only, that can be used: EDUCATION.'

At the very outset, while reforming education, it has to be realised that provision of skills and competencies to fuel economic growth is an important function, but it cannot be the overriding function of education. The intrinsic value of education–embedded in the inculcation of values of life in the young minds and in the moulding of the character of the children, in addition to the creation of joy of learning, ability to communicate with others, read, understand and enjoy simple pamphlets to literature and sciences, the joy of acquisition of knowledge etc.–is undoubtedly of prime importance. This is not altogether new. After all, this was considered for long as the traditional aim, function, and the very fundamental purpose of education.

Role of Education

While the traditional value of education could be regarded as the internal or intrinsic value of education, the materialistic developmental role of education could be regarded as an external one. Both are important and are mutually related. It is not only the materialistic aspects of education that lead to human resource development, but also the intrinsic values of education that lead to high-quality human resource development. As the human development specialists have underlined, the instrumental role of education is only secondary; the primary function is the constitutive role of education, performed by the inculcation of intrinsic values in such a way that people feel elevated with education and enjoy a better quality of life. But in the changing socio-economic circumstances, the materialistic aspects of education are dominating the world's education scene.

The administrators, policy planners, and scholars, consider education as an instrument for development, and believe that the materialistic benefits of education are most important. This way of thinking has assumed undue prominence, and it has invaded the thinking of the common people to such an extent that the traditional function of education is being forgotten altogether.

In the context of the recent economic reform policies introduced in many parts of the world, including India, that include liberalisation, privatisation and globalisation, and focus on *Programme for International Student Assessment* (PISA) scores and international competition, the danger of completely ignoring traditional values of education tends to be much higher. Globalisation has brought in western liberal values that conflict with traditional national values in many societies, including India. Western liberalism emphasises on materialistic development, whilst traditional Indian values focus on spiritualism. The rapid growth in the current types of privatisation of education, which focus mainly on profits and are not based on philanthropy or on any educational consideration, has led to rapid erosion in human values in the society. The current type of private education, which is diametrically opposite to the private education institutions established during the pre- and post-independence periods, which were characterised by noble values of charity, philanthropy and human care, seems to be seriously damaging the long well-cherished noble values and functions of education, marking a big shift from philanthropy to profits, and from social /national to individual interests and values. In the process of privatisation of education, not only equity-social, economic and regional–but also quality and ethical values in education are at stake.

Education–a Business?

In school education, civics, languages, history, moral education, crafts (e.g. gardening work), and even programmes like scouting, physical education, social/community service, etc. are fast going into oblivion; and the focus has shifted to 'core' academic subjects like science, technology, engineering and mathematics (STEM). The focus is not on the dissemination of knowledge in these subjects, but on the examination scores in these subjects. In higher education, it is clear: academic disciplines that involve study of languages, humanities, liberal arts and social sciences, which are important in making good citizens and human beings with better understanding of diverse cultures, languages, and ways of living, are getting displaced by the growth of substandard marketable programmes, which produce incomplete human beings and lop-sided personalities. Further, with the invasion of forces of globalisation and market forces in education, new value-loaded terminology entered into policy discourses on education, such as 'consumers' (for students), 'products' (for graduates), 'suppliers' (for schools and teachers), 'delivery' (for teaching), 'cost and profit centres' (for school activities), 'prices,' 'returns', 'profits', 'surplus', 'export', 'business', 'trade', 'enterprise' or 'business' and 'education markets' or 'education bazaars.' Current educational discourses consider these aspects as welcome developments.

With corrupt and unfair practices starting from setting up of the educational institution, to the awarding of certificates/ degrees, including admissions, fees, recruitment, payment of salaries, scholarships, examinations and evaluations, these profit-centred commercial private institutions–that do not see a distinction between education and cheap business–inculcate dangerous values in the students, as the school environment necessarily and automatically imparts many values among the students and even teachers.

High fee charging profit-mongering private education makes:

- Parents to focus on marketable stochastic values and money-value of education;
- Students selfish and career-centric; and
- Society greedy, possessive, and consumerist, with lack of social awareness and social concerns.

With an alarmingly high rate of growth of such private institutions, in the whole process, not only public sector in education is getting displaced, but also national, social, democratic and educational values are being replaced by narrow, personal, money-centric, career-centric, values like arrogance, greed, possessiveness, consumerism, cut-throat competition, rivalry, hatred, 'killing instincts', personality development and not personal development, contempt for national concerns and so on. These poor values assume prominence over long cherished values. Thus, the public good character of education is rapidly getting buried deep, leaving no trace of it anywhere.

Privatisation or commercialisation of education–as there is no difference between the two–is not a simple phenomenon. The exploitative, commercial markets in education or simply, the '*educational mercantilism*' impart several values that are incompatible with good education values, and not to speak of larger universal human values. For example, appetite for employment-oriented skills and competencies is preferred over quest for knowledge and truth, and commercially viable disciplines of study are preferred over sound academic disciplines of study, which are necessary for the progress of societies. At best, private institutions may be able to produce skilled manpower, but not critical and creative thinkers and humanists. In short, growth in private education with cheap motives of pecuniary benefits and erosion in values in education seem to be strongly related. The materialistic values that profit-motivated private education institutions produce are too dangerous to afford by any society. It appears, as the Hicksian (market and commercial) value for education increases, human values in education tend to disappear. The problem is human values are non-cognitive, and non-tangible, whereas commercial values are tangible and attractive. Exclusive emphasis on the latter could be detrimental to the progress of society and to the growth of individual personality as well.

Educational Reforms for Inculcating Human Values

In the 1960s, Phillip Coombs had forecasted the world education crisis. The crisis continued in several forms, which led many scholars in India, including AK Sen, JP Naik, KN Raj, and Suma Chitnis, among many, to observe it as "the continuing education crisis" in India. Unfortunately, the crisis continues even today and perhaps the nature and intensity of the crisis is more complex and severe today than ever, affecting the basic foundational characteristic features of education.

This, along with the need to reform the education system, is often recognised in India in the recent past. For example, the Government of India observed in the *National Policy on Education* (1986), 'the growing concern over the erosion of essential values and an increasing cynicism in society has brought to focus the need for readjustment in the curriculum in order to make education a forceful tool for the cultivation of social and moral values. In our culturally plural society, education should foster universal and eternal values, oriented towards the unity and integration of our people. Such value-education should help to eliminate obscurantism, religious fanaticism, violence, superstition and fatalism.' The core idea behind value education is to cultivate essential core human values.

Almost all education commissions and committees constituted in independent India have emphasised the importance of value-education, and more specifically of imparting of values through education. The commissions include, among others, the *Radhakrishnan Commission* on higher education (1948-49), the *Mudaliar Commission* on secondary education (1952-53), the *Kothari Commission* (1964-66) and the *Acharya Ramamurthy Committee* (1990).

The *Kothari Commission* warned, 'illiteracy and ignorance with goodness may be ok; but education without values is dangerous'. The *Mudaliar Commission* on secondary education has observed that religious and moral instructions play an important role in the growth of character of the children. Several committees, that were constituted specifically to look into the problem of value education (e.g. *Sri Prakasa Committee* on Religious and Moral Instruction, 1959; and *Kireet Joshi Committee* on Value Education, 1981-82), have clearly recommended that:

- Value orientation should be the main focus of education;
- The teachings of moral and spiritual values in education institutions are desirable; and
- The value-oriented education should be provided throughout the country.

Thus, many earlier committees and commissions, and policy statements on education in India have recognised the importance of imparting spiritual and moral education to children, so that human values are formed with a strong foundation. In today's age, spiritual kindling and awareness can be the only way forward.

Value-education for a Better World

Education does promote values. The question is: What kind of values education ought to promote? There are various kinds of values that any good education system has to give importance to. Some values that education is expected to create and sustain may be changing along with the changes in the socio-economic environment, but some remain unchanged forever and universally valid.

The core values are those which encompass universal human values. They are: *Satya* (truth), *Dharma* (righteousness), *Shanti* (peace), *Ahimsa* (non-violence) and *Prema* (love).

The *Parliamentary Standing Committee* on *Human Recourse Development* in its 'Eighty-First Report on Value-based Education (1999)' has highlighted these as the core universal values, which needed to be identified as the foundation on which the education programme can be built up. These are also considered as eternal human values. They do not change over time, and are not context or location-specific. Most societies cherish these values. They are widely respected and least controversial. All other values–national, social, religious, spiritual, environmental, physical, personal, intellectual, emotional–spring from these eternal values.

Not only these human values, but also certain national, social and political values, remain unchanged and these too could be universal in nature. These are: equity, social justice, patriotism, freedom, citizenship, dignity of labour, cleanliness, compassion, respect for others (particularly the women, the aged, children, disabled, backward communities), empathy, and concern for the poor, etc. These are also widely shared social, cultural and national values. All human values are captured by the *International Commission on Education* for the Twenty-first Century, familiarly known as the *Delors Commission* in its report, *Learning: The Treasure Within,* when it described the following four pillars of learning:

- *Learning to Know*
- *Learning to Do*
- *Learning to Be* and
- *Learning to Live Together*

The values that may be subject to change are context and location specific and they depend upon socio-political environment. For example, values relating to communism and socialism, freedom, democracy and authoritarianism etc. may vary from society to society and change from time to time. Democracy, secularism and social justice have been enshrined in the Indian Constitution as the three most important national values. But democracy and secularism may not figure favourably in authoritarian societies and in religion-based societies. Similarly, communism or socialism were important national values in the erstwhile Soviet Union and communist countries, which may not be important in the countries of the Commonwealth of the Russian Federation, or in the capitalist societies. Thus, some of these values become 'negotiated' values for a given time and context. They are not static; they are dynamic in nature, and may mean differently in different contexts.

Above all, there are spiritual values, which are considered more important for the very survival and sustenance of societies. Spiritual values are also believed to be those that lay basic foundation for the development of character of individuals, stressing moral and ethical values, such as sincerity, empathy, honesty, integrity, and truthfulness.

Spiritual values are considered above religious values. Rather religious values draw their strength from spiritual values. Accordingly, people may find it difficult to impart spiritual values without relating to any religion and vice versa. Only at higher levels, religious values may completely get submerged with spiritual values and lose their individual specific identity. So, in practice, imparting of spiritual values in many contexts takes place through religion. This is not necessarily an undesirable method of imparting human values, unless certain religious values conflict with human and spiritual values.

The Kothari Commission observed: 'A serious defect in the school curriculum is the absence of provision for education in social, moral and spiritual values. In the life of the majority of Indians, religion is a great motivating force and is intimately bound up with the formation of character and the inclusion of ethical values. A national system of education that is related to the life needs and aspirations of the people cannot afford to ignore this purposeful force.'

There may be no conflict between religious and human values, or between religion and science. As the famous quote of Albert Einstein goes, 'Science without religion is lame [and] religion without science is blind.' After all, most religions, in their original form, preach humanistic values, such as tolerance, compassion, non-violence and love. They preach spiritual values of righteousness, truthfulness etc. Most of the values–universal, spiritual, national and social–have emerged from the fundamental classical epics with emphasis on respect for humanity and life in all its forms. Common heritage of great religions includes respect for all religions and corresponding traditions and practices. Religious values *versus* spiritual values, spiritual values *versus* secular values, moral/ethical values *versus* development values, etc. are indeed false dichotomies. Simultaneous respect for secular and religious values can be noted in a good number of societies, both in ancient periods and the contemporary period, as secularism does not mean irreligion, but respect for all religions.

Similarly, economic development and moral principles can go hand in hand. For instance, the first Economist, Adam Smith, was profoundly linked to ethics; he was a professor of Moral Philosophy and author of *Theory of Moral Sentiments*, in which he stated, '*Ethics is the soul of economics. An economics without ethics inevitably becomes an economics of greed and avarice ... An economy without ethics means a continent without development.*' So development and ethics must go together. Development should be based on the foundation of ethical principles. Thus, there is no conflict between many of these values, though some tend to argue that religious and spiritual aspects come into conflict with national and even human values. In fact, as argued earlier, they mutually support each other.

Most of these values are not mutually exclusive and do not necessarily conflict with each other. Spiritual values lay basic foundation for character building; and social values promote social harmony, and help in building a desirable 'social order'. National values help in the national renaissance. Human values stand much above all these values and help in creating a better humanity and a better world order. It is important to note that no values could be neutral, nor could they be imparted through a value-neutral education system. As somebody remarked in a somewhat punching tone, the value-neutral education system, if any, may turn out to valueless education system. After all, '*education without values serves none*' (Sathya Sai Baba).

It is the basic function of education to promote these values. '*Education with values*' is regarded as the only solution for all kinds of problems that the societies are nowadays confronted with. It is unfortunate that even universal core values are ignored or overlooked, not only in our social, economic and political lives, but also in our education system in schools. Education has an important function in nurturing and promoting human values in a society. The *National Policy on Education 1992* states: 'It is the task of education to critically explore the ethical environment, identify human/central/core values, reflect on their preferability to others, resolve the conflicting and contradictory values, and inculcate right values. Education should be a forceful tool for the cultivation of social and moral values.' Important values that the schools should inculcate include universal human values like truth, peace, righteousness, love, and non-violence, which form the basis for social, national and personal values. Social values, such as concern for fellow beings, reduction in poverty, equity, justice, and non-discrimination; national values like patriotism, secularism, democracy and national integration; and personal values like honesty, loyalty, integrity–all can be seen as derivatives from universal human values.

It may be a misnomer to think that value-based education is abstract, teaching only morals, and is bereft of practical use. Value-based education includes knowledge of the humanistic foundations of society, as well as of natural, biological and physical sciences, philosophy and ethics that support the growth of good personality of the students with integrity and responsibility and excellence in knowledge. Sciences are not anti-theatrical to intrinsic values of education. Good education provides a balanced diet of material and spiritual values–a healthy blend of the worldly and spiritual knowledge. After all, academic education is shallow and useless, if it has no value orientation.

Educationists tend to believe, probably rightly, that introduction of value-education at any level of education requires a considerable re-look at the load of curriculum and the nature of curriculum. The *Radhakrishnan Commission* spelt out the methods of providing value-education; for example, (a) at school level, stories which illustrate great moral and religious principles may be used to inculcate values; and (b) at college level, ideas, events and leading figures associated with social and religious movements should be studied to reinforce the values further. All this may be necessary to revise the curriculum so as to make value education an integral part of the education system. Curriculum has to be developed that focuses on family values, societal values, universal values, including spiritual values. Value education in schools should aim at the development of the children and young adults, whilst focusing on virtues like simplicity, honesty, humility, cooperation, love, peace, unity and happiness. It is important that value-education is not treated like a separate subject of study, to be taught in fixed timings. Value inculcation should be an integral and central part of the entire schooling process. It should be thoroughly integrated into the whole curriculum, the method of instruction, and the whole education process. It should be noted that values are neither inert beliefs to be memorised, nor are they just rules and regulations to be adhered to. Just like inert knowledge of physics is no knowledge at all, values that are learnt by rote have little use; and may even be dangerous. All this may also require: (a) training, both preservice and in-service; (b) orientation programmes in value-education for school teachers; and (c) refresher courses for college teachers. Value-oriented teacher education programmes need to be developed. Teaching about values is not a matter of teaching the good ones; it is about harmonious development of the person, and helping young minds to become 'full' human beings for a humane society.

Education Reinforced with Extra-Curricular Activities

Along with many mechanisms of imparting value-based education, educational planners in India had introduced, in the past, certain specific mechanisms of creating good values among the students. Some important ones include the *Bharat Scouts and Guides*, the *National Social Service* (NSS), the *National Cadet Corps* (NCC), Yoga, *Socially Useful Productive Work* (SUPW), arts, crafts, gardening, etc., besides daily programme of prayers, flag hoisting, singing national anthem, etc. Many of these programmes and practices seem to be rapidly disappearing in all schools–both public and private, but more rapidly in private school. In fact, some of them have become defunct, if not disappeared altogether. There is a need to lay special emphasis on some of these activities, including sports and physical education in schools. 'Sports form an integral part of the scheme of studies in all our institutions, along with various academic subjects like Maths, Physics and Chemistry. Not only should there be participation, but there should also be a greater awareness and appreciation of the philosophy and principles governing the sports and games.' (*Sathya Sai Baba).*

- Firstly, it is necessary that special initiatives are made to revitalise/reintroduce such programmes. It is not proper to view that these mechanisms are important only to a given level of education and need to be introduced in one specific level of education or in specific schools. They are important at all levels of education starting from primary to higher, including higher professional education and in all schools–government and private. Some initiatives are already being made; they need to be scaled up; and institutionalised.

- Secondly, enrolment in these programmes needs to be made compulsory for all students and teachers. In fact, the participants in such programmes at local levels should cover not only the students and teachers, but also the parents and the entire community at large, including the government officials.
- Thirdly, it is not just instruction of values to the students, but creation of an environment to put them into practice is more important. Extra-curricular activities need to be designed in such a way that they create opportunities for practice of the values inculcated. There are several institutions in India, such as the *Sri Sathya Sai Institute of Higher Learning* (and the campus of schools), and the schools run by the *Ramakrishna Mission* all over India that demonstrate that, not only preaching, but also practice of the human values is possible. Many valuable lessons can be learnt from such experiments, which are in fact, ceasing to be small micro level experiments having immense potential to become great movements.
- Fourthly, it has to be realised that only strong and well-planned good public education systems alone can foster true universal human values and lay strong foundations for building a humane society. Philanthropy-based

special institutions can add to these public efforts with experiments and demonstrations.

- Lastly, careful planning is needed to see that the great traditional fundamental values that India stands for are not swayed away by the forces of globalisation; while at the same time, we learn from the experiences of other countries.

Conclusion

To conclude, the challenge is to reorient our education system to a humanistic vision of education and to resurrect the noble human values that India stands for. In the current era, these need to be strongly restated and defended. A UNESCO Report (*Rethinking Schooling for the 21st Century*, New Mahatma Gandhi Institute of Education for Peace and Sustainable Development, UNESCO, New Delhi, 2017), reasonably argued: '*We need to rethink the fundamentals priorities of our education policy.*'

Specifically, first, we need to improve our public education system in a massive way. It is widely regarded to be in shambles. In a note, titled '*Rejuvenation of Public Schools*' (*II C Quarterly*, June 2017), which the author has submitted to the Sub-Committee of the Central Advisory Board of Education to devise pathways, to improve condition of government schools (MHRD 2015), outlined below are a number of measures on how to rejuvenate the public school system:

First, strong public school system that places heavy emphasis on value-based education is critical on its own, and it will also reduce the growth of profit-seeking cheap quality private education institutions that do not care for any values.

Second, genuine philanthropy-based and service-oriented

private education efforts need to be encouraged to supplement public efforts.

Third, major curricular reforms in school and higher education are needed that focus on value-based education.

Fourth, major reforms are needed in the teacher training system, including in the curriculum of the teacher training institutions. They should promote creative pedagogic practices.

Sufficient emphasis must be placed on the training system on teachers' moral and ethical role in teaching. A recent report of Campaign for Popular Education (CAMPE) in Bangladesh (2018), titled '*Ethics and Values in School*', has outlined, *inter alia*, several measures on how to nurturer the idealism among young minds and make teacher a role model. After all, a teacher, having a direct effect on the character-building of the pupils, plays a pivotal role in the creation of generations of citizens with great character.

Why our Textbooks do not Tell Us about the Sarasvati River

Arpita Mitra

Many issues related to the writing of the history of the Indus Valley Civilisation (IVC), the oldest civilisation of India, have come to the fore in recent times. Some of the early interpretations of the IVC, like the Aryan invasion theory and related ideas, were based on pure hypothesis and informed by racism. In the past few decades, such baseless theories have been challenged. However, while the idea of an invasion has been given up, some scholars continue to argue about Aryan immigration. In the light of evidence that point towards the importance of the River Sarasvati to this civilisation, the hypothesis of an immigration stands challenged. While it takes time for long-standing beliefs and deeply-entrenched prejudices to get erased from higher academics, it takes even longer for this change in views to be reflected in the school-level curriculum. The result is that our students always lose out on latest research outcomes and debates. The purpose of this article is twofold: to inform the reader about the history of the Aryan invasion/immigration theory to demonstrate how untenable it is; and to draw the attention of concerned authorities to make immediate amendments in our history textbooks in the light of findings of the latest research.

Beginning of India's Civilisation

A major debate in Indian historiography is around the question of the beginning of India's civilisational history. The Indus Valley Civilisation (IVC) (also known as Harappan Civilisation) is the oldest civilisation of India. In the light of recent research findings, it is perhaps also the oldest civilisation of the world.

Today, Harappan sites number about 1,022, of which 406 are in Pakistan and 616 in India. About 97 Harappan sites in India have been excavated so far.[1] The discovery of this civilisation in the early twentieth century was quite dramatic. In those days, when India was under the British rule, the discovery of a civilisation of such antiquity pushed India's civilisational history back to the 3rd millennium BCE (this dating has been pushed further back by subsequent discoveries and debates). The Independence of India, however, also brought about the Partition of the country, and some of the best IVC sites discovered till then–such as Harappa and Mohenjodaro–fell within Pakistan's territory. In fact, to this day, the only IVC site listed in the UNESCO World Heritage Sites is Mohenjodaro in present-day Pakistan. Archaeologists in independent India continued to excavate other IVC sites. Gradually, the socio-politics related to the writing of the history of the IVC came to the fore, and many established beliefs were challenged. The discovery of the Sarasvati River was especially a game changer in the narrative about this past. As rightly pointed out by Dilip K Chakrabarti, 'The socio-political issues of the Indus civilisation are fought on a number of fronts: the issue of its name, the problem of its origin, the question of its 'Aryan' or 'Dravidian' identity, and its place as the fountainhead of the mainstream Indian culture.'[2]

This article discusses some of this socio-politics and its broader implications. Finally, it also demonstrates how the NCERT (National Council of Educational Research and Training) textbooks for history, first published in 2006 and still in use, are problematic with regard to representing this chapter of Indian history.

The objective behind writing this article is to create public awareness regarding the politics of writing about our past and to draw the attention of the concerned authorities regarding the need to attend immediately to the glaring problems in our textbooks. This essay is organised into two sections:

In the first part we discuss the high points in the story of how the history of the IVC came to be understood and the larger implications of this understanding. The section discusses the important debates related to the IVC. It also discusses the recent findings that could alter the history written so far.

In the second part we discuss what is represented in the NCERT textbooks of classes VI (first edition 2006, reprint 2016)[3] and XII (first edition 2007, reprint 2017)[4] regarding the IVC.

The Aryan Hypothesis

It is important to discuss briefly the history of the Aryan hypothesis, as a run-up to the interpretation of the archaeological findings at the IVC sites once they were discovered, as the former greatly informed this interpretation.

In the 1580s, the Italian Jesuit Filippo Sassetti, who lived in Goa, noted that Sanskrit shared a lot of common words with the European languages. Subsequently, this observation was made time and again by many others as well. Finally, it was Sir William Jones's proclamation, in 1786, which received much attention. Jones pointed out the unmistakable likeness between languages like Sanskrit, Greek, Latin, etc. and suggested that these languages must have originated from the same ancestor language. This ancestor language, however, no longer existed, and could only be re-constructed hypothetically. Later-day linguists came to call this language Proto-Indo-European, and the current family of languages, to which Sanskrit, Greek etc. belong, came to be known as Indo-European. It must be noted that this idea of a language family and a common ancestral language was purely hypothetical and a way of explaining the apparent resemblance between languages.

It was due to the pioneering comparative philological work of Franz Bopp, with publications starting from 1816, that the concept of the Indo-European language family was consolidated (although Bopp himself used the term 'Indo-Germanic' for these languages; the term 'Indo-European' was coined by the linguist Thomas Young). Subsequently, it was Max Müller who popularised the term 'Aryan' to denote the Indo-European family of languages. He believed that the original homeland of the Aryans was located 'somewhere in Asia' from where they must have branched off in two directions–one group in the North-Western direction, eventually reaching Europe, and the other in the South-Eastern direction, reaching Iran and India.[5]

Max Müller believed, '*Aryans were originally strangers in India*' and the '*first conquerors and masters of India*'. It should be noted that there were many European intellectuals, who believed the contrary to be true–that is, according to them, India was the cradle of civilisation and the original homeland of the Aryans, who migrated from the Indian territory to other places.[6] However, this view got suppressed in course of time, and the idea of the Aryan invasion of India gained ground, mainly due to false notions of racial superiority of the Europeans.

In the meantime, in 1816, the College of Fort St. George, Madras, published a textbook of Telugu grammar, written by AD Campbell, for junior civil servants. FW Ellis, a civil servant and the founder of the College, wrote the 'Note to the Introduction', where he argued that on the one hand, Telegu, Kannada and Tamil have a mutual relation with one another, and on the other hand, they are very different from Sanskrit. In 1856, a missionary, Robert Caldwell, published his *Comparative Grammar of the Dravidian or South-Indian Languages*, which formalised the concept of 'Dravidian' languages.[7] Thus, on the one hand, the concept of Aryan came to take shape and on the other, that of Dravidian.

Max Müller clarified several times that Aryan was a language and not a race. But soon, the scenario changed and the Aryan theory came to be articulated in racial terms. HH Risley was a British administrator, who was also known for his ethnological work on India. In his book, *Tribes and Castes of Bengal* (1892), he arrived at a racial classification of Indians based on the measurement of their nose. He categorised Indians into seven racial categories, of which five bore the terms Aryan or Dravidian: Indo-Aryan, Scytho-Dravidian, Aryo-Dravidian, Mongolo-Dravidian and Dravidian.[8] Gradually, these racial concepts developed more fully. This was also the time of the rise of the pseudo-science of racial ethnology in Britain.

Subsequently, the racial concepts of Aryan and Dravidian

were uncritically accepted by many Indians as well. In the nineteenth century itself, the theory of the supposed Aryan/Dravidian animosity was interpreted in terms of caste dynamics by the Dalit ideologue, Jyotirao Phule, who claimed that Brahmins were the descendants of the Aryan invaders (that is, they were not the indigenous people of India), who usurped the land and rights of the natives. Phule's ideas were, in fact, deeply influenced by writings of Christian missionaries, especially John Wilson's *India Three Thousand Years Ago* (1858).[9] These ideas have got so entrenched in both academic and political discourses on India that, for us today, the Aryan-Dravidian clash of cultures is the gospel truth and we never even pause to interrogate its premise and validity.

It is important to note here that the later-day social reformer, BR Ambedkar, however, never subscribed to the Aryan invasion theory and questioned the racial turn that the definition of the Aryan concept had taken. He wrote: 'What evidence is there of the invasion of India by the Aryan race and the subjugation by it of native tribes? So far as the *Rig Veda* is concerned, there is not a particle of evidence suggesting the invasion of India by the Aryans from outside India.'[10] He called the theory of Aryan invasion an invention, which he attributed to the 'gratuitous assumption' of Western theorists that they are the purest representatives of the Aryan race.

The Discovery of the IVC

By 1914, for Edward Rapson, a Cambridge University Sanskritist, who wrote the book, *Ancient India*, the Aryan-Dravidian divide and the Aryan invasion of India were the given facts. Thus, by the first quarter of the twentieth century, the theoretical framework for Aryan/Dravidian language/

race being antithetical to each other was already in place. When the ancient sites of Harappa and Mohenjodaro were excavated in 1921 and 1922, respectively, it was just a matter of superimposition of concepts like Aryan and Dravidian onto the newly discovered IVC. *It should be noted here that the theory of an Aryan invasion was formulated long before the actual discovery of the sites took place, and, as delineated above, behind this formulation was no evidence but pure hypothesis informed by racism.* Once the sites were discovered, this pre-existing theory shaped the interpretation of the archaeological findings.

Ever since the nineteenth century, people were aware of the existence of the mound of Harappa. In 1920-21, Daya Ram Sahni started his first season of excavation at Harappa. Sir John Marshall, the then Director-General of the *Archaeological Survey of India* (ASI), was quick to grasp the importance of these sites. In 1922-23, seals of the Harappan type were discovered in Mohenjodaro by Rakhaldas Banerji. The reports of the archaeological excavations conducted in Harappa and Mohenjodaro were published in the Archaeological Survey *Annual Report* of 1920-21 and 1922-23, respectively, and more extensively in the ASI Report of 1923-24.

Nature of the Civilisation

Based on the reference to the possible religious components of the civilisation in the ASI Report of 1923-24, Subrata Chakrabarti notes that 'there was no mental barrier to seek the reflection of the religion of this civilisation in the prevailing rituals of Hinduism.'[11] This tendency was, however, quickly subverted in the next few years. In December 1924, *The Modern Review*, published from Calcutta, carried an article, *Dravidian Origins and Beginnings of Indian Civilisation*, by a famous linguist, Suniti Kumar Chatterji. In this article, Chatterji presented quite a number of flawed arguments[12] and concluded that the civilisation discovered in Mohenjodaro and Harappa was non-Aryan.

Ramaprasad Chanda was the Superintendent of the Archaeological Section of the Indian Museum, Calcutta. In his memoir, *The Indus Valley in the Vedic Period* (1926), published by the ASI, Chanda argued that the civilisation discovered in Harappa and Mohenjodaro appeared to be pre-Vedic and non-Vedic, and that it was destroyed by successive waves of Aryan invaders. According to Chakrabarti, 'the idea of the Indus civilisation being pre-and non-Vedic became from now on a well-established part of the archaeological thought. The idea of the Aryans destroying the cities of the Indus civilisation is also firmly rooted in this publication.'[13] However, Chanda also mentioned the possibilities of interaction between the Aryans and the Indus civilisation people. In his second memoir, *Survival of the Prehistoric Civilisation of the Indus Valley* (1929), it is this theme of interaction and co-existence of the Aryans and the Indus people that gained ground.

By his 1931 report on Mohenjodaro, Marshall had developed the view that the Indus and Vedic cultures were 'unrelated'. Sir Mortimer Wheeler, later-day Director-General of the ASI, in the report on his 1946 excavation of Harappa, completely accepted that the IVC was a non-Aryan civilisation that was destroyed by 'Aryan invasions'. This entire discourse received a definite twist at the hands of Wheeler. So far, whosoever was arguing for an Aryan invasion was doing so either on the basis of pre-formed notions of racial groups or notions about continuity or discontinuity of cultures. But now, Wheeler managed to find a positive proof of the invasion.

And what was this proof? Numerous skeletons unearthed at the sites, which constituted Wheeler's infallible evidence for a large-scale 'massacre'.

Dating of the Civilisation

The method of dating archaeological finds on the basis of radioactive clocks that give absolute calendrical dates was discovered only during World War II. Hence, when the early excavators of the IVC, in the 1920s, were faced with the task of dating objects, they resorted to a different method for dating, which was not absolutely fool-proof. Marshall was certain from the very beginning that the Harappan civilisation represented 'a development reaching back incalculable centuries on Indian soil'.[14] When he saw Sahni's finds from Harappa, his initial conclusion was that these were 'pre-Mauryan' or perhaps older. Finally, they arrived at an agreeable date for the IVC based on seals that were found there. Seals of a similar type had been found in Mesopotamia in a datable context of 3rd millennium BCE. Based on this correlation, it was concluded that the IVC could be safely placed in the same millennium.

On the other hand, way back in the nineteenth century, Max Müller had already suggested a date for the *Rig Veda*–1,200 BCE. He had clarified that he was suggesting a minimum date and that it was difficult to determine with certitude the precise date of the *Rig Veda*.[15] However, certain ideas cling so stubbornly to our minds that to this day, most people still talk about *Rig Veda* being datable to 1,200 BCE, without interrogating (or perhaps even knowing) the basis for this dating. Secondly, as discussed above, the entire discourse of Aryan/Dravidian language/race and of Aryan invasion of India was already in place. Thirdly, the *Rig Veda* was the 'Aryan' text *par excellence*, depicting Indra, the Aryan God, destroying cities and forts. And the evidence of this destruction was found by Wheeler in a host of skeletons lying scattered in the Harappan sites. All these taken together, what else was required to prove that the IVC was the earliest known civilisation of India, datable to the 3rd millennium BCE, and that it was destroyed by hoards of invading Aryans, who subsequently set up a new civilisation–the Vedic civilisation–in India?

The Myth of the Aryan Invasion Challenged

In 1954-55, BB Lal challenged Wheeler's interpretation of the existence of skeletons by pointing out that there were clues in Wheeler's own report that suggested that the culture of the Citadel area in the site and that of the Cemetery H area belonged to two different periods.

In 1964, George F Dales published an article titled, *The Mythical Massacre at Mohenjo-Daro,*[16] in which he argued that the existing evidence of skeletons is not sufficient to prove infallibly that any massacre took place in Mohenjo-Daro. Dales wrote: '...what is the material evidence to substantiate the supposed invasion and massacre? Where are the burned fortresses, the arrowheads, weapons, pieces of armour, the smashed chariots and bodies of the invaders and defenders? Despite the extensive excavations at the largest Harappan sites, there is not a single bit of evidence that can be brought forth as unconditional proof of an armed conquest and destruction on the supposed scale of the Aryan invasion.' It is interesting that Sir John Marshall himself, the Director of the Mohenjodaro excavations that first revealed the 'massacre' remains, separated the end of the Indus civilisation from the time of the Aryan invasion by two centuries. He attributed the slayings to bandits from the hills west of the Indus, who carried out sporadic raids on an already tired, decaying, and defenceless civilisation.[17]

In his recent book, *The Rigvedic People*, BB Lal has discussed in detail why the skeletons are not proof of any massacre.[18] To put it in simple words, these skeletal remains do not belong to the same chronological period; hence, they cannot be treated as evidence of any large-scale massacre. So, we see that some archaeologists have been arguing convincingly for decades now that there is no archaeological evidence for an Aryan invasion. It is amazing to note how, in spite of such a basic fact related to the skeletons, and in spite of voices of dissent from the 1950s onwards, the myth of an Aryan invasion continued to hold sway over generations of readers. Perhaps even today, many, who have studied history decades ago in textbooks that mention an Aryan invasion, still hold this misconception to be true.

The Case against Aryan Immigration

Now, of course, as described above, we have finally officially given up the idea of an Aryan invasion. However, a group of scholars still cling to the idea that the Aryans came from outside. These scholars now talk about an Aryan immigration instead of invasion. A key question in this regard is: '*If the Aryans really came from outside, where did they come from*?' Opinions have varied on this count. A recent argument is that they came from the Bactria-Margiana Archaeological Complex (BMAC), also known as the Oxus Civilisation in Central Asia, discovered by the Soviet archaeologist, Viktor Sarianidi, in the 1970s. This argument is based on the apparent similarity between cultural motifs found in the BMAC and in the IVC. Once again, Lal demonstrates in details the weaknesses of this argument.[19] To summarise his views: The distribution maps of

BMAC cultural motifs across various civilisations, prepared by Sarianidi himself,[20] clearly show that these characteristic BMAC elements did not at all enter the Vedic region, which was east of the Indus.[21] Moreover, whatever few items were found to the east of the Indus, may simply indicate trade contacts, and not the immigration of the BMAC people into India. More importantly, Sarianidi's mode of reasoning does not offer any direct and concrete evidence in support of the case that BMAC people migrated to India.

Continuity in Indian Culture

Another matter to be taken seriously is the issue of discontinuity in Indian culture. While there were many who argued in favour of discontinuity between the Indus and the Vedic civilisations, there are equally many scholars arguing in favour of continuity. I shall briefly summarise some of the key arguments in this respect. Marshall himself was more inclined to accept the discontinuity thesis. In 1931, he very succinctly summarised the perceived difficulty in accepting that the Indus and the Vedic civilisations could be the same: '…we are wholly at a loss to explain how the Indo-Aryans came to relapse from the city to the village state, or how, having once evolved excellent houses of brick, they afterwards contended themselves with inferior structures of bamboo; or how, having once worshipped Siva and the linga and the Mother Goddess, they ceased to do so in the Vedic period, but returned to their worship later…'[22]

In recent times, a strong case has been made in favour of continuity between the Vedic and the Indus cultures. Lal's book, *The Sarasvati Flows On*, has an entire chapter devoted to the theme of continuity, where he meticulously documents all those aspects which are common between the

IVC and the present Indian culture; thereby, suggesting that no cultural discontinuity ever took place as a result of the arrival of foreigners.[23] This similarity can be noted in quotidian things, like type and pattern of ornaments (especially in Rajasthan and Haryana), the practice of wearing vermillion on the parting of the hair, games and recreation activities (objects like pottery discs used in the *pittu* game, gamesmen probably for chess, cubical dice, toys etc. have been found), cooking and feeding utensils to more large-scale things, like town planning, wells and reservoirs, religious artefacts, craft practices and so on. Particular note might be taken of two artefacts–*Shiva linga* and sacrificial fire altars that have been found in various sites like Kalibangan and Lothal. The *linga* found at Kalibangan is complete with the *yoni-patta,*[24] it is unmistakably a *Shiva linga*. It is difficult to argue–in this case at least–that we are wrongly reading ancient objects through the modern lens. The case for sacrificial fire altars is equally strong (Lal shows evidence against the suggestion that these were not fire altars but cooking hearths[25]). SR Rao, Chakrabarti, Amarendra Nath and many others argue for continuity of the Indus culture right up to our present times.

If the thesis for continuity is accepted, then the alternative that remains open for us is to accept that the Indus Valley and the Vedic cultures were the one and the same civilisation. They could either be coeval, or the Harappan culture could be a later phase of the Vedic civilisation itself. The particulars of this thesis are yet to be decided conclusively, but the general idea that 'the IVC and the Vedic culture were the same' is accepted by many archaeologists. Finally, there is a powerful *internal* and *positive* evidence in support of this argument–a river that once existed and is now part of India's lore–the Sarasvati.

Sarasvati Enters the Scene

The present-day Ghaggar is a seasonal river, rising in the Shiwaliks, entering the plains near Pinjore, and then flowing through Sirsa in Haryana and Hanumangarh and Suratgarh in Rajasthan. Once it enters Pakistan, it is called the Hakra. This river finally disappears into the Cholistan Desert. Its upper course is fed by monsoon waters, while its lower course is now mainly a dry bed. But this was not the case always.

In his *Annals and Antiquities of Rajasthan* (1832), Lt Col James Tod records, 'the tradition of the absorption of the Caggar [Ghaggar] river, as one of the causes of the comparative depopulation of the northern desert'.[26] The fact that there was a history of depopulation in this area, owing to the drying up of a river bed, was observed by various people since ancient times. Overlooking the Ghaggar, lies an important Harappan site–Kalibangan. This seasonal river, when once active, was part of the Harappan civilisation. A large number of the IVC settlements (a conservative estimate states 400 settlements, other estimates give a higher number) have been found in the Ghaggar-Hakra region. In fact, there are more sites in this region than in the Indus Valley proper. Furthermore, the decline of the IVC is often attributed to the drying up of rivers–the Sutlej and the Yamuna changed their course for certain;[27] thereby, causing the drying up of rivers in this region (as the water supply from Sutlej and Yamuna got re-directed to other rivers).

The *Imperial Gazetteer of India* of 1885 gave the following description of the river Ghaggar: 'In ancient times the lower portion of the river seems to have borne the name of its confluent the Sarasvati or Sarsuti, which joins the main stream in Patiala territory. It then possessed the dimensions of an important channel…'[28] The same *Gazetteer* described the

'Sarasvati (Sarsuti) as rising "in the low hills of Sirmur State, emerges upon the plain at Zadh Budri [Adi Badri—near the Haryana-Himachal Pradesh border], a place esteemed sacred by all Hindus" and "passes by the holy town of Thanesar and the numerous shrines of the Kurukshetra, a tract celebrated as a centre of pilgrimages…." before joining the Ghaggar. 'In ancient times, the united stream below the point of junction appears to have borne the name of Sarsuti [Sarasvati], and undiminished by irrigation near the hills, to have flowed across the Rajputana plains…'[29] Louis Vivien de Saint-Martin, the nineteenth-century French geographer who studied the region, was of the opinion that "the totality of the streams [for example, Ghaggar, Markanda and Sarsuti] flowing down from the mountain close to each other before they unite in a single bed" appears to have received the designation of 'Sarasvati'.[30]

A NASA satellite launched in 1972 found a huge dried-up river bed in India, flowing from the Himalayas to the Rann of Kachchh. This is now believed to be the dried-up River Sarasvati. A remarkable feature of the region is the host of numerous palaeo beds criss-crossing Sutlej-Yamuna interfluves. In 1995, scientists from Bhabha Atomic Research Centre (BARC) drew samples from wells in various parts of Rajasthan and found that even in such a desert area, groundwater was available at the depth of 50 to 60 m below the ground surface. These 'fossil waters' have been dated to c. 3,700-3,200 BCE based on radiocarbon methods.

A host of other scientific evidence also prove that a gigantic river once flowed in this region.[31] This river could be none other than the Vedic Sarasvati and further reasoning suggests that the once active Ghaggar must have been the upper stream of the River Sarasvati.

Thus, we see that the River Sarasvati is not a mythological river but a real river that originated in the Himalayas. It entered the plains at Adi Badri and then flowed in almost south-westerly direction through the present-day states of Haryana, Rajasthan and Gujarat before finally joining the Arabian Sea through the present-day Rann of Kachchh, which was probably an estuary that got silted later. The Sarasvati lost most part of its water due to various geological, hydro-geological and climatic factors, such as tectonic movements, tributary diversions and climate change. It, thus, literally became a subterranean river, with only a dry bed now as evidence of its course at one point of time.

The Sarasvati River & Theory of Aryan Immigration

What we know today as the IVC is, thus, the Indus-Sarasvati or Sindhu-Sarasvati Civilisation. There are more sites in the Sarasvati Valley than in the Indus Valley. The older sites are concentrated in the lower reaches of the Sarasvati, while the later sites in the upper reaches, as there was migration upwards after the drying up of the river in the lower reaches. In the light of recent excavations, Indian archaeologists are arguing that Rakhigarhi in Haryana is the largest IVC site unearthed so far and it shows settlements of all the phases, that is, early, mature and late Harappan phases.[32] Rakhigarhi lies in the valley of what was once the Drishadvati, a river closely related to the Sarasvati drainage system.

Now, the *Rig Veda* abounds in references to the River Sarasvati. It refers to it as a mighty river, 'abounding in waters' (*maho-arnah*, RV 1.3.12) and flowing 'from the mountains to the sea' (*giribhyah asamudrat*, RV 7.95.2). It was 'roaring' (*charati roruvat*, RV 6.61.8) and 'fierce' (*ghora*, RV 6.61.7), 'possessing unlimited strength' (*yasyah amah ananto*, RV, 6.61.8). It flowed 'rapidly' (*pra-sasre*, RV 7.95.1) and moved 'faultlessly' (*akavari*, RV 7.96.3), and was thus 'the most impetuous of all other streams' (*apasam-apastama*, RV 6.61.13).

Not merely its physical description, but the *Rig Veda* also mentions that the Sarasvati was a giver of material as well as spiritual wealth. She is extolled as 'the best among mothers, the best among rivers, the best among goddesses' (*ambitame naditame devitame*, RV 2.41.16). In one of its verses (RV 10.75.5-6), the text also names the rivers of the northern and north-western region in order from right to left. This verse clearly indicates that the Sarasvati flowed between the Yamuna and the Shutudri (Sutlej).

Some important questions:

(1) Did Sarasvati and Indus together form what is known today as the Harappan Civilisation?

(2) Did Sarasvati dry up by the end of this civilisation, thereby causing its decline?

(3) If the *Rig Veda* describes the Sarasvati in full vigour, can we continue to say that the Harappan Civilisation preceded the Vedic Age?

An answer to all above questions is plain and simple: 'No, we cannot.'

Two NCERT History Textbooks

As mentioned in the Introduction, two NCERT history textbooks will be analysed here, in this section–one for Class VI and another for Class XII–with regard to their content on the IVC.

The fourth chapter of the Class VI textbook deals with the IVC. There is no mention of the River Sarasvati, and there is no mention of the Indus either. Hence, the name Indus Valley

Civilisation (IVC) is not uttered at all. The chapter manages to tell children about this great civilisation of the world using only the appellation 'Harappan civilisation'. The whole chapter is pivoted around the fact of the 'city'. Hence, the chapter is titled 'In the Earliest Cities' and it discusses houses, drains, streets, life in the city, new crafts in the city, food for people in the cities and so on. The chapter ends with the following: 'New cities emerged about 1,400 years later. You will read about them in Chapters 6 and 9.'[33]

This is a reference to the growth of the *janapadas* and *mahajanapadas*. A kind of discontinuity is implicitly suggested by such a statement, but the silence is not filled up with any explanations. It may also be noted here that the depiction of the IVC in this chapter presents it as an urban settlement and this is what the predominant identity of this civilisation has been since the days of its very discovery. However, recent archaeological research also throws light on town and village settlements belonging to this culture.[34]

Curiously, Chapter 4 does mention that sites, such as Kalibangan and Lothal, had fire altars where sacrifices may have been performed, but it does not join the dots of the fact of fire altars and sacrifices with that of the larger IVC/Aryan question. This chapter also discusses briefly the end of the Harappan civilisation. Thankfully, the author(s) do not mention the 'coming of the Aryans' as the cause of the downfall.

It is mentioned that some scholars think the civilisation came to an end because rivers dried up. The next chapter launches directly into Vedic civilisation. Neither the fourth nor the fifth chapter mentions the relationship (whatever the authors accepts that to be) between the Harappan and the Vedic civilisations. Chapter 5 dates the *Rig Veda* at c. 1,500

BCE (p. 43)–giving only a 300-year concession to the date suggested by Max Müller.

A textbox talks about Sanskrit belonging to the Indo-European family of languages (p. 44), but does not state explicitly the implications of Sanskrit belonging to the same language family as English, German, Greek, Italian etc. Curiously, the chapter also includes a textbox with a dialogue between the sage Visvamitra and the rivers Beas and Sutlej (p. 45). In this text, the River Sarasvati is mentioned as it is part of the Rigvedic hymn that has been quoted. There is, however, no discussion on the Sarasvati.

Now, let us turn to the textbook for Class XII. As one would expect, the chapter on the Harappan civilisation (Chapter 1) is in much greater detail compared to the textbook for Class VI. But, even this one does not make any mention about the River Sarasvati. In twenty-five pages, it covers almost every other aspect of the civilisation except the Aryan debate. In fact, it even avoids using the term 'Aryan'. This word is mentioned only in an excerpt from Wheeler. This excerpt appears in a textbox, which is titled, *Evidence of an 'invasion'* (p. 18). Note how cleverly the entire Aryan question is elided. While the title of the textbox might lead one to believe it presents an argument in favour of an invasion, the purpose of this particular textbox is, on the contrary, to inform the readers that the idea of an invasion has now been given up. By tracing the rise and fall of this notion of invasion, from Marshall to Wheeler to Dales (without, however, entering into the details of it), the textbox also aims to demonstrate how historical conclusions can be revised in the course of time. If people have been schooled in a certain wrong belief, they need to be explicitly de-schooled as well, instead of adopting a calculated silence.

Again, the author (s) is clever enough to mention that we should not read religious symbolism into ancient artefacts from the standpoint of our own times (p. 23). And then on the next page, one finds another clever move of showing *linga*-like structures on a chess board accompanied with an excerpt from an archaeologist, Earnest Mackay, who doubted if these were *lingas* or gamesmen (p. 24). There is no mention of the *linga* with *yoni patta* that was discovered at Kalibangan. Partial representation of truth is also, in a way, distortion of truth.

The next chapter moves straight to 600 BCE. Only the introductory paragraph mentions: 'There were several developments in different parts of the subcontinent during the long span of 1,500 years following the end of the Harappan civilisation. This was also the period during which the *Rigveda* was composed by people living along the Indus and its tributaries.'[35] This clearly indicates that the authors do not take cognisance of the debate on the identity of the Harappan and Vedic civilisations, and present only a one-sided view, which is in all likelihood erroneous. Even if the authors do not accept the thesis of continuity, to be fair, they should at least mention both sides of the debate.

Finally, it is only in Chapter 4 that the *Rig Veda* is discussed, that too strictly as a background to the critique posed by the Buddha. The *Rig Veda* is said to have been compiled between c. 1,500 to 1,000 BCE and the Upanishads are placed in 600 BCE (p. 84). Then, there are all kinds of false generalisations that Buddhism and Jainism stressed on individual agency, while the 'Brahmanical position' (whatever that is supposed to mean) considered individual agency to be determined by 'his or her birth in a specific caste or gender'.[36] Furthermore, there are random verses quoted from the Upanishads in textboxes

(p. 85) that would hardly mean anything to an eighteen-year-old who is not aware of the broader context of these verses. Needless to say, the chapter itself does little to enlighten the reader about the Upanishads in a comprehensible manner.

Conclusion

There has been much hue and cry over the politics of history textbooks, but a politics of the kind discussed above has received less attention. What is important to note is that the NCERT books do not even mention that a debate exists. There may be and there are disagreements among scholars, but the sign of a good text book is that it introduces the reader to the debate in a non-partisan manner. For a long time, the debate on the Aryan invasion/immigration has been suppressed in the name of being 'Right-wing propaganda'.

The issue of the River Sarasvati has been suppressed even more in mainstream academic circles, as it provides infallible proof that the Harappan and the Vedic cultures are one. Perhaps, the nineteenth-century European geographers and scholars, who record the folklore related to the River Sarasvati, were also party to a 'Right-wing propaganda'! And, perhaps, the authors of the numerous ancient texts, that mention the River Sarasvati, were lunatics to have given such importance to a non-existent river!

If one looks at the entire issue in a non-partisan way, one cannot fail to note that many areas pertaining to our earliest recorded history need serious re-thinking and reconsideration. Not only are the present textbooks partisan and deficient in important perspectives, they also need to be updated, as new archaeological data related to sites, such as Bhirrana and Rakhigarhi, need to be taken into account. Given the importance of the Sindhu-Sarasvati/Vedic Civilisation as the very fountainhead of our culture, the sooner this revision takes place, the better.

References

1 Upinder Singh, A History of Ancient and Early Medieval India: From the Stone Age to the 21st Century, Dorling Kindersley, Delhi, 2009, p. 137.

2 Dilip K. Chakrabarti, The Battle for Ancient India: An Essay in the Sociopolitics of Indian Archaeology, Aryan Books, New Delhi, 2008, p. 51.

3 Our Pasts-I: Textbook in History for Class VI, NCERT, Delhi, 2006 (http://ncert.nic.in/textbook/textbook.htm?fess1=0-12). Social Studies, including History, is introduced only from the sixth standard—this is one of the changes that the National Curriculum Framework (NCF) 2005 effected.

4 Themes in Indian History Part-I: Textbook in History for Class XII, NCERT, New Delhi, 2007 (http://ncert.nic.in/textbook/textbook.htm?lehs1=0-4).

5 Friedrich Max Müller, Lectures on the Science of Language, vol. 1, Longmans Green & Co., London, 1885; Friedrich Max Müller, Biographies of Words and the Home of the Aryas, Longmans Green & Co., London, 1888.

6 For details, see Edwin Bryant, The Quest for the Origins of Vedic Culture: The Indo-Aryan Migration Debate, Oxford University Press, New York, 2001, p. 18.

7 Thomas R. Trautmann, ed., The Aryan Debate, Oxford University Press, New Delhi, 2005, pp. 6-7.

8 Chakrabarti, The Battle for Ancient India, p. 53.

9 Rosalind O'Hanlon, Caste, Conflict and Ideology: Mahatma Jotirao Phule and Low Caste Protest in Nineteenth Century Western India, Cambridge University Press, Cambridge, 1985, p. 141.

10 B. R. Ambedkar, Who were the Shudras? How They Came to be the Fourth Varna in Indo-Aryan Society, Thacker & Co., Bombay, 1946, p. 68.

11 Chakrabarti, The Battle for Ancient India, p. 57.

12 For details, see ibid, p. 65.

13 Ibid, p. 60

14 Cited in ibid, p. 57.

15 See B. B. Lal, The igvedic People: 'Invaders'?/'Immigrants'? or Indigenous? Evidence of Archaeology and Literature, Aryan Books, New Delhi, 2015, pp. 10-11.

16 George F. Dales, 'The Mythical Massacre at Mohenjo-daro', in Expedition, vol. 6, issue 3, 1964, pp. 36-43. https://www.penn.museum/sites/expedition/the-mythical-massacre-at-mohenjo-daro/

17 Ibid, p. 38.

18 Lal, The igvedic People, pp. 14-15.

19 Ibid, pp. 19-33.

20 Reproduced in ibid, pp. 30-31.

21 Ibid, p. 30

22 As cited in Chakrabarti, The Battle for Ancient India, p. 69.

23 B. B. Lal, The Sarasvat Flows On: The Continuity of Indian Culture, Aryan Books, New Delhi, 2002, pp. 82-135.

24 For picture, see ibid, p. 118.

25 Lal, The igvedic People, pp. 135-143.

26 As cited in Michel Danino, The Lost River: On the Trail of the Sarasvati, Penguin Books, New Delhi, 2010, p. 9.

27 For details, see chapters in S. Kalyanaraman, ed., Vedic River Sarasvati and Hindu Civilisation, Aryan Books, New Delhi, 2008.

28 As cited in Danino, The Lost River, p. 21.

29 Ibid, p. 22

30 Ibid, p. 19

31 For details of the evidence discussed and more, see Kalyanaraman, ed., Vedic River Sarasvati.

32 http://www.tribuneindia.com/news/sunday-special/kaleidoscope/the-lost-world-of-hisar-s-mohenjo-daro/72296.html

33 Our Pasts-I: Textbook in History for Class VI, NCERT, Delhi, 2006 (http://ncert.nic.in/textbook/textbook.htm?fess1=0-12) p. 41.

34 Singh, A History of Ancient and Early Medieval India, pp. 135-36.

35 Themes in Indian History Part-I, p. 28.

36 Ibid, p. 85.